The Dilemma
of Modernity

PETER LANG
New York • Washington, D.C./Baltimore • Bern
Frankfurt am Main • Berlin • Brussels • Vienna • Oxford

John A. McCulloch

The Dilemma
of Modernity

Ramón Gómez de la Serna
and the Spanish Modernist Novel

PETER LANG
New York • Washington, D.C./Baltimore • Bern
Frankfurt am Main • Berlin • Brussels • Vienna • Oxford

Library of Congress Cataloging-in-Publication Data

McCulloch, John.
The dilemma of modernity: Ramón Gómez de la Serna
and the Spanish modernist novel / John A. McCulloch.
p. cm.
Includes bibliographical references.
1. Gómez de la Serna, Ramón, 1888–1963. 2. Authors, Spanish—
20th century—Biography. 3. Spanish fiction—20th century—
History and criticism. I. Title.
PQ6613.O4Z7735 863'.62—dc22 2006038099
ISBN 978-0-8204-8183-8

Bibliographic information published by **Die Deutsche Bibliothek**.
Die Deutsche Bibliothek lists this publication in the "Deutsche
Nationalbibliografie"; detailed bibliographic data is available
on the Internet at http://dnb.ddb.de/.

Cover design by Joni Holst

The paper in this book meets the guidelines for permanence and durability
of the Committee on Production Guidelines for Book Longevity
of the Council of Library Resources.

© 2007 Peter Lang Publishing, Inc., New York
29 Broadway, 18th floor, New York, NY 10006
www.peterlang.com

Printed in Germany

For Annette, Esther and Anna

Creo que al mundo no se le ha dado aún el sentido
de arbitrariedad y desfachatez que merece.

Ramón Gómez de la Serna (1888–1963)

Contents

Acknowledgments

I would like to express my thanks to the British Academy and the Carnegie Trust for the award of grant monies to assist in the publication of this book, and also to the School of Modern Languages at Strathclyde University for granting me research leave. My thanks is also due to Robin Warner at Sheffield University for his help and patient guidance in the early stages of my research. I am also grateful to Ana Avila for her assistance in finding some of the first editions of Ramón's novels, to Dorita Osorno for her hospitality during my visits to Madrid, and to my wife Annette for her support throughout.

Chapter 1. The Making of a Bohemian (1909–1918)

Let's break out of the horrible shell of
wisdom and throw ourselves like
pride-ripened fruit into the wide,
contorted mouth of the wind!
>   Filippo Thomaso Marinetti (1876–1944)

Avant-tout, les artistes sont des humains qui
Veulent devenir inhumains.
>   Guillaume Apollinaire (1880–1918)

Melancólico—pero ya no frenético—me volví un monomaníaco literario, me
compré una bufanda y un monóculo, y me lancé al Madrid del atardecer, ya sin
ideales políticos, ya solo con el sediento ideal del arte.
>   Ramón Gómez de la Serna. (1888–1963)

Introduction

Born in Madrid in 1888, much of Ramón Gómez de la Serna's childhood years were spent in the Spanish capital. His early childhood memories are closely associated with the streets and buildings of Madrid, which were to leave an indelible mark on his narrative fiction and occupy a central place in his formation as a writer. Brought up in a middle class family, Gómez de la Serna benefited from a relatively privileged start in life amongst the emerging urban bourgeoisie of Madrid. He came from an educated family, and his aunt Carolina Coronado was one of the few female Romantic authors who had had some degree of literary success. Gómez de la Serna was soon to follow in her footsteps and devote himself to literature, and become one of Spain's most important modernist writers.[1]

The years spanning from 1909 to 1918 are of central importance to understanding the early influences which come to bear on his work, not least because it was during these early years that he formulated various theoretical essays on the art of writing, and also published his seminal novel *La viuda blanca y negra* (1917). This chapter will trace the main influences on Gómez de la Serna at this time, in an attempt to come to a fuller understanding of his early beginnings. Understanding his life in Madrid as a young author im-

mersed in the literary scene of the cafés and *tertulias* is essential to coming to
a greater understanding of his peculiar narrative style and challenging novels.
Living in the Spanish capital, with frequent trips to major European cities,
enabled him to access new emerging ideas from Europe and beyond, whilst
remaining deeply entrenched in the Spanish literary tradition.

Growing up in Spain's capital at that time must have been full of contradictions. Politically Spain was in turmoil, slowly embracing modernity when
compared to her European neighbours, whilst traditional ways of life per-
sisted. Spain's internal political conflicts and chronic economic decline not
only ensured relative isolation from major international conflicts such as
World War I, but served to reinforce the perception that Spain was a pariah
state, with limited relevance to a rapidly modernising Europe. The nature of
this decline does not feature in Gómez de la Serna's fiction, immediately setting him apart from his predecessors, the so-called Generation of 1898.
Despite his fascination with the new emerging literary and artistic ideas, he
does however share a certain nostalgia for Spain's past which is expressed
through his love of historic city streets, objects in the *Rastro* market, old cafés and bars; but at no time does he indulge in philosophical questioning
about the reason for Spain's decline, nor does he seek to search for any remedy. This apparent aesthetic detachment is essential for understanding both
his work and the critical flak he was to receive as an author. It is not surprising that such political failure caused the Spanish philosopher (and close
friend of Gómez de la Serna) Ortega y Gasset to call for political change
linked to reform, to argue for an enlightened and educated minority to take
increasing political responsibility for the governance of Spain. Spanish political life had become a gross distortion of democratic normality, and
according to the satirical author Valle Inclán, could therefore only be portrayed through the monstrous contortions of the *esperpento*. It is revealing
that Gómez de la Serna referred to Spain several years later as 'este gran
valle de las Hurdes',[2] conjuring an image of inward looking isolation:

> Parece que este gran valle de las Hurdes que es toda España, se ha cuajado de sangre
> y el espíritu, y no corre ningún viento y todo es más ingente y más fiero y una
> pesadez creada por la complicidad de todos lo ha malogrado todo. La frase de Larra:
> 'Suponte que eres español y no te aflijas', y la frase de Cánovas cuando redactaba el
> Art. 1. de la Constitución: 'Son españoles…¡ Los que no han podido ser otra cosa!',
> son dos frases cada vez más formidables y más precisas.[3]

Similar to other modernist writers of the time, Gómez de la Serna's disenchantment with politics led him to follow an impulse not that dissimilar to
Schopenhauer's prescribed remedy to life's ultimate meaninglessness; namely the pursuit of aesthetic contemplation as the only means for the individual

to momentarily escape from the absurdity and futility of everyday life. Much of Gómez de la Serna's fiction therefore relies on the poetic abstraction of the immediate world in an attempt to transcend mundane reality. The aesthetic takes on a central and determining role both in terms of characterisation and the development of narrative. Reminiscent of Brentano's idea that in art the boundaries between subject and object are broken down, abstracted, through a heavy reliance on poetic transformation and distortion, Gómez de la Serna's aesthetic of the *greguería* is predicated on a similar foundation. The modernist poetic of fragmentation and broken images, so powerfully evoked by Eliot in *The Waste Land* (1922), although distinct in nature to Gómez de la Serna's *greguería*, asserts the importance of the part over the whole. The *greguerías* have often been seen as little more than and individual literary quirk of an eccentric author, but clearly need to be understood as part of the aesthetics of European modernism in their insistent exaltation of poetic fragmentation.

Gómez de la Serna encapsulates a deeply entrenched 'Spanishness'—similar to Goya he portrays a vibrant and multifaceted picture of Madrid—whilst at the same time posing as the literary connoisseur of ideas emerging north of the Pyrenees. In this sense his work is of central importance in order to come to a fuller understanding of Spain's cultural dilemma: its ideological 'tug-of-war' between a historical tendency for extreme introversion, whilst simultaneously striving to be outward looking on a par with her European neighbours. This 'dilemma' brought about by the progressive arrival of modernity in a country which was, outside the major cities, largely a barren agricultural back-water, is, to some extent mirrored in Gómez de la Serna's fiction. His fictional characters are very modern by nature, but never ultimately fit in with their surrounding society, remaining instead at the margins of a society which makes little sense. There is an uneasiness and incongruity about them, and on the whole they seem out of place. They inhabit a bizarre hinterland where everyday events and occurrences do not follow a particular pattern or logic. These modern characters stand out from the crowd and do not merge in with the homogenised society around them. They are out of kilter with their world.

Of all the fleeting images which make up Gómez de la Serna's fiction, one constant preoccupation which unifies all his novels and stands out is the depiction of modern man: the aloof, rootless wandering aesthete, roaming at will through a changing world, encountering situations through a mixture of chance and serendipity. Gómez de la Serna's characters are drawn from the emerging urban bourgeoisie, and therefore remain rootless, all atavistic ties having been severed. As such, they share in the modern condition, engaging in an existence which lacks any real depth or purpose, driven by an aesthetic will to live. However, these characters are not representative of mass man, marked by a profound sense of pessimism and corporate despair; instead they are individuals who stand out from the crowd. It might be argued that this is a deliberate move on the part of the author, as a kind of protest against the rise of mass society, which had been prophesied by historians and thinkers such as Oswald Spengler and Ortega y Gasset. Whilst it would be wrong to suggest that Gómez de la Serna's fictional characters embody angst-ridden individuals attempting to break out of what Max Weber called 'the iron cage of modernity,'[4] their often frivolous and quirky behaviour does not mask their failures nor lessen their existential plight, even though this is seldom dealt with explicitly. The assumption that Gómez de la Serna's novels are simply humorous and shallow, largely consisting of layers of random *greguerías* which engage the reader on a superficial level but tell us very little about the human condition itself is an oversimplification which has become commonplace because of his use of humour. Gómez de la Serna's use of humour has to be understood as a rebellion against the absurdity of existence, a cry of individuality in a world where individual values are on the wane. With this in mind, the picture inevitably becomes more complex.[5]

Regardless of how we perceive Ramón Gómez de la Serna's fiction, and whether we write him off as a clown-like figure, more important for his avant-garde rhetoric than for anything of more substance, there is no doubt that there has been a revival of interest by readers and critics alike over the last two decades. In a novel as contemporary as *Las máscaras del héroe*, the writer Juan Manuel de Prada introduces the figure of Ramón Gómez de la Serna in the following fashion:

> [...] era rechoncho, cejijunto, como un Napoleón de paisano; tenía cara de niño que se atiborra de barquillos y merengue, hacía como que fumaba en pipa sin tabaco: se llamaba Ramón Gómez de la Serna, y se tiraba eructos que olían a horchata de chufa. Abstemio y caprichoso, hablaba a gritos, como un pavo real o una gaviota obsesa [...] Acababa de terminar la carrera de Derecho con apenas veinte años y su papá le financiaba una revista para mantenerlo entretenido y que así no diese mucho la lata. Ramón aborrecía las imposiciones del clasicismo, y, para contrarrestarla, se inventaba una vanguardia cada día.[6]

Despite de Prada's deliberate parodic intent and humorous poetic licence, this description of Ramón Gómez de la Serna in a novel as recent as *Las máscaras del heroe*, would suggest that the figure of Ramón is deeply entrenched in the Spanish psyche. Most young Spanish readers would be familiar with the name of Ramón Gómez de la Serna, although relatively few would be able to claim that they had read any of his novels, whilst much of the older generation would have undoubtedly come across his *greguerías* and articles in the press. Ramón's gregarious public persona—on which de Prada draws in his novel—has ensured that Ramón's name is arguably as well known as those of the great Spanish classical authors such as Lope, Calderón, and Galdós, despite the experimental nature of many of his works. This is remarkable, given the relatively recent critical acclaim for his novels, and highlights one of the difficulties faced by any reader interested in approaching Ramón's work: that of establishing the delimitation between his flamboyant public persona, and the essence of the man himself. There is no doubt that Ramón himself deliberately cultivated his own public persona —one only has to read his autobiography *Automoribundia* to realise the extent to which he deliberately presents himself as an eccentric and unconventional individual. The task, therefore, for the critic is to go beyond the myth, and unravel the real nature of Ramón and the particular vision of society portrayed in his works.

Like many of the great Spanish authors of old, Ramón is clearly influenced by the European literary tradition. He lived in Paris between 1909 and 1911, and travelled extensively through all the major European capitals both before and after the First World War. His association with the European literary scene of the day, however, did not lead him to forsake his Spanishness, but provided him with the opportunity to assert what he had learnt from his literary heritage within the wider European context. His years in Paris brought him into contact with a variety of avant-garde writers and movements, including a brief encounter with Apollinaire, which was to influence him deeply. He remembers seeing Manuel Machado writing in a Parisian café, although he dared not interrupt him. He also remembers encountering Baroja, which is recounted in *Automoribundia*:

> Coincidí alguna vez con Baroja en aquel Paris encantador, y como vulgarmente se dice, 'me dio la cena'.
>
> Yo vivía de pequeñas ilusiones, de mucha buena fe literaria, de oler las violetas de la admiración esparcida por los poetas y los bohemios—de lo que sigo viviendo al cabo de los años—cuando Baroja se empeñaba en ensombrecer la vida. [7]

During his two year stay in Paris he had led a bohemian lifestyle, roaming the streets and flea market and writing through the night. It was during that time that Carmen de Burgos had visited him. Gómez de la Serna remembers how they travelled to London in the winter and then down to Italy, before returning to Paris where they parted:

> [...] Volvimos a Paris, y allí nos despedimos como dos artistas que han de sacrificarse para seguir ganando con qué vivir mientras con nuevo material ardiente habían de fundir nuevas concepciones. (*AM*, p.221)

From an early age Gómez de la Serna was interested in Paris not least because his father had told him about his trips to Paris and London. Paris was to become the backdrop to several of his novels including *La viuda blanca y negra* (1917) and *El chalet de las Rosas* (1923)—for at least part of the novel—and was a city he memorably evoked through poetic one-liners such as 'Paris está hecho de cemento de niebla de siglos'. But despite any influence he might have received from living in Paris for two years it is clear that, beneath the surface preoccupations of the avant-garde, the deeper objectives of subverting and questioning were essentially Spanish attitudes which can be traced in numerous Spanish authors down the years, from the witty and sardonic Quevedo to the soul-searching Unamuno. What differentiates Ramón from his literary forebears is that he disengages literature from sentimental, ideological and moral constraints.

The absence of traditional humanistic preoccupations in Ramón's work makes it difficult for the reader to reach any degree of empathy with his fictional characters, although, paradoxically, the main theme of his work (the persistent search for companionship in a changing world) could be understood as a universal human concern which transcends time and place. This quest on the part of characters generally meets with failure, although there is little attempt on the part of the author to draw attention to the tragic condition of man. Instead, potentially serious issues are gilded in avant-garde humour. It is clear that Ramón does not believe in society, but in the individual, and in the importance of asserting one's individuality—his eccentric lifestyle is proof in itself—and yet, paradoxically, all of his characters speak the same language and share similar concerns.

Ramón's bleak vision of society was undoubtedly influenced by his solitary and reclusive lifestyle. Locked away for days on end in his apartment which was to become his ivory tower, surrounded by a plethora of *bric-a-brac* and bizarre objects and keeping unsociable hours to enable him to write through the night, it comes as little surprise that he developed a detached attitude towards society. At the same time, the immediate surroundings of his study account for his obsession with describing the tangible world, even though the aesthetic process deployed to achieve this converts the real world into a poetic construct, constantly recreating itself in the mind of the beholder. His *modus operandus* is largely Kantian, in that objects are not simply important for their material nomenclature, but for what they represent, for the visual and poetic images they suggest in the mind of the beholder. 'Things' are fashioned through the author's mind and his idiosyncratic poetic vision of life. His numerous *greguerías* operate on this principle.

Reflecting his rich cultural background, Ramón's works resist strict classification within any one literary paradigm, whilst evincing traits which simultaneously derive from both traditional and modern narrative practice. The author's own commentaries on literary figures such as Quevedo,[8] Lope de Vega,[9] Galdós and even John Ruskin[10] confirm his strong link with the literary tradition at large, a fact which is frequently forgotten in the emphasis by critics on his preoccupation with the avant-garde. His dealings with the world of art betray a similar pattern: despite his friendship with figures such as Picasso, Dalí and Juan Gris, his extensive work on El Greco,[11] Velázquez and Goya[12] is a constant reminder of his rich cultural heritage. Given that Ramón wrote on figures as diverse as Ibsen, Apollinaire, Kafka, Oscar Wilde, Bernard Shaw, Marinetti, Charlie Chaplin, Jean Cocteau and Maruja Mallo (to name but a few), it is difficult to summarise the diverse influences which come to bear on his literary productions.[13] A constant feature of his work is an equal fascination with the old and the new. It is important therefore, both to establish the extent to which his fiction represents a break with pre-existing literary paradigms and at the same time to give due recognition to the persistence in his work of traditional influences.

The key to Ramón's success during the 1920s was his ability to present himself as the key figure of the Spanish avant-garde, whilst simultaneously embodying deeply entrenched Spanish literary sensibilities which he intertwined with his modern subversive aesthetics. It is widely accepted that his work was a defining statement of the direction being taken by literature during the nineteen-twenties, yet, despite the recent interest in his work, his fiction still requires thorough analysis, as much of the recent critical interest has centred on clarifying editorial ambiguities rather than analysing the works themselves.[14]

Given the sheer quantity of novels and short-stories by Ramón, a full analysis of his complete works would run into many volumes. For the purposes of this study, I have therefore decided to limit my commenting to the author's most representative narrative fiction in each decade spanning from his early beginnings in 1909 and his death in Buenos Aires in 1963. I do not claim to provide an exhaustive study of the works produced during this period, but aim to provide an understanding of how his fiction evolved in the context of the European avant-garde, and the extent to which his fiction echoes the big ideas of his time. As the reader will note, considerably more works from the 1920s are analysed to reflect Gómez de la Serna's most productive decade (although not necessarily his best). There is no doubt that Gómez de la Serna's work in a sense championed avant-garde and experimental aesthetics beyond the confines of the 1920s when the novel at large was reverting to a more social-realist style.[15]

Ramón himself gives ample warning of the difficulties facing anyone at-tempting to define and classify his extensive corpus of work. He openly admits to the playful nature of his writing, and constantly plays with the reader's expectations as to what to expect from a novel. In an interview with the French critic Federico Lefève, published in the Parisian journal *Les Nou-velles Littéraires* (1928) and later recorded in his autobiography *Automoribundia*, Ramón states:

> Mi péndulo oscila entre dos polos contradictorios, entre lo evidente y lo inverosímil, entre lo superficial y el abismo, entre lo grosero y lo extraordinario, entre el circo y la muerte. (*AM*, p.805)

The extent to which the author adheres to this and indeed many other self-characterisations can only be ascertained through a close examination of the works themselves. However, although such comments are important, any analysis based exclusively on Ramón's literary self-characterisations would be inadequate. It is all too easy to paper over difficult or contradictory as-pects of his work by appealing directly to his own expressed theories. To arrive at a balanced interpretation it is essential to compare his words with the evidence of the texts themselves. Ramón's theoretical formulations, how-ever, do suggest that he took writing very seriously. This conscious need to define the process of writing does not really accord with the prevailing view that he wrote spontaneously with little care and attention. It is unlikely that someone who had taken the time and effort to write numerous theoretical essays on the nature of creative writing such as 'El concepto de la nueva lit-eratura' (1909), 'Mis siete palabras' (1910), 'Novelismo' (1931) and 'Las palabras y lo indecible' (1934), would not be concerned with the nature of his literary output. Furthermore, it is not a coincidence that what is arguably Ramón's most important work, *El novelista* (1923), clearly takes as its main theme the process of writing itself. In his theoretical writings Ramón argues that even the most unlikely and improbable situations should be included in the novel, as Nature itself is ever-changing and fluctuating. He argues that the novel should break with all traditional constraints and be 'el sitio ideal en que unos cuantos sintamos la libertad'.[16] This contention is based on the idea that it is the duty of the novelist to liberate himself from prejudices through clear, audacious images, in order to escape from what he describes as 'a con-fined and limited world':

> En este mundo en que todo lo que sucede sucede limitado, confinado, en plena asfixia, debía de haber novelas en que la vida estuviese resuelta con mayor amplitud, en mayor libertad de prejuicios, en imágenes audaces y claras.[17]

Far from offering support for the generally held view that Ramón's novels are a fortuitous assemblage of narrative material, his ideas expressed in 'Novelismo' would suggest, to the contrary, that he had thought about the nature and techniques of writing in some depth. It is true to say that many of Ramón's novels give an impression of disjointedness and fragmentation, but there is a strong argument that Ramón was very much aware of what he was doing. For Ramón, writing became the only way through which he could momentarily escape from the limitations of society, a way of making sense of existence itself. This may to some extent account for Ramón's day-to-day lifestyle, isolated from society and keeping unsociable hours writing through the night. As with his alter-ego in *El novelista* (1923) Andrés Castilla, the line between literature and existence was one which was to become extremely blurred and difficult to distinguish.

In addition to any light which might be shed on his works by his theoretical views on writing, Ramón's esoteric and bohemian life-style provide us with a picture of the man himself. In the already mentioned interview with Federico Lefève, Gómez de la Serna tells of how he installed a street lamp in his study. This anecdote is highly revealing of the complex relationship of the writer with his surrounding world: on the one hand he deliberately attempts to break with realist and naturalist aesthetics, on the other he betrays a deeply entrenched love for *costumbrista*-like detail. Poet Luis Cernuda argues that:

> Gómez de la Serna, quizá por ser el último gran escritor en rango de importancia de nuestros grandes clásicos, como Lope o Quevedo, es un realista. Quiero decir que el mundo donde su fantasía se mueve es el de la realidad material inmediata, mundo al que además juzga bien hecho tal como está, tanto desde el punto de vista estatal como desde el provincialista; y aunque lo transforme a su antojo respeta siempre sus límites establecidos, que van de lo posible a lo monstruoso, pero se detienen ante lo imposible y lo imaginario. [18]

Gómez de la Serna does not hide away in a world of complete abstraction and unrestrained fantasy, but on more than one occasion he reminds the reader that much of his inspiration derives from observing the flux of life in the streets, and is prepared to set up a street lamp in his study to bring an element of street life into the space where he spent the nights writing:

> Para trabajar, me es necesaria la calle; necesito en cierto modo trabajar en la calle...Pero no salgo más que los sábados... ¿Cómo iba a arreglármelas? De pronto tuve una idea genial: si tuviese un farol de gas en mi torreón, no necesitaría ya ir a la calle. Me costó mucho trabajo realizar mi proyecto. Los accionistas de la compañía de gas se empeñaban en no comprender. El caso no estaba previsto en el Reglamento. Pude triunfar al fin. Mi proyecto realmente podía parecer incongruente

a aquellos burgueses, aunque les hubiera sido difícil demostrar su 'inmoralidad'. Por
eso desde entonces escribo en mi despacho, que es bastante espacioso, a la luz de un
auténtico farol. Como todos los faroles madrileños, indica hasta la calle. La calle
Ramón. (*AM*, p.807)

The presence of the gas lamp in his study is a useful image to better understand the principles behind his writing as a whole. Objects of the real
world are removed from their usual sphere of use, and brought into a highly
stylised setting, where they acquire aesthetic value.[19] The new setting (the
author's study) creates a false impression of a street, a street of imaginary
qualities, enabling the author to extol the virtues of a stylised and artistic existence. His day-to-day lifestyle is that of a man devoted to literature. The
immediate surroundings of his study thus reveal a fascination with finding
new combinations of elements taken from the everyday world.

Many of his novels depict characters who share similar traits with the author, and are undoubtedly inspired by incidents and experiences in his own
life. There are no simple formulas to explain Ramón's work, and many questions still remain as to why he has remained such an enigmatic figure for so
many years, despite unequivocal endorsement from eminent writers and critics alike.

The success and influence Ramón enjoyed in the twenties and early thirties subsequently went into decline; a loss of interest caused in part by the
increasing politicisation of literature in Spain, compounded by the self-
imposed exile of the author to Argentina until his death in 1963. Nevertheless, the long-standing view that Ramón Gómez de la Serna's work suffers
from critical neglect has been challenged by the relatively recent resurgence
of interest in his narrative fiction.[20] The recent re-edition of his complete
works clearly attests a desire to unearth and explore one of the most elusive
and misunderstood authors of twentieth-century Spain, an enterprise which
will, and has already started to open up new critical insights into his works.

A brief overview of the critical reception of Ramón Gómez de la Serna's
work is both useful and enlightening prior to embarking on a close analysis
of the novels themselves. According to Julio Cortázar, one of the most respected Hispanic writers of the twentieth century, Ramón Gómez de la Serna
deserves to be placed: 'en lo más alto de nuestras letras hispanas',[21] a judgement borne out by Octavio Paz, whose well-known admiration for Ramón
and belief that he was one of the greatest Spanish authors of all times, has
been cited on many occasions. Writers such as Pablo Neruda, Azorín and
Ortega y Gasset not only admired Ramón's work, but were proud to consider
themselves his personal friends. Other of his contemporaries, such as Ben-
jamín Jarnés, stated that his narrative prose was the writing of the future,

whilst Borges compared him to Whitman and added that only the Renaissance could have produced an author of similar gifts. Waldo Frank compared him to Proust, whilst the poet Pedro Salinas greatly admired him and argued that his writing represented a kind of 'anti-creación'.[22] Other contemporary figures such as Cansinos Assens, Guillermo de Torre and José Bergamín, despite any ideological differences they might have had with Ramón, recognised his central importance to the literary scene of the day.

The endorsement he received from his peers prior to 1936 stands in stark contrast to the largely indifferent reception of his works thereafter, although it is true that the anniversaries both of his birth and his death gave rise to numerous articles and reviews, which despite centring on general aspects of his life and works, are nonetheless enlightening and useful. Establishing an adequate critical perspective, however, is no easy task. In addition to the very favourable reception of his work by most of his contemporaries; a number of subsequent critics and commentators have enthusiastically endorsed the quality of his writing (Gaspar Gómez de la Serna, Cardona, Camón Aznar, Granjel, Ponce, Nora). All of these authors—with the exception of Rodolfo Cardona, who continues to publish articles and re-editions of Ramón Gómez de la Serna's works—were the main standard bearers for the author's work during a period of relative neglect which lasted until the late seventies. During the last two decades there has been a noticeable revival of interest in Ramón's work, although this has mostly taken the form of articles, reviews and critical editions rather than full-length studies. Important names in this last group include Ricardo Senabre (1967, 1988), Alan Hoyle (1972, 1988, 1996, 2001, 2004), José Carlos Mainer (1975, 1988), Francisco Umbral (1978, 1988), García de la Concha (1984), Nigel Dennis (1988), Carolyn Richmond (1988), Antonio del Rey Briones (1988, 1992), Amancio Sabugo Abril (1988), whilst Derek Harris (1995, 1996) has placed the avant-garde as a whole in context. The list of critical articles is too extensive to comment on here. As well as the continuing work of such figures, numerous isolated contributions to Ramonian studies have also appeared in recent years.

One way of achieving a coherent overview of the different critical approaches to Ramón's work over the years is to divide it into the comments on his work prior to 1936, the relatively scarce work carried out between 1936 and the late seventies, and the recent resurgence of interest in his work over the last two decades, during which numerous critical articles, reviews, books, re-editions of his works and theses have appeared. A brief and selective summary of the critical attention his work has received is necessary before going on to analysing the works themselves.

The corpus of critical studies carried out in the period up to the nineteeneighties starts with Rodolfo Cardona's pioneering study (1957),[23] setting out,

for the first time in the English language, an analysis of the main aspects of
Gómez de la Serna's work placed in the context of the vanguard movements
of the day. He confesses that his first encounter with the work of Ramón
Gómez de la Serna was 'one of the greatest revelations' he had had in the
field of Spanish literature.[24] He links Ramón's works to aspects of cubism,
Dada, surrealism and even expressionism, whilst highlighting Ramón's
deeply entrenched *españolismo*. Due to the broadly-conceived scope of this
work and the formidable extent of the opus to be covered, Cardona's commentaries on individual novels, although perceptive, are understandably con-
cise in nature, whilst the short stories are not examined at all.

Several years after Cardona's ground-breaking work, Luis Granjel
(1963)[25] produced an informative synopsis of Ramón's novels, outlining the
main features of his idiosyncratic style in a chapter entitled *Ramonismo*,
whilst painting a useful picture of Ramón's social milieu. Less rigorously
analytical than Cardona's work, Granjel's study undoubtedly served to popu-
larise Ramón's work and introduce it to a wider audience. Gaspar Gómez de
la Serna (1963)[26] makes good use of his privileged position as cousin of the
author to provide an insightful account of the life and works, with a predicta-
bly heavy dose of biographical detail. Fernando Ponce's (1968)[27] sketch of
Ramón's work, broadly covers the same issues as Granjel and Gaspar, adding
little new in the way of critical analysis. Both Camón Aznar (1972)[28] and
Eugenio de Nora (1973)[29] produced substantial works on Ramón, but any
attempt to cover Ramón Gómez de la Serna's work in its entirety runs the
risk of allowing only limited analysis of each work, and it cannot be honestly
claimed that these studies manage to overcome this problem. Camón Aznar
provides an overview of Ramón's biographical details and broad stylistic
traits. Nora, ambitious in his attempt to cover the whole range of Ramón's
work, argues that his narrative method had serious limitations, amounting to
what he believed to be little more than 'un escamoteo de la realidad'. He
criticises the absence of character-psychology in the novels, and the general
lack of social commentary on the Spain of the day. However, Nora fails to
give Ramón credit for his complex notion of literature, and makes little attempt to consider the ways in which he compensated for the attenuation of
character-psychology and lack of a social dimension.

In addition to the monographic studies of this period, we find a considerable number of articles by eminent authors and critics devoted to aspects of
Ramón's life. It is not strictly necessary at this stage to focus in such detail
on this growing corpus of articles and press cuttings. While many of the
shorter centenary articles are useful in that they give some attention to the
various features of Gómez de la Serna's work, they do not give an in-depth
account. Furthermore, many of these articles repeat well-worn clichés about

the author rather than opening up new critical perspectives. They merely serve the purpose of introducing Ramón as an author, whilst highlighting his ongoing influence on the Spanish literary scene.

The centrality of Gómez de la Serna's writing to the avant-garde enterprise has been emphasised by numerous critics. Frenk, Perrian and Thompson, for instance, state that Ramon's writings are a 'key site for the avant-garde adventure'.[30] Whilst there can be little doubt that the importance of Gómez de la Serna in bringing the perspectives and techniques of the avant-garde to Spain, his works remain somewhat of an enigma to most readers. Many of Ramón's novels draw on aspects of the cosmopolitan modern age, without renouncing the profound influence of Madrid and the traditional images of Spain and her landscape. This apparent contradiction lies at the heart of much of Ramón's work, and is essential to understanding it. Ramón, many years later compared writing to 'una esponja',[31] a useful analogy to bear in mind when considering the syncretic nature of his literary style, which although was used with specific reference to his surrealist prose, nonetheless helps shed light on his early fiction and the multi-layered approach he adopts, not least in arguably his most important 1920s work *El novelista* (1923). In many of his works imagery is drawn from the world of sport, cinema and technology in an attempt to shake off images which had become associated with outdated romantic or realist literary paradigms. Many of his *greguerías* attest a new fragmented perception of the world, in line with the modernist vision at large. In Ramón's fiction the world is presented as broken into its essential components, and new relationships between objects are established through a mixture of poetic imagination and humour. In Gómez de la Serna's own theoretical formulations writing is defined as a process which constantly challenges conventional notions of what to expect from a novel: 'Hay que agitar la vida, mezclarla con verosimilitud a circunstancias inverosímiles e inconvencionales'.[32]

The avant-garde side of Gómez de la Serna, represents, however, only one facet of his work. It is significant that he himself stated 'Somos del pasado más que el porvenir', an attitude which is strongly evident in much of his fiction.[33] There is no doubt he attempted to present an avant-garde persona (his notorious lectures from a trapeze and the top of an elephant are cases in point) in an attempt to identify himself with the new. His Saturday night *tertulias* in the 'Pombo' crypt were to become 'el promotor de lo nuevo', attracting eminent figures such as Borges, Picasso and Neruda over the years.[34] Analogous to the sentiments which had fuelled Dada during its early days at Café Voltaire, the atmosphere of *Pombo* was largely a response to a general sense of emptiness and ambiguity:

En el ambiente incorruptible de Pombo, rodeados del vacío absoluto, nos damos más absoluta cuenta de este ardite vivo que la intemperancia de lo social—inorgánico, ambiguo, inhumano—sume más en nosotros y nos lo hace asumir más. (p.226)

During the First World War Gómez de la Serna had visited many European capitals, and in a letter to *Pombo* he denounced the war and argued for Spain's continued neutrality. He talks of 'esos viajes tristes y llenos de obstáculos por la Europa sombría',[35] conveying a sense of the pervasive absurdity of the war, a mood which in part fuelled the reactionary cast of mind prevalent in the nineteen-twenties. Gómez de la Serna's journeys through Europe are significant not only for introducing him to the various art movements of the day, but also for persuading him to share in a general mood (expressed most forcibly by the Dadaists) of despair at the instrumental-rationalist view as a way of explaining the world, and a tendency to replace it with absurdity. Gómez de la Serna's avant-garde playfulness has to be understood in this context as a desire to promote optimism in the face of uncertainty and all-pervasive emptiness. The influence of these two moods is very evident in much of his fiction. Whilst many of his characters inhabit a world where human pain and suffering is largely ignored, they seldom manage to shake off the sombre side of life, although this is never dealt with in an existentialist manner. Whilst much of Gómez de la Serna's fiction is in tune with themes of Ortega y Gasset's *La deshumanización del arte* (1925) in its rejection of human emotion, it still reflects, at least in part, Ramón's personal fears about life, his sense of the loneliness of living in a big city, his suspicious attitude to women, and the tendency of his rambling imagination to transform the immediate world around him. This fusion of avant-garde playfulness with personal angst, accounts, to some extent, for the instability of mood and the combination of optimism, with a foreboding sense of death in many of Ramón's novels.

Gómez de la Serna himself dates his first real contact with the avant-garde to the year 1911, whilst he was living in Paris. It was at this time that he came into contact with the first European avant-garde movements, most notably through the exhibition at the 'Salon des Independents'.[36] Amongst others, Marcel Duchamp exhibited some of his early work here together with Picasso and other cubist artists. This initial contact with the avant-garde was to prove central to his own aesthetic *modus operandus*. In 1909 Gómez de la Serna translated Marinetti's futurist manifesto into Spanish, and some years later he organised the first exhibition of cubist art in Spain in 1915, entitled 'Exposición de los íntegros',[37] a venture which was in itself further evidence of his pivotal role in bringing the avant-garde to Spain.

The nature of Ramon's avant-gardism cannot be fully understood without reference to his ideas expressed in *Ismos* (1931), a work in which he explores different schools of thought—some of them of his own invention—which must be taken into account in order to make sense of his fiction. It is significant that Apollinaire and Picasso feature strongly. He devotes large sections of *Ismos* to these two figures, openly admitting their influence on his own approach. His interest in both would suggest the importance he placed on intellectual concept over emotion, on fragmentation over narrative integrity, and for the tangible world of objects which is central to their works. His admiration for Apollinaire also stemmed from the way in which the French writer combined both modern and old, a trait equally recurrent and just as central in his work. For instance, he considers that Apollinaire's narratives 'tienen, al mismo tiempo que su vorágine modernísima, una sombra de relatos medievales'.[38] One of the features of Gómez de la Serna's work which most forcibly strikes the reader is precisely this duality. The importance placed by Apollinaire on what he termed 'concept over imitation' was indeed part of the modernist attempt to shake off nineteenth century aesthetics—an objective pursued by Ramón also. But it is not only Apollinaire who is mentioned in *Ismos*, Ramón also writes about his friendship with Marinetti, expressing interest in the futuristic dances advocated by the Italian: the 'shrapnel' dance or 'la bailarina del aeroplano'. The inclusion of this material reveals Ramón's familiarity with the major trends of the avant-garde. Ramón's interest in simultaneism (a crucial development for understanding the formal changes of the novel at this time) is confirmed in the chapter 'Simultanismo'. He recounts his visits to the home of Robert and Sonia Delaunay, who resided in Madrid between 1917 and 1921 and became good friends of his. The Delaunays were friends with Huidobro, and had worked with Apollinaire and other poets such as Blaise Cendrars, exploring the influences of the plastic arts on poetry, which is why they were also well known to the Spanish ultraist poets of the day. References to Charlie Chaplin, Cocteau and extensive passages on Picasso's cubism clearly confirm Ramón's interest in diverse strands of the avant-garde. His notion of humour—perceptively analysed by Hoyle—underlines the importance of avant-garde humour in challenging the preconceived values of the world and the need to rearrange things according to new hierarchies. Alan Hoyle states:

> No se trata de la clásica risa de comedia, ni de la sátira social, ni de la agudeza metafísica del barroco, ni de la ironía romántica, ni del famoso y civilizado humor inglés, sino que se trata de un nuevo tipo de humor que desarrolla la vanguardia como forma de ruptura del sistema, como arma para rebelarse contra la sociedad convencional y para crear un nuevo punto de vista de minoría avanzada para minar, y de alguna manera transformar, la realidad que vive la gran mayoría de la gente.[39]

However, it is significant that Ramón claimed considerable importance of individual movements such as *maquinismo, luminismo, klaxonismo, jazz-bandismo* over and above any one all-encompassing theory. By creating and drawing attention to a variety of movements, Ramón is asserting the efficacy of the part over the whole, of the importance of a fragmented rather than organic vision of the world. It is essential to give due importance to this viewpoint if we are to understand his aesthetics. Nigel Dennis argues that Gómez de la Serna tended to 'deconstruct', moving 'insistently away from wholeness towards the isolated, self-contained fragment'. Dennis attributes this tendency to the author's journalism, and goes on to argue that his writing 'assumes the provisional, unfinished form of a rough copy: an endlessly extended and extensible preliminary text that he is forever unable to revise and polish and prepare adequately for publication'.[40]

Much of Gómez de la Serna's literary renewal lies in his ability to write poetically and humorously about almost any kind of object, in an attempt to demonstrate that the artist need not be influenced by traditionally established subjects, but can make poetry out of anti-poetic themes.[41] Anthony Leo Geist argues that 'Los elementos de la nueva poesía concuerdan en una orientación hacia el objeto',[42] in a direct attempt to renounce images which had become clothed in a particular sensibility or style. This ethos, in part, accounts for the *ultraist* poets, who attempted to create a literary world governed by its own internal laws, with no need to take account of ethical, moral or political issues:

El Ultraísmo deseaba más que ir simplemente más allá; también quería crear ultra-objetos, inventar poemas y mundos más allá de la realidad inmediata. Por eso Ortega celebra el hallazgo de la palabra ultra.[43]

However, any attempt to create a kind of literature completely cut off from the outside world is an impossible venture, and doomed to failure. The 'purity' of form which both the *creacionistas* and the *ultraists* sought, should rather be understood in the sense of an attempt to write poetry which was no longer premised on the need to transmit a particular ideology or feeling, but which existed in its own right, needing no justifying motive.[44] Guillermo de Torre's ultraist manifesto 'Estética del yoísmo ultraísta'[45] captures this mood of a world which exists purely for the individual:

El óvulo de mí mismo.
    El circuito de mí mismo.Yo soy:
    Y el vértice de mí mismo.
    En el umbral de la gesta constructiva que inicia el Ultraísmo potencial Yo afirmo: la alta jerarquía y la calidad insustituible del Yoísmo: Y su preponderancia

eterna sobre las restantes virtudes espirituales de las personalidades subversivas e innovadoras.[46]

The stark individualism so characteristic of this epoch was born from a mixture of Nietzsche's philosophy and a desire to explore the inner recesses of the mind in the wake of Freudian theories of the unconscious and Dadaist automatism. Literature was no longer to derive from external forces, nor should it replicate nature in any way. The obsessive interest in man-made machinery in much of *ultraist* poetry, was included in an attempt to eschew all transcendentalism, spirituality and sentimentality.[47] As Geist states:

La ausencia del sentimentalismo en esta literatura no responde a una aversión por la emoción en sí, sino a la firme creencia de que la experiencia estética es principalmente intelectual.[48]

Although Gómez de la Serna rejected any association with ultraism, his work bears similarities to some of the characteristics of this movement, sharing many affinities at various levels, most notably in the attenuation of anecdote and its replacement with poetic imagery. However, the elimination of anecdote and the importance of concept over emotion, had already been advocated by the cubists, almost a decade before ultraism emerged as a movement. Cansinos Assens himself recognised the important link between cubism and Gómez de la Serna's work when he observed:

Ramón Gómez de la Serna vuelve a encenderse una nueva antorcha de entusiasmo puro y a manifestarse una nueva voluntad de arte [...] Su obra literaria se corresponde con las nuevas tendencias pictóricas de cubistas e integrales. Es algo que supera ya nuestra más alta ambición estética y hasta podría decirse nuestra más amplia facultad de comprender. Es una obra verdaderamente pánica, de cuyo afán de representación nada queda excluído y en que ningún aspecto de las cosas es olvidado por el artista.[49]

This formulation is analogous to Huidobro's characterisation of poetry:

Crear un poema tomando a la vida sus motivos y transformándolos para darles una vida nueva e independiente. Nada de anecdótico ni descriptivo. La emoción ha de nacer de la única virtud creadora.[50]

Although it is easier to attenuate narrative in poetry, many of Gómez de la Serna's novels rely in a similar way on attenuation of narrative and of plot causality, in a direct attempt to break with traditional literary practice. The widespread feeling among intellectuals that art and literature should undergo radical change, geared to the appreciation of an enlightened minority in order to escape from the populism of realism and romanticism, is undoubtedly present in Gómez de la Serna's work. The elitism attached to modern art is clearly evident in Ortega y Gasset's *La deshumanización del arte*, which depicts modern art moving towards a 'dehumanised' form, where the human elements are replaced by concept and ideas, and a heavily stylised expression. Ortega provides a good example of the conceptual nature of modern art, remarking that whenever painters are commissioned to paint a portrait, they always paint their subjects' physical appearance. However, Ortega argues that it would be more appropriate to portray the person's ideas. This is, of course, by no means new: the importance accorded to ideas over reality itself is in some ways reminiscent of Platonism.

Before going on in a little more detail about the influences on Ramón's work it might be useful to look at his first novel. As with all experimental fiction, reminded to us by Max Jacob:

> El arte muy moderno deja de serlo cuando el que lo hace comienza a comprenderlo, cuando aquellos que podrían comprenderlo y los que lo han comprendido aspiran a un arte que jamás comprenderán.[51]

La viuda blanca y negra *(1917)*

Ramón Gómez de la Serna's narrative fiction cannot be reduced to a neat historical scheme. The numerous novels and short stories written after the publication of his first short story *El Ruso* in 1913, vary not only in terms of theme, but also in the extent to which they are influenced and shaped by contemporary developments in the world of science, art and literature. Both permeable to the new aesthetic influences of the day, and yet rooted in the Spanish literary tradition, Ramón's work is difficult to classify and can be easily misunderstood. Simply viewing him as an avant-garde innovator would prevent understanding his work within the greater context of its literary precedents, and would ignore his complexity as an author. The fact that he does not sit comfortably with any particular literary generation be it that of 1898, 1914 or 1927, highlights the problem with subsuming authors under a particular literary movement or generation. Their work runs the risk of being approached with certain preconditions and the reader is predisposed to look out for certain traits and common stylistic trends, often resulting in an artificial understanding of an author's work as a whole.

The decision to focus on this seminal work, stems from the need to address the question of how Ramón Gómez de la Serna evolved as a writer, and to what extent his early work sets a precedent in terms of style and theme for his later works. To answer this question *La viuda blanca y negra* (1917)[52] needs to be considered as it represents the author's fiction at its birth. The date of publication is of interest, not least because it precedes influential movements and schools of thought which were to leave their mark on much of Ramón's work during the nineteen-twenties, even if its actual publication date is as late as 1921, as suggested in Zlotescu's *Obras Completas*. Whatever the date, it nonetheless represents the first serious attempt by Gómez de la Serna to produce a novel, as *El doctor inverosímil* (which first emerged in embryonic form in 1914) is more akin to a humorous experimental and essayistic depiction of the medical profession.

At first sight the style of *La viuda blanca y negra*[53] is cautious rather than experimental. The narrative structure is largely conventional, with a heavy reliance on plot and story, and although the technique of the *greguería* is not absent, by no means does it constitute the basic recourse of the narrative. Whilst this novel is not experimental to the same degree as many of Ramón's later works are, it foreshadows similar traits and themes which were to become central to much of his fiction: his erotic fantasizing about women, the use of objects as the starting point for the aesthetic digressions of the characters within the narrative, the theme of obsessive love, the importance of urban spaces, and the pervasive sense of death. At the same time there is little attempt to address socio-political problems, despite the turbulent years in which these works were written, a trait which was to characterise Ramón's work throughout the nineteen-twenties and eventually contribute to the decline of interest in his works, when, towards the end of the decade, many of the 1927 Generation of writers reverted to relatively realistic forms of writing. Certainly in theme *La viuda blanca y negra* foreshadows much of what was to follow in later years, whilst the relatively conventional style of its narrative was to gradually disappear.

Prior to the publication of this novel Ramón had already written numerous *greguerías*. The poetic and humorous deconstruction of the world brought about by these short fragmentary constructs undoubtedly permeated his fiction from early stages, breaking with traditional narrative conventions through an imagistic prose, although in *La viuda blanca y negra* they do not truncate the flow of Ramón's prose to the same extent as they do in later novels. Ramón's use of the *greguería* is, in part, an attempt to bring about a lyrical transformation of the world coupled with avant-garde humour and a re-ordering of moral and aesthetic hierarchies. He deploys the *greguería* to create a provisional rather than a stable literary form, in keeping with the tendency of modernist fiction to reject realist and naturalist aesthetics.

La viuda blanca y negra is set in Madrid, although Paris also features towards the end, and it depicts the obsession of a male protagonist with a woman, described largely in aesthetic terms through colour rather than with any in-depth exploration of character. Much of the narrative follows the protagonist as he seeks some form of companionship in a sensual and erotically charged world, where more importance is placed on the mechanisms of perception than on reality itself. The picture of the world which emerges is one made up of transient sensations, where human relationships are shown to be problematic and ephemeral.

The critical attention this novel has received can be summarised briefly. Cardona claims that this novel 'evinces' many 'surrealist traits'. His main premise is that there is a 'mysterious veil' enveloping Rodrigo's and Cristina's lives, 'the constant presence of the supposedly dead husband', Cristina's 'aloofness' and 'masochism'. He compares *La viuda blanca y negra* to André Breton's *Nadja*, published a decade later when surrealism was well established as a movement, although Ramón does not employ the use of characteristic surrealist trends such as automatic writing, or the untrammelled promotion of disjointed images. However Cardona re-examines this novel more than thirty years later, in his introduction to the 1988 Cátedra edition, arguing that *La viuda blanca y negra* requires several readings at different levels, as it lends itself to different interpretations. In his first reading, Cardona examines it in conjunction with Ramon's autobiography and links it to *El ruso*. He considers *La viuda blanca y negra* to be a reflection of Ramón's relationship with the author and suffragist Carmen de Burgos. In his second reading, his analysis centres on how the city of Madrid is portrayed, and points to the paradox which was to affect Ramon's nineteen-twenties fiction at large, that despite its avant-gardism, the novel is rooted in Madrid: a real city with which the author had strong emotional ties. The third reading deals with the themes of love and death in the novel, arguing that Cristina is a 'medio ser', in that she hides the other side of herself, namely the existence of her husband. Antonio del Rey Briones's draws attention to its 'denso eroticismo' and accuses it of 'falta de agilidad narrativa', whilst Camón Aznar comments on its sensual theme, and highlights its lack of plot and failure to engage the reader on an emotional level: 'No hay trama, no hay interés argumental, no hay emoción diluida en episodios laterales'. He goes on to argue, in my view erroneously, that it is very different in style to other works of his: 'Digamos que su estética es precisamente la contraria de la habitual: la persistencia en el mismo tema, la monotonía como fórmula expresiva, el agotamiento de una situación cuya persistencia le presta interés alucinante'. The similarities to other works of his in terms of themes and plot are not mentioned, and the novel itself is not examined in any depth at all. Iona Zlotescu cites Jean Cassou's vision of the novel, arguing that *La viuda blanca y negra* represents 'Une étude qui a rarément été tenté avec autant de précision et de ferveur'.

La viuda blanca y negra narrates of how the protagonist 'Rodrigo' is attracted to a woman by the name of 'Cristina', whom he sees for the first time at a church mass marking the tenth anniversary of a deceased relative of his. Her black garments which contrast with her pale complexion bestow her the title of 'la viuda blanca y negra', and there is no doubt initially in Rodrigo's mind that she is a widow, and therefore free from the constraints of marriage. The exploration of human relations was to become a familiar theme in Ramón's work, but in this novel interest is sustained through the obsessive psychology of the main character Rodrigo and the exploration of space as a way of compensating for lack of action. With a slow pace and heavy reliance on sensual and erotic descriptions of Cristina, the novel deals with the familiar themes of obsessive love, jealousy and transient relationships; playing with the traditional themes of 'engaño' and 'desengaño'.

In one sense it constitutes a prime example of a character-novel, in that events in the story are clearly a result of the main character's thoughts and actions. Outward situations and incidents do not drive the plot forward or change the characters in any way. Instead, the slow pace of the narrative, digressive in its incursions into Rodrigo's erotic obsessions, imbues the novel with a heavily charged atmosphere described by Ramón himself in *Automoribundia* where he describes how he wrote it: 'Escrita en el verano madrileño con la obsesión del crimen, los celos y el aire trasnochador y verbenero'.[54]

However, Rodrigo's jealousy and obsession with Cristina's apparently dead husband is not entirely ill-founded. His suspicion of her leads him to eaves-drop on a conversation Cristina has with the 'portera', where he learns that her husband is in fact alive. With the realisation of her deceitfulness (the 'desengaño' referred to earlier) his idea of Cristina changes completely: 'Le pareció que su traje era rojo en vez de negro, y su blancura no era blancura, sino lividez de mentirosa' (p.111). She is presented exclusively through the subjective mind of Rodrigo. His fear and paranoia is fuelled by an ominous story in the press recounting how a judge in Madrid had killed his wife and her lover after having discovered that he had been cuckolded. Suspicion and suspense is further fuelled when the husband of Cristina enters the house one afternoon, and enigmatically leaves a mask on the table, only to depart. Following this event, Rodrigo, in part through hearsay and in part through his direct conversations with Cristina, begins to piece together the various pieces of information regarding Cristina's mysterious relationship with her husband, suspecting violence and consensual sado-masochistic practices. Much of the remainder of the work evokes the heavily charged atmosphere of Rodrigo's world, his walks at night, and his fear that at any time Cristina's husband would return and seek revenge. After a trip to Paris with Cristina in an at-

tempt to get away from Madrid to a city where they would have some degree
of anonymity, the remaining chapters consist of conversations between Rodrigo and Cristina after they return to Madrid, culminating in Rodrigo's final
departure, marking the end of the furtive and ephemeral relationship in what
would become a familiar ending of many of Ramón's later works.

La viuda blanca y negra evokes Rodrigo's sensual appetite for Cristina,
whilst the religious imagery, colour and the poetic style of language draw
attention to the beauty of language itself. The way in which experience and
perception are conveyed acquires more importance than the plot itself. Despite its marked divergence from realist literature, there is, compared to
Ramón's later novels, a general lack of experimentalism, and certainly less of
an avant-garde feel to the work. Light, and the symbolic use of colour and
space are prominent: the shafts of sunlight illuminating the darkness of the
church, the description of the confessionals ingeniously described as shadows 'llena de pecados estancados, con telarañas negras en los rincones en
los que trabajaba la araña del pecado...' (p.80), and the resplendent face of
Cristina, which contrasts with the sombre surroundings. Much of Rodrigo's
erotic fascination with Cristina is couched in an aesthetic appreciation and
description of her beauty. At the beginning of the novel when he sees Cristina in the church he describes her pallid complexion in the following
flattering terms: 'La blancura de usted pone el día como una de esas lunas de
la mañana que se atreven con el sol' (p.84). At every stage in the novel there
is a heavy reliance on description which slows down the pace of the narrative
in what was going to be a recurrent trait in much of Ramón's fiction. At one
juncture, her voice is described as 'aquel kaleidoscopio de sonidos de distinto
color que se rompía en cada palabra que pronunciaba' (p.197). Cristina is a
poetic creation removed from the plane of the everyday, and as such, is ultimately unattainable.

The poetic descriptions of Cristina set a precedent for numerous female
characters in later works. Cristina is not drawn from life, but is a product of
aesthetic creation. She is not framed in a social context; the reader knows
little of her origin or family background. She herself never discloses any information which reveals anything about her. She is the first of many
Ramonian female characters who embody an aesthetic and erotic ideal. The
very titles of many of Ramón's later novels suggest the aestheticization of
the female character. Lucía is described as 'La mujer de ámbar' in the novel
of that title because the tone of her skin resembles the lava flowing down
from Mount Vesuvius. The central figure of *La nardo* (1930) Aurelia is
known as 'la nardo' because her white complexion resembles the spikenard
flower evoked in the title. Colour is used expressionistically, in that it does
not necessarily represent the natural complexion of a character, but conveys a

certain mood or feeling. This is one of the many ways in which the author departs from realist aesthetics in favour of aestheticism, creating a fictional world according to his artistic ideas. The obsessive behaviour of the male character Rodrigo also sets a precedent for the male characters, encountered in numerous short stories and novels written by Ramón in later years. His obsession stems from an irrational jealousy of others. Rodrigo is not only jealous of Cristina's ex-husband, but of unknown men sitting in cafés and even of Cristina's own brother. The surroundings and atmosphere are shaped by his feelings, and to depict them becomes a standard way of expressing the characters' emotions. On one occasion when he sees a man sitting in the drawing room of Cristina's house, the space of the house itself becomes the most important element: '¡Que pronto se vuelven contra uno toda una casa! pensaba Rodrigo. Todo había dejado de ser de él, todo le era hostil, todo lo que le encubría hacía unas horas.' (p.63). Rodrigo is imprisoned by his own obsession, irresistibly attracted to the secretive and shadowy world in which Cristina lives. Bewitched by the furtiveness of Cristina, his surrounding world closes in around him. Little is said about other characters in other places, and virtually all of the narrative takes place in the mind of the pro-tagonist. This pattern of the lonely individual consumed by human passions is repeated in much of Ramón's fiction. Rodrigo's world is a self-reflecting one, made up of confusing images which combine to convey a sense of mys-tery, clearly seen in a passage which describes Cristina's house:

> Y la casa tenía grandes espejos como una casa puesta a la antigua, con un gusto un poco viejo. Le molestaba hasta verla venir hacia él desde el fondo del espejo, cuando estaba sentado ante el gran espejo colocado frente a la puerta; le parecía que ella venía del pasado, de otra habitación que no correspondía con la puerta verdadera, sino con otra más pequeña y de intimidad más estrecha. (p.135)

The underlying preoccupation with perception lies at the heart of much of the author's fiction, and is in keeping with the wider tenets of modernism at large, and the difficulty with viewing the world from an objective view-point. The mechanisms of perception become as important as what is being observed. This approach anticipates the technique of later novels such as *El secreto del acueducto* (1922) and *La mujer de ámbar* (1927).

The obsession of Ramón's characters with perception, transforming the immediate landscape into an unstable construction of myriad images allows the author to remain within his narrative material, at the cost of moving away from history.

Although *La viuda blanca y negra* is not experimental to any great de-gree, there are episodes which display incongruity, hints that are to be fully realised in the later novel *El incongruente* (1922). Although Rodrigo is

driven by obsession and jealousy rather than by serendipity and chance, some
of the characters he meets reveal Gómez de la Serna's penchant for quirky
and incongruous personalities whose behaviour borders on insanity compounded with Dadaist absurdity. One night, when Rodrigo is sitting outside a
café, he meets the highly elusive Alberto. His speech is a toned-down forerunner of the absurdist speeches found in later novels such as *El
incongruente* (1922) and *Cinelandia* (1923): '—Yo creo—decía Alberto—
que en estas noches que se quedan un poco frescas andamos por las
alcantarillas de la vida, por el fondo de las catacumbas' (p.186). His way of
talking is symptomatic of a gradual departure from rationality. After a brief
conversation between Alberto and Rodrigo, the narrator informs the reader:

> Se fueron muy simpáticos y cuando todos se separaron aquella madrugada, ellos
> solos se quedaron unidos y comenzaron a seguir un rumbo incongruente que iba a
> dar a los desmontes de la incongruencia. (p.186)

Whilst in later works, incongruity not only governs characters' actions
but sets the pace of the narrative itself, in *La viuda blanca y negra* it plays
only a limited role. The lack of development of this theme leaves many questions in the reader's mind. Alberto is little more than a fleeting presence,
removed from the central sphere of Cristina and Rodrigo's relationship, but
significant nonetheless for having something of the avant-garde character
who wanders alone, in an open-ended existence of chance encounters, detached from history and unconcerned by ideology. *La viuda blanca y negra* is
a mere precursor, if an important one, of later treatments of this motif, whilst
retaining a fairly straight-forward narrative style. It fuses the idealised erotic
fantasies of the main character with the author's own experience of life itself—his sojourn in Paris, his jealousy and aesthetic depiction of women. In
this sense, it is central to the author's development as a writer. Its highly
charged prose would re-emerge in later works: the lyrical transformation of
landscape and characters as a way of evading the harsh reality of the everyday world and escape to an idealised literary fantasy. There are signs of a
new approach to writing, rejecting symbolism in favour of a renewed exploration of metaphor and imagery, to some extent removed from 1898 angst
and yet not fully integrated into the world of avant-garde aesthetics. *La viuda
blanca y negra*, resisting strict classification, occupies a position between
aestheticism and the avant-garde, and looks forward to some central concepts
of Ramón's work in the nineteen-twenties.

The closing lines of *La viuda blanca y negra* depict Rodrigo as a man
who has lost all hope and has nothing left, and therefore decides to leave.

This was to become a familiar ending to many of the author's later novels. The process of 'desengaño' has reached its culmination:

> Y de pronto, raudo como un ladrón, echó a correr y se sintió en la calle, sin nada, vacío, deshecho, viudo de sí mismo, todo perdido...pero libre [...] Y Rodrigo se fue a su casa como el muerto que, a raíz de su muerte, comienza a ver el mundo de una manera muy distinta. (p.290, 91)

Thematically, the ending of *La viuda blanca y negra* is a blueprint for later novels in that it depicts a protagonist who searches for companionship as a way of giving his existence some meaning in an ever-changing and unstable world. The central character, the recurrent 'hombre perdido', was to become the protagonist of Gómez de la Serna's most important 1940s novel which deals with this same theme but in a much more existential way, more than twenty-five years later in the novel entitled *El hombre perdido* (1947).

Notes

1 I use 'modernist' in the Anglo-American sense of the term, i.e. literature written broadly between the turn of the century and WWII which is characterised by a breaking away from established norms and conventions, heavily relying on experimentation. This is to be distinguished from the Hispanic term *modernismo*, the movement closely associated with Nicaraguan Poet Rubén Darío, and arguably more akin to what would be known as a mixture of aestheticism and symbolism to Anglo-American readers.

2 Ramón Gómez de la Serna, *Pombo* [1918–1924] (Barcelona: Editorial Juventud, 1960) p.211.

3 ibid.

4 Charles Harrison and Paul Word, *Art in Theory 1900–2000: An Anthology of Changing Ideas* (Oxford: Blackwell, 2003) p.128.

5 For those interested in exploring Ramón Gómez de la Serna's humour further, see Alan Hoyle's insightful study *El humor ramoniano de vanguagrdia* (Manchester: Working Papers 2, 1996)

6 Juan Manuel de Prada, *Las máscaras del heroe*, 7th edn (Madrid: Valdemar, 1997) p.53.

7 Ramón Gómez de la Serna, *Automoribundia*, (Buenos Aires: Editorial Sudamericana, 1948) p.223. To avoid the repetition of detail, *Automoribundia* will be referred to as *AM*, with the appropriate page number beside it.

8 Ramón Gómez de la Serna, *Quevedo* (Madrid: Espasa Calpe, 1962).

9 Ramón Gómez de la Serna, *Lope viviente* (Buenos Aires: Espasa Calpe, 1954).

10 Ramón Gomez de la Serna, *Nuevos retratos contemporáneos y otros retratos* (Madrid: Aguilar, 1990).

11 Ramón Gómez de la Serna, *El Greco: el visionario de la pintura* (Buenos Aires: Losada, 1945).

12 Ramón Gómez de la Serna, *Goya* (Madrid: Espasa Calpe, 1958).

13 Ramón Gómez de la Serna, *Nuevos retratos contemporáneos y otros retratos*, (Madrid: Aguilar, 1989).

14 Ramón Gómez de la Serna, *Obras completas: Novelismo I (El doctor inverosímil y otras novelas 1914–1923)* ed. by Iona Zlotescu (Barcelona: Galaxia Gutenberg-Círculo de Lectores, 1997).

15 *La Gaceta Literaria*, 83 (1930) published a questionnaire where prominent literary figures were asked about their thoughts regarding the avant-garde. Gómez de la Serna's well known words '¡Viva la vanguardia, ¡Viva el vanguardismo!' (p.32) affirm his strong allegiance to the avant-garde throughout.

16 Ramón Gómez de la Serna, *Ismos* [1930] (Madrid: Ediciones Guadarrama, 1975) p.353.

17 Ibid, p.358.

18 In 'Gómez de la Serna y la Generación Poética de 1925', *Luis Cernuda: Prosa Completa*, ed. by Derek Harris and Luis Maritsany (Barcelona: Barral Editores, 1975) p.407.

19 Francisco Umbral argues that *El Rastro* is 'La asociación fortuita, azarosa y poética de los objetos, liberados ya de su utilidad y de la escala de valores que les da el rito', *Ramón y las vanguardias* (Madrid: Espasa Calpe, 1978) p.172.

20 It is not my intention to rehearse the reasons as to why Ramón Gómez de la Serna has been largely neglected as an author until fairly recently, as they are well known. Critics such as Cardona (1957) Hoyle (1972) Dennis (1988) and Harris (1995) have offered a number of convincing reasons for Ramón Gómez de la Serna's relative neglect.

21 Julio Cortázar, 'Los pescadores de esponjas', *Lateral*, 24 (1996) 1–2, (p.1).

22 References to all of these author's opinions regarding Gómez de la Serna can be found in the Appendix of *AM*, pp.784–803.

23 Rodolfo Cardona, *Ramón: A study of Ramón Gómez de la Serna and his works* (New York: Eliseo Torres and Sons, 1957).

24 Cardona, p.7.

25 Luis Granjel, *Retrato de Ramón* (Madrid: Ediciones Guadarrama, 1963).

26 Gaspar Gómez de la Serna, *Ramón: obra y vida* (Madrid: Taurus, 1963).

27 Fernando Ponce, *Ramón Gómez de la Serna* (Madrid: Unión Editorial, 1968).

28 José Camón Aznar, *Ramón Gómez de la Serna en sus obras* (Madrid: Espasa Calpe, 1972). Prior to the appearance of this book, Camón Aznar had already demonstrated an interest in Gómez de la Serna. On the 23 of April, 1968 at a conference celebrating 'La fiesta del libro', he read out a lecture entitled 'Los libros de arte en la obra de Ramón Gómez de la Serna' (Madrid: Editorial Maestre, 1968) pp.5–18. Camón Aznar comments both on Gómez de la Serna's *Ismos*, and his similarities with Goya.

29 Eugenio G. Nora, *La novela española contemporánea: 1927–1939* (Madrid: Editorial Gredos, 1973).

30 Sue Frenk, Chris Perriam and Mike Thompson, 'The Literary Avant-garde: A Contradictory Modernity', in *Spanish Cultural Studies: an introduction*, ed. by Helen Graham and Jo Labanyi (Oxford University Press, 1995) pp.63–69 (p.66).

31 Ramón Gómez de la Serna, 'Las cosas y el ello' (1936) in *Una teoría personal del arte: antología de textos de estética y teoría del arte de Ramón*, ed. by Ana Martínez-Collado (Madrid: Tecnos, 1988) pp.25–34 (p.27).

32 Gómez de la Serna, *Ismos* [1931] (Madrid: Ediciones Guadarrama, 1975) p.353.

33 Ramón Gómez de la Serna, *Pombo* (Barcelona: Editorial Juventud, 1960) p.222.

34 Ramón, *Pombo*, p.61.

35 Ramón, *Pombo*, p.147.

36 Ramón, *Pombo*, p.47.

37 Ramón, *Pombo*, p.66.

38 Ramón, *Ismos*, p.38.

39 *El humor ramoniano de vanguardia*, (Manchester: Working Papers 2, 1996) p.5. Pío Baroja argued that humour was 'el surco nuevo y tiene el encanto de lo imprevisto; la retórica es el surco viejo y tiene el encanto de la repetición necesaria para el ritmo. El humor necesita inventar, la retórica se contenta con repetir. El humor tiene el sentido místico de lo nuevo, la retórica el sentido respetuoso de lo viejo'. In *La caverna del humorismo* (Madrid: Colección Selecta, 1919) p.92.

40 Nigel Dennis, *Studies on Ramón Gómez de la Serna*, Ottawa Hispanic Studies 2, Dovehouse Editions, Canada (1988) 18–19.

41 Andriano del Valle wrote a poem entitled 'La apoteosis del cohete', in *Grecia*, 10 (1919); José María who composed a futuristic poem 'Canción del aeroplano', in *Grecia*, 13 (1919); whilst Xavier de Bóveda in a similar vein composed 'Un automóvil pasa', *Grecia*, 13 (1919). These poems are representative of a new found aesthetics based on modernity and the advent of technology.

42 Anthony Leo Geist, La poética de la generación del 27 y las revistas literarias de la vanguardia al compromiso: 1918–1936 (Barcelona: Guadarrama, 1980) p.60.

43 Geist, p.54.

44 Derek Harris argues that: 'All artistic endeavour since the Renaissance had been based on the Aristotelian concept of art as the imitation of nature and the neo-Platonic concept of art and beauty as the reflection of the divine ideal. The avant-garde rejects these fundamental

bases, art and literature are set free from the requirement to copy and reflect something outside of itself'. In *The Spanish avant-garde* (Manchester: University Press, 1995) p.3.

45 Guillermo de Torre, 'Estética del yoísmo ultraísta', *Cosmópolis*, 29 (1921) 51–61.

46 Guillermo de Torre, *Estética...*, 50–51.

47 In the literary journal *Grecia*, Luis Sallés de Toledo states: 'El hombre es demasiado metafísico', 'El fracaso de la filosofía: apuntes para un libro de filosofía intranscendental', *Grecia*, 1 (1918) 15.

48 Leo Geist, p.152.

49 Cansinos Assens, *La nueva literatura* (Madrid: Editorial Paez, 1925) p.372.

50 Vicente Huidobro, cited in Cansinos Assens 'Huidobro y el Creacionismo', *Cosmópolis*, 1 (1919) 68–73 (p.69).

51 Max Jacob, cited in Ramón Gómez de la Serna, 'Realidades', in *España*, 24, August, 1923, p.73.

52 According to Ignacio Soldevila *La viuda blanca y negra* was written around 1914, although no first edition with this date or with the later date of 1917 has been found. After having consulted the Biblioteca Nueva edition which does not include any indication of its date, and comparing it to Rodolfo Cardona's edition (Madrid: Cátedra, 1988) I have decided to cite from the latter, as the two are identical. The Biblioteca Nueva edition was the edition on which Cardona based his 1988 edition, although the copy which I consulted in the 'Biblioteca Nacional' in Madrid, was Catalina de Burgos' personal copy.

53 Ramón Gómez de la Serna, *La viuda blanca y negra* (Madrid: Cátedra, 1988). In the most recent re-edition of *La viuda blanca y negra*, Ignacio Soldevila points to the novel's relation to the life of the author, and argues that the references to bullfighting in the text are representative of Gómez de la Serna's mysogenistic treatment of women, but fails to analyse any of the main themes of the work or the narrative devices employed. Ramón Gómez de la Serna, *Obras Completas: Novelismo I (El doctor inverosímil y otras novelas 1914– 1923),*ed. by Iona Zlotescu (Barcelona:Galaxia Gutenberg-Círculo de lectores, 1997) XII, (p.28).

54 Ramón Gómez de la Serna, *Automoribundia* (Buenos Aires: Edición Sudamericana, 1948) p.292.

Chapter 2. The Banquet Years I
(1919–1923)

Yo no era más que un transeúnte un poco más consciente que los demás transeúntes, pero con menos presente y porvenir que ellos, aunque podía elegir como nadie el rumbo del paseo de la tarde.

Ramón Gómez de la Serna (1888–1963)

Being no longer controlled by the powerful impulses of 'common sense', and the 'normal', the valves of our unconscious open (...) Thus a world of new sensations and awareness comes into being.

Amédée Ozenfant (1886–1966)

The age demanded an image of its accelerated grimace, something for the modern stage (...)

Ezra Pound (1885–1972)

The 1920s ushered in Gómez de la Serna's most productive period in his career as a writer, although not necessarily his best. During this decade he wrote more than ten major novels and numerous short stories, whilst contributing to the major literary journals and newspapers of the day. Such a prodigious output inevitably raises questions regarding the quality of such a large corpus of work written in a relatively short space of time. Whatever conclusions are reached regarding the literary worth of his work, there is no doubt that the decade of the 1920s is crucial to understanding Gómez de la Serna's work as a whole. In the novels and short stories he wrote during this time he experimented with the genre of the novel and established the themes and character types which were to become emblematic of his writing. As the quote cited at the beginning of this chapter suggests, the image of Gómez de la Serna roaming the streets of Madrid in the early evening as a kind of literary 'transeúnte' is a useful one to bear in mind. It is, by and large, the changing patterns of life in the city of Madrid and its architecture which Gómez de la Serna poetically transforms and re-combines in his fiction. A world similar to that which Amédée Ozenfant suggests above 'of new sensations', set loose by the workings of a creative mind relying on poetic freedom rather any attempt to document. If any author of 1920s Spain presents an 'image of the age' (to borrow Ezra Pound's stanza) it is Gómez de la Serna. In this chapter I intend to examine several of his early novels from the first phase of his 1920s literary enterprise.

Apart from an interlude in Estoril (Portugal) and Naples during the 1920s, most of Gómez de la Serna's fiction written during this decade was written in Madrid. Although Paris of the 1920s was undoubtedly the centre of European cultural and intellectual activity, Madrid, with its proliferation of cafés and *tertulia* bars provided fertile ground for intellectual discussion and bohemian lifestyle. It is therefore not surprising that it attracted numerous young artists and authors, not least through the *Residencia de Estudiantes*, where Salvador Dalí, Luis Buñuel and Federico García Lorca met. Although Ramón Gómez de la Serna was never a part of the Generation of 1927, he was in contact with many of its members some of whom were regulars at the literary *soirées* at Café Pombo. Over the years the Saturday night gatherings at Pombo drew a wide-range of bohemian artists, important essayists and journalists, novelists and poets, including figures of international renown such as Borges, Huidobro, Jean Cassou and of course Sonia and Robert Delaunnay, who had emigrated to Madrid during the War to escape from France. In its initial phase, parallels with Café Voltaire in Zurich are not all together unfounded, not least in the underlying sense of the absurdity and emptiness which underpinned and informed many of its activities: 'Pombo no sirve, pues, para nada, nada, nada, nada más que para encontrarse'—the repetition of he word 'nada' echoing the opening lines of Tristan Tzara's Dadaist manifesto (whom Gómez de la Serna had met whilst in Switzerland). (*PB*.12) In the early pages of *Pombo* Gómez de la Serna taps into the pervasive feeling of angst sweeping through Europe during and after the War, which was to inform and shape the modernist aesthetic throughout post-war Europe:

Ya no hay mundo, ya no cree nadie en el mundo; no se puede creer en el mundo; solo tenemos estos pequeños lugares íntimos en que encontrarnos.[1]

Many of the evenings took the form of a literary *soirée*, with readings, discussions and debates. Other evenings were spent commemorating literary figures whilst drinking copious amounts of black coffee to combat tiredness in the small hours. Sometimes these discussions would continue well on into the night, and those taking part would walk out onto the Plaza Mayor to see the sunrise, or take a ride on an early morning tram. It is clear from reading Gómez de la Serna's diaries of Pombo that he was fascinated by cafés and taverns in Madrid; in fact many of the early pages provide a history and inventory of cafés in Madrid, gathering interesting anecdotes in the process. Café Iberia, for example, was famed for having a blind orchestra and was often frequented by politicians and authors. One particular summer a group of aristocratic women danced naked in the garden, whilst the orchestra played on. Adjacent to the Puerta del Sol and originally designed as a *bo-tellería*, Café Pombo was to become of central importance to Gómez de la Serna's contact with the outside literary and artistic world, and essential in understanding his literary output during his most productive years as a novelist.

Ramón Gómez de la Serna's nineteen twenties works cannot be taken as a single entity, although all share a desire to explore, both thematically and stylistically, central facets of the modern world. Similar to his contemporaries, there is an initial fascination with fashionable themes in vogue at the time such as sport, travel,[2] cosmopolitanism,[3] cinema and technological innovation in a deliberate attempt to shake off perceivably traditional topics and position himself with what was perceived as being 'new'. But beneath this avant-garde veneer Gómez de la Serna's works deal with themes of universal concern such as loneliness, the nature of human relationships and the effects of landscape on an individual whilst poetically exploring the material world in an attempt to re-fashion and remould it. This interest in drawing on themes and aspects of the modern world was of course not exclusively a Ramonian trait. In much of the early poetry of the 1927 Generation sport is of central importance, although, as the poets matured their writing took on more universal themes which they intertwined with the Spanish literary tradition and influences from the avant-garde.[4] The critic Antony Leo Geist argued that the lyrical poetry of the avant-garde period chose elements of the modern world (like sport), which were devoid of 'sentimientos tradicionales y creaciones hechas'. Anyone who has read early poems by Rafael Alberti such as 'Nadadora', or Gerardo Diego's 'El balón de fútbol' or Guillermo de Torre's 'Skating-ring', will no doubt be familiar with this kind of imagery. It would, however, be erroneous to suggest that the avant-garde stage in the work of the poets of 1927 simply amounted to an exploration of modern-day life. Towards the end of the nineteen-twenties Rafael Alberti in *Sobre los ángeles* (1929), Luis Cernuda in *Un río, un amor* (1929), and Lorca in *Poeta en Nueva York* (1929) give voice to their feelings of uncertainty, discontent and uneasiness through a poetic discourse that draws on surrealism as a means of liberating the creative experience. Gómez de la Serna's works follow a similar evolution, as will become clear when we consider his more mature works written in the 1930s and 1940s.

As critic-historian Christopher Innes argues, modern art and literature is difficult to classify as it 'appears fragmented and sectarian, defined as much by manifestos as imaginative work, and representing the amorphous complexity of post-industrialised society in a multiplicity of dynamic but instable movements focussed on philosophical abstractions'.[5] We must, however, remember that Innes is not writing specifically about Spain here, which could

not be described as a post-industrial society by any stretch of the imagination, although was undergoing a process of modernisation which was unparalleled in any other decade. The complexity of modern society referred to by
Innes in this passage would clearly provide any author with a challenge to re-
examine the very generic conventions of the novel and poetry, increasingly
rejecting traditional practice and gradually adopting what critic Victor
Fuentes argues is 'una nueva novela basada en los descubrimientos científi-
cos, tecnológicos y artísticos de la nueva época'.[6] In other words, the new
ideas in the world of science, technology, cinema and sport become part of
the fabric of the new novel, drawing on a modern social context and thus departing from the influences of aestheticism: 'las novelas vanguardistas se
estructuran sobre la vida urbana moderna, su dinamismo maquinista y su
estridente cosmopolitanismo: aglomeración de gente, automóviles, bancos y
hoteles'.[7] The avant-garde novel is informed by its surrounding world, but
the world portrayed is one which is undergoing a process of change and
therefore demands a new aesthetic medium, through which modern art seeks
to expand and transgress the boundaries of classical art. The recurrent obsession in Spain at the time with the attempt to create 'arte puro' can be misleading. The progressive weakening of what Díaz Plaja refers to as 'the
human element',[8] not altogether dissimilar to Ortega's idea of 'dehumanised
art', is debatable. It is virtually impossible to divest literature of its human
dimension, or indeed block out references to the outside world. This is not
what Ramón, or any other writer of that time, was trying to do. Vela's notion
of 'arte puro' has to be understood as a general mood and direction in literature, rather than a prescribed set of ideas or an accurate definition of
literature during the period as a whole.[9]

The deliberate attempt on the part of Gómez de la Serna to dismantle realist and naturalist aesthetics is achieved at various levels. Structurally, plot
causality is weakened, releasing narrative events from the constraints of an
organic narrative structure. The cubists had already experimented with these
ideas in art almost a decade earlier, freeing the picture from the need to
communicate anecdote to draw attention to its formal structure by viewing
objects from different angles and superimposing different shapes on the canvas to show that: 'things exist in multiple relations to each other and change
their appearance according to the point of view from which we see them'.[10]
Wylie Sypher argues that the modern world is dominated by ambiguity
which is best expressed through cubism, which comes to be an underlying
feature of modernism as a whole.[11] Gómez de la Serna's disregard of narrative places him at the centre of the modernist literary enterprise. Thus, in the
works to be examined in this chapter, fictional events appear to be tenuously
linked to each other, rather than by any organic determination. Emerging

cinematic techniques became important influences on the novel in their promotion of a fragmented vision of reality. Gómez de la Serna's novel
Cinelandia (1923) is part of a growing interest among Spanish writers in this
new art form. In 'Cinema y la novísima literatura', Guillermo de Torre, exploring the influences of cinema on literature, argues that in the cinema the
fragment takes precedent over action, thereby weakening the narrative
thread.[12] In 'Kinescopio: el elogio de lo pasajero', which appeared as an article in the journal *España* in 1921, Mauricio Bacarisse proposes that the speed
of the camera in capturing transitory images, prevents the viewer experiencing reality too directly and painfully:

> Todo es más pasajero y dura menos aún que en la realidad, y así nos priva del dolor
> de padecer los trances angustiosos y en su inverosimilitud veloz nos priva de
> sumirnos en la lógica y en el ritmo lento, que es la otra forma de caer en el dolor.[13]

Although his theory is plausible, a fragmented and accelerated vision of
reality does not necessarily play down the seriousness of the events encountered in a film or novel. It is precisely the breaking away from all sense of
order and sequence which proves to be disturbing, and the rejection of preconceived ideas which poses searching questions about the nature of
existence itself. But these ideas and questions are not necessarily depicted in
the novels of the period in a cause and effect relationship, but through a new
medium no longer predicated on rationality. G.G. Brown argues that 'The
decline in prestige of the scientific rationalism which had conferred authority
on literary realism in the nineteenth century was accompanied by a widespread waning of interest in representational art'.[14] Guillermo de Torre had
vociferously argued for a kind of art which promoted ilogicality as a way of
avoiding traditional rhetorical patterns and forms, arguing that: 'La evasión
del realismo objetivo de su transcripción literaria, implica el ilogismo, o
manumisión del control realista, y el anti-intelectualismo cenestésico de la
nueva lírica'.[15] This is not dissimilar to Luis Fernández Cifuentes' view that
the vanguardist novel sees logic as a repressive constraint on the creative
process:

> La lógica externa, común al realismo se reveló así no sólo falaz sino también
> represiva, una precaución contra el inconsciente individual, una forma de reducir o
> sofocar la imaginación propia.[16]

At a time when the theories of Freud were fuelling a growing fascination
with the unconscious both in art and in literature, and the emergence of surrealism which championed the demise of logic and rationality as a means of
better understanding the human condition, it is not surprising that Gómez de

la Serna writes novels such as *El incongruente* in 1922. Living in Madrid and chairing the *tertulias* in the café Pombo, whilst travelling to Paris and beyond brought him into contact with all the major figures of the literary avant-garde world. These influences are important to bear in mind when considering the novels about to be discussed, as they all mark a clear departure from the traditional novel. Not only do they make reference to modish fashions from the contemporary world (jazz, sport, travel, cosmopolitanism), but they also prioritise concept over emotion in a deliberate attempt to move away from the emotionally-infused prose of romanticism. A renewed interest in experiences outside the normal is stimulated both by the emerging theories of surrealism and a general disenchantment with realism.[17] On a structural level, traditional notions of plot are swept away, replaced instead by a series of fragments strung together in a tenuous structure. The novels considered in this chapter comprise a modern style of writing tailored to depict an emerging modern world. In each of them there is a breaking away from the panoply of rules which governed traditional fiction, resulting in a determined attempt to re-define the novel as a genre according to new sensibilities. Despite Gómez de la Serna's firm grounding in the Spanish literary tradition, his open defence of the avant-garde is substantiated by the contents of the novels themselves. Some of the novels of this period are set outside Spain: *El Gran Hotel* (1923),[18] *Cinelandia* (1923),[19] *El caballero del hongo gris* (1928)[20] in step with the widespread interest in cosmopolitanism[21] at large, and with Hollywood in the case of *Cinelandia* (1923). In *El doctor inverosímil* (1921)[22] and *El incongruente* the exact location of the action is deliberately left unclear, as Ramón is not interested in drawing attention to a particular setting, but to the eccentric thought-patterns and behaviour of his main characters. Regarding Gómez de la Serna's avant-garde writing Cansinos Assens argues:

> Aspira a interpretar el dinamismo de la vida como un torbellino de átomos materiales o sentimentales. Su mundo de la representación es así un mundo abigarrado e inquieto en el que todas las cosas se manifiestan casi simultáneas, casi como se ofrecerían a la vista de los nautas aéreos. Su obra es como una ciudad en la que todas las avenidas pudiesen verse con una sola mirada y el transeúnte no tuviese nunca delante un muro aislador.[23]

The Decline of Scientific Rationalism: El doctor inverosímil

El doctor inverosímil (1921), described by Ortega y Gasset as 'Un prototipo de prosa vanguardista',[24] recounts the experiences of the main character Dr Vivar as he goes about curing his patients through a peculiar and idiosyncratic kind of medicine, which is as much a product of humour and chance as of his own quirky personality. The novella is interesting on a thematic level because it deals with the subject of medicine, a topic which was becoming increasingly fashionable during the period of the nineteen-twenties.[25] Although the themes of illness and medicine have been treated before in literature, Freud's ground-breaking theories on the unconscious published in 1901 coupled with later developments in surrealism fuelled a renewed interest not only in psychoanalysis, but in areas pertaining to illness and its effects on the mind of the patient. According to Poggioli, both Nietzsche's and Baudelaire's exaltation of malady stemmed from a belief that malady brought about a state in the individual which was no longer treated 'metaphysically', but as a 'physical and objective phenomena', therefore breaking with emotion.[26] Poggioli goes on to suggest that this view 'establishes a totally determined link between art and neurosis, obviously a consequence of Freudian doctrines of psychoanalytic theories'.[27] By writing a novel on a theme of such contemporary interest Gómez de la Serna once again reaffirms his commitment to the avant-garde enterprise. *El doctor inverosímil* is a good example of Ramón's capacity to take a given topic, and to re-create it through a heavy reliance on humour and imagination. Structurally, it reads as an amalgamation of independent episodes, the only connecting thread being the character of Dr. Vivar.

Readers of his autobiography *Automoribundia* will have been struck by Ramón's fascination with illnesses and medical cures. Not only does he refer to the 1918 influenza epidemic which spread with devastating effects through Europe (Spain included), but recounts how he had ordered a long list of medicines for his own consumption prior to giving a conference in Montevideo (*AM*, p.310). For Ramón medicines were not simply a way of bringing a particular cure to an illness, but a way of provoking particular states of mind: 'En las medicinas hay un sonambulismo que abre compuertas con llaves especiales' (*AM*, p.687). For Ramón, most illnesses stemmed from a mixture of superstition and incongruity. A humorous acceptance of the ailment, was, in his view, the best possible cure. It therefore comes as no surprise that the promotion of humour and consequent rejection of tragedy lies at the heart of *El doctor inverosímil*. The reader is expected to be interested in the characters' ailments for what they reveal about the character, but the patients do not elicit any great degree of sympathy, as most of the episodes are humorous and do not depict any serious suffering.

The first edition of *El doctor inverosímil* appeared in 1914, but as is the case with much of the author's fiction, the work was amended and updated at a later date, which to some extent accounts for its fragmentary nature.[28] It is useful to take the 1921 edition of the work into consideration, as it includes important photographic material which is not included in later editions.[29] The importance of the photographs within the novel is worth looking at in detail. From a superficial point of view, it would appear that the inclusion of photographic material within the novel adds a sense of realism, in the same way that photographs in newspapers do. However, it would be naive to assume that Ramón is attempting to dupe the reader into believing the stories he is telling are factual or true in some way; he rather obliges the reader to consider what truth is in an ironic and playful manner. In the 1921 edition there is a photograph of an x-ray, possibly included due to a fascination with the aesthetics of medical technology, and a photograph of a deranged woman before and after treatment. Surrounding the photographs of the woman are drawings of enlarged cells and chromosomes, under which are the words 'Células del sistema nervioso, normales y trastornadas, alrededor de una loca y de la misma después de curada' (p.257). Ramón's treatment of madness here is deliberately humorous, and this example by no means constitutes the first time Ramón deals with this particular theme. He is not only interested in madness as a kind of modern post-Dadaist phenomenon; his ideas about madness are also firmly embedded in the Spanish literary tradition. The fact that Ramón dedicates an entire chapter to 'Juana la Loca' in *Automoribundia* is evidence of his interest in this theme. His interest in this quintessentially insane figure first arose when he saw a picture of her in his grandmother's house. Ramón was fascinated not only by her insanity but also because she was a widow. Both his grandmother and great aunt (the Romantic writer Carolina Coronado) were widows, a fact which is interesting to bear in mind when considering the treatment of women in his novels. However, Ramón did not believe that 'Juana la Loca' was actually mad. For Ramón, madness is an extreme manifestation of passion and obsession, and Juana la Loca was no exception. He saw her as essentially passionate in nature, but the expression of her feelings transgressed the social norms of the day (*AM*, p.366–369). It would appear that Ramón does not necessarily see madness as a congenital condition, but rather as a manifestation of eccentricity which often transgresses the social norm. This would account for the behaviour of many of his fictional characters, don Pablo in *El secreto del acueducto* (1922) being a case in point.

Plot and suspense are sacrificed in *El doctor inverosímil* and replaced by over two-hundred pages of rambling, *greguería*-littered prose, depicting a typically Ramonian world of droll characters who display bizarre behavioural patterns. Written in the first person, its structure is that of a diary-novel—at this level it is hardly experimental—which suggests that Ortega's remarks about its avant-gardist qualities are inspired by the thematic nature of the work rather than in its structure. Its aberrant depiction of science and heavy dependency on irrationality as a key to explaining the world, confirms its status as one of the author's avant-garde novels, although its literary worth is limited.

The critical view of this novel tends to confirm its avant-gardist quality.[30] Dr. Vivar's rejection of scientific fact coupled with his independence and uniqueness of personality, sets him at odds with society at large, and he emerges as a quintessentially modern-day hero. In this respect, Patricia Waugh argues that in eighteenth and nineteenth-century literature the author attempted to create characters who fitted the normal conventions of society, whereas in modern fiction 'The struggle for personal autonomy can be continued only through opposition to existing social institutions and conventions. This struggle necessarily involves individual alienation, and often ends with mental dissolution.'[31] If Dr. Vivar represents a departure from the rational world of science, in the process achieving some form of personal autonomy in his inability to fit in with society at large, he shows no traces of alienation, as the humour and ingenuity which he displays allows no room for individual angst. Dr. Vivar is not an existential hero: his medicine is made up from a blend of humour, chance and imagination. His lack of belief in what Waugh terms an external authoritative system of order,[32] foreshadows aspects of postmodernism. The fragmentary structure of the narrative in conjunction with the attenuation of causality and rejection of traditional plot devices, represent clear departures from established narrative norms. Furthermore, the world evoked in *El doctor inverosímil* is deliberately strange, to ensure that the reader does not take the novel as relevant to his or her experience of the world. Thus, both thematically and structurally, *El doctor inverosímil* should be regarded as central to our understanding of the development of Ramón's work in the nineteen-twenties.

Much of the narrative centres on Dr. Vivar's clinic, charting the various patients' consultations. Many of the ailments derive from an aesthetic idea. There is a man who is diagnosed as having 'La espina de rayo de luz clavada en el alma' (p.66), prompting Dr. Vivar to keep him in a dark room for fifteen days, thus successfully alleviating the patient's condition. This cult of the image was of course central to ultraism and creationism in their attempt to break away from 19th century realism. Images disassociated from narrative were to become the main thrust of literature. This works better with poetry as it destroys the main premise of the novel. *El doctor inverosímil* does not work as a novel, it is little more than an assemblage of humorous fragments. The anti-scientific premise on which Dr. Vivar's medical knowledge is based is sustained throughout the novel. Dr. Vivar believes that certain objects cause particular illnesses. Without explaining why, he claims that mirrors cause cancer, whilst raincoats kill because their tedious colour converts the individual into a monochromatic insipid street colour. One woman-patient always dresses in tartan. She informs Dr. Vivar of her conviction that she is constantly saying good-bye to the world. Dr. Vivar's diagnosis rests on the curious belief that it is the tartan skirt which is causing this problem: 'Ese traje es el traje de la que se despide de la vida, de la que aspira a ser la compañera de los muertos del pasado, de la que quiere irse al limbo de los personajes de novela que ya han servido' (p.56). His brand of medicine fuses humour and imagination with traces of superstition mixed in with avant-garde aesthetics. The narrator never pauses to consider, assess, or draw conclusions about society at large. The outside world is barely depicted at all, with much of the action taking place in the mind of the characters.

Many ailments are treated humorously, such as that of a woman who is experiencing mid-life menopausal symptoms. She finds that she cannot stop laughing when she sits in her rocking chair. Her friends and neighbours believe that she has succumbed to insanity, and call for Dr. Vivar. After examining her, his advice to her friends is not to lock her up, but instead to join with her in celebration:

> Únanse a la fiesta que celebra hoy...Pobrecilla. Hoy se despide de su vida pasada, hoy ha acabado su vida genésica...la naturaleza celebra su última fiesta, lo que en medicina se llama menopausia...Traigan dulces, pastas y unas botellas de jerez...hay que emborracharla y que tenga el largo y restaurador sueño de los borrachos. (p.120)

The episode ends, depicting a contented Dr. Vivar as he has helped cure another patient. There are numerous episodes which feature a similar prophylactic use of humour, whilst in other passages Dr. Vivar warns against the danger of certain objects. He advises against sewing-boxes because 'No hay nada más estancado que un costurero' (p.224) and warns about spending too much time looking at animals in the zoo. He mentions the case of a woman who had developed 'La enfermedad del antílope' (p.226), because she had spent too much time reading her book by a cage. Typically Ramonian preoccupations such as the importance of space and the idea that objects conceal hidden properties (which are often revealed through the use of a *greguería*) are brought to the fore. On one occasion Dr. Vivar diagnoses the cause of a patient's illness as residing in the gloves that he wears. His diagnosis relies on the imaginative insight often encountered in *greguerías*: 'En su fondo (el de los guantes) está el pasado hipócrita como ellos...El pasado se corrompe y sienta mal, como un pescado con la espina negra... ¡Tíralos!' (p.21).[33] Ramón's fascination with gloves is undoubtedly linked to their erotic properties and their association with the stereotype of frivolous and hedonistic bourgeois womanhood. Gloves serve a very visual purpose, as seen in Giorgio de Chirico's well-known 1914 oil canvas depicting a pair of gloves nailed to a board alongside other objects. The importance accorded to objects does not exclusively stem from a fascination with the material world, but bears similarities with aspects of Freud's theories. Freud would frequently take patients back to memories of specific incidents which, in his view, had instigated the mental neurosis. When re-visited in the right therapeutic context, the patient would be able to free themselves from the incidents which had produced neurosis. To some extent, aspects of Dr. Vivar's treatment bear resemblances to Freudian therapy. It is hardly surprising that Ramón admits in *Automoribundia* that his medical ideas stem from a fusion of reality and fantasy.[34] The illnesses depicted in *El doctor inverosímil* are psychosomatic, rather than clinical conditions. The patients never appear to be undergoing any pain. Many of the cures are brought about by a joyful acceptance of the illness on the part of the patient, thus rejecting all tragedy which according to Ramón is linked to death:

> Hay que convivir alegremente con la enfermedad y así nos salvaremos, pues el origen de la tragedia patológica está en la seriedad, ya que como la muerte es lo más serio que existe, se cuela en el cuerpo del hombre serio al primer descuido que tiene. (*AM*, p.689)

As is the case with the majority of Gómez de la Serna's characters, many of Dr. Vivar's inscrutable patients display absurdist tendencies. One such patient feels that he is being buried by time passing: 'Yo solo siento que me van enterrando los días, que la tierra y el polvo me envuelven, que la caspa del tiempo cubre mi cabeza y me abruma' (p.46). Dr. Vivar traces this problem to the fact that his patient had spent too many days enclosed in dusty and claustrophobic libraries. On a different occasion Dr. Vivar visits an aristocratic family whose son Manolín suffers from a compulsion to throw stones into the garden pond, despite the efforts made by his parents to stop him doing so. Dr. Vivar tells the parents that they must allow him to continue throwing stones until he becomes aware that he has finished his task, and then he will come to his senses and be cured. Following the doctors advice they allow him to continue his activity, until he has built a pyramid which arises out of the pond. Upon its completion, Manolín sits back to admire his work of art, and comes to his rightful senses. The idea behind this episode is not too dissimilar to Freud's account of neurosis and repression, where the individual constructs a particular object out of a repressed desire. However, Ramón presents the reader with a gleeful world where suffering is reduced to a humorous experience which bears little resemblance to reality.

Other patients of Dr. Vivar are described in purely aesthetic terms, such as the Arab immigrants who suffer because of the cold of Madrid's winter. Described as 'Unos tipos de color ámbar' (p.166), they accept Dr. Vivar's recommendations that they travel to Andalusia in order to drink from a well situated in the Alhambra palace, in order to be cured. There are Biblical overtones here (the idea of water giving life), whilst mention of the historic city of Granada and the presence of the Arabs shows his capacity to take historic and cultural aspects of Spain, and adapt them to the ethos of the avant-garde.

Overall, it is clear that *El doctor inverosímil* corresponds to the author's desire to move his fiction to the centre of the avant-garde world. Its interest lies in its avant-gardist theme, coupled with the detached and objective style in which it is narrated, whilst eschewing all emotion and sentimentality. Although it lacks the structural innovation of *El novelista*, it clearly belongs in the category of Gómez de la Serna's experimental fiction.

Ramón's ideas about medicine are clearly paradoxical. He playfully claims that 'Soy un pobre enfermo que vive gozando de la salud' and recommends that we should all take medicines which are derived from the soil, as we are formed from dust and will return to it when we die.[35] In his view, the consumption of prophylactics is what differentiates man from animals, although he does not intend the reader to take him seriously and openly admits that his sole objective in taking medicines is to 'divertirme curándome' (p.77). He describes a collection of bottles of medications placed on his desk, and claims that he is not the only person to be fascinated with medicines, but that Ortega y Gasset also had a drawer full of different sized bottles.

Untainted as it is by emotion, the world of medicine provided Ramón with a perfect subject matter through which to channel his imagination, and create characters who were recognisable for their curious medical condition, rather than for any deeply entrenched human values.

Experimenting with Surrealism: El incongruente

El incongruente (1922)[36] represents Ramón Gómez de la Serna's avant-garde fiction at its most thought provoking. It is a profoundly modern work in that it questions the hegemony of order and unity, suggesting a world where all rational order has been disrupted. The sociologist David Bell defined modernism as 'A rage against order'.[37] He goes on to suggest that in the modernist work 'The emphasis is on the self, and the unceasing search for experience [...] Rationalism is seen as devastating'[38], and therefore counter-effective to the flow of creativity. *El incongruente*, far from merely constituting the digressive ramblings of a slightly deranged character, encapsulates the *zeitgeist* of the age in its promotion of fragmentation and the exaltation of self through a deliberate attempt to differentiate between the individual and the mass. Bell sees modernism as central to this change in emphasis, arguing that it aims to bring about:

> [...] A shift in emphasis from 'character', which is the unity of moral codes and disciplined purpose, to an emphasis on 'personality', which is the enhancement of self through the compulsive search for individual differentiation. In brief, not work but 'life-style' became the source of satisfaction and criterion for desirable behaviour in the society.[39]

Similar to much of Gómez de la Serna's fiction, *El incongruente* does not provide the reader with a convincing picture of society but deliberately focuses in on the individual—the protagonist becomes the only unifying force in an otherwise disparate and fragmented narrative. The protagonist of *El incongruente* militates against the norm, against that which has become the defining trait of common society in an attempt to achieve mental liberty through the poetic exploration of human experience. The plot of *El incongruente* centres on the experiences and adventures of the highly elusive character Gustavo, who governed by a random and inexplicable force, lives in a world where the logical laws of science have given way to absurdity and incongruity. His behaviour is one which is not constrained by limits and is reminiscent of the prototypical modernist character described by Bell as one which cannot be subjected to 'aesthetic limits' or 'moral norms', as in his view 'The crucial insistence is that experience is to have no boundaries to its craving, that there is to be nothing sacred'.[40] There are no boundaries to Gustavo's world, he is presented as a character who is out of step with normality, living in a world of aesthetic possibility outside the constraints of morality and rationalism. At the age of four he asks his father to provide him with a walking stick on his birthday. On another occasion, Gustavo releases some goldfish into the air, suspecting that they are a bad omen. Defying the law of gravity, the fish carry on swimming through the air whilst the tank floats upwards. He has singular difficulty in determining his own fate, as the characters he encounters and the places he arrives at are as much a product of blind chance, as of purposive actions or the working out of destiny. The various episodes which constitute the novel portray a world which has been turned on its head, where the line between reality and fantasy has become increasingly blurred. It is a world where wax figures and knights of armour come to life, populated by quirky characters who have lost their power of reason. The spaces in the novel frequently convey a sense of the fantastic: palaces with many rooms, labyrinthine corridors and theatre stages with changing decors. Gustavo's world is one which is in confrontation with normality, presenting an alternative vision of human existence. It has been compared by some critics to the world of Kafka's fiction.[41] Although there may be some parallels (a world governed by strange laws, a protagonist engulfed by loneliness, and a lack of human emotion); the tone of *El incongruente* is humorous throughout, and there is no evidence to suggest that the author is deliberately interested in exploring existential questions.[42] However, the lack of a psychological and human dimension in the characters can be unsettling, even though it is a feature of Ramón's work in general, although the novel's ending—unusually for Ramón—is optimistic: Gustavo regains his congruence after marrying a woman he meets in the cinema.

The episodic structure of *El incongruente* through which the events governing Gustavo's life unfold, enmesh the reader in the day-to-day life experiences of Gustavo. It is a device used by Gómez de la Serna in an attempt to witness Gustavo's life for ourselves, and is similar to Bell's notion of the 'eclipse of distance', which he defines as:

> Stylistically, there is a common syntax in what I have called 'the eclipse of distance'. This is the effort to achieve immediacy, impact, simultaneity, and sensation by eliminating aesthetic and psychic distance. In diminishing aesthetic distance, one annihilates contemplation and envelops the spectator in the experience. By eliminating psychic distance, one emphasises (in Freudian terms) the 'primary process' of dream and hallucination, of instinct and impulse. In all this modernism rejects 'the rational cosmology' that was introduced into the arts during the Renaissance and codified by Alberti: of foreground and background in pictorial space; of beginning, middle, and end, of sequence, in time; and the distinction of genres and the modes of work appropriate to each genre. This eclipse of distance, as a formal syntax, cuts across all the arts: in literature 'the stream of consciousness'; in painting, the elimination of the 'interior distance' within the canvas: in music the upset of the balance of melody and harmony; in poetry, the disruption of the ordered meter. In the broadest sense, this common syntax repudiates mimesis as a principle of art...[43]

Gustavo is highly individualistic and unrestrained by any over-arching hegemony or restrictive code of behaviour. It is therefore not surprising that critics are in general agreement regarding the surrealist qualities of *El incongruente*.[44] Even a superficial reading of the text will confirm this view; salient features include the workings of the unconscious mind, non-logical development of plot, the liberation from logic, the pervasive influence of chance, and a strong interest in dreams. *El incongruente* shares a surrealist interest in dreams, not only because they allowed momentary evasion from everyday reality but because at the same time opened up another realm of human understanding. André Breton recounts the story of 'Saint-Pol-Roux', who, before going to bed, would place a placard on the door of his manor house which read 'THE POET IS WORKING'.[45]

In both style and structure *El incongruente*, together with *Cinelandia*, represents the most topical of Ramón's 1920s novels. It is similar to other works of his in its depiction of a socially marginalized figure, and touches on many of his habitual themes, such as loneliness, the futility of human relationships, the effects of modernisation, combining them with avant-garde humour and imagery. The forays into the world of fantasy and the surreal are particularly noteworthy, given that it was published before the appearance of André Breton's Surrealist Manifesto. Structurally, *El incongruente* is designed to reflect the incongruity of the main character Gustavo, and is therefore fragmented and lacking coherence. The reader is warned of this lack of continuity early in the novel, when the narrator states: 'Todo lo que estaba en el mundo estaba como un cabo suelto de rota continuidad' (p.11). The narrative structure is thus tailored to convey disjointedness:

> Ni en la novela de esta misma época ni en la de después se pueden seguir con cierta cronología las peripecias. Tiene que ser una incongruencia la misma historia de su vida y la de la elección de capítulos. (p.15)

The fragmentary nature of the narrative is further compounded by the fact that Gustavo is writing a diary, where he pens his thoughts and recounts his adventures. Entitled 'Libro mayor', his diary contains incongruities and images of his surrounding world which reinforce both the disjointed thought-pattern of Gustavo and the vividness of his imagination. On one occasion he affirms that odd-numbered pages are better than even ones, concluding that all even pages should be removed from books. Other passages are related through the mechanism of the *greguería*, re-inventing the world through witty analogies: 'Hay árboles histéricos, de sistema nervioso muy engarbitado…Se les nota sobre todo en otoño, cuando su sistema nervioso se queda al descubierto' (p.20). Similar to other of Ramón's characters (don Pablo in *El secreto del acueducto* and to a greater extent Andrés Castilla in *El novelista*), Gustavo is both a character and an author. However, in *El incongruente* the process of creating a novel within a novel is not explored in much depth, but rather serves to reinforce the protagonist's disjointed train of thought. The contribution of Gustavo's writings to the novel as a whole are limited, amounting to little more than an opportunity for Ramón to invest one of his characters with an untrammelled array of *greguerías*. It could hardly be claimed that this subtext adds any complexity (nor indeed quality) to the overall narrative, since it simply serves as a diversion, a device for holding up the flow of narrative. The structure of *El incongruente*, therefore, does not make excessive demands on the reader, but takes the form of self-contained episodes (forty-one in total),[46] the order of which—except for the opening and closing chapters[47]—is largely arbitrary. Most of the episodes narrate the various adventures and chance-encounters of the main character paying little attention to the secondary characters who appear in the novel. For that matter, even the character of Gustavo is shrouded in enigma, as the narrator seldom describes his mood, preferring to narrate his adventures and bizarre encounters rather than making psychological forays into his mind. Gustavo does not undergo great emotional upheaval, nor does his fate rise and fall in heroic fashion. His adventures are narrated impassively, with little emotion, and the detached and un-realistic nature of Gustavo's world makes it difficult for the reader to reach any degree of empathy with him. The author seems to be more interested in concepts and ideas, rather than feeling and the de-piction of human traits. Gustavo's character has something of the wandering *pícaro*, but who is living in an age of rapid modernisation, and whose fate is controlled by an inexplicable force of incongruity.

It is unclear where Gustavo's incongruity stems from, although early in the novel there is a suggestion that it is a state of mind, a way of coping with difficult existential questions such as that of death:

> Para mí, la muerte será una incongruencia más, y, por lo tanto, carecerá de esa importancia que otros la dan. Yo no he ligado mi vida a nada. Yo no tengo lógica, y, por lo tanto se desatan todas esas cosas apretadas y muy ligadas que tienen los otros, las cosas que les obligan, les conducen, les llenan de dolor. (p.18)

Gustavo's incongruity constitutes an inherent part of his character and is symptomatic of his rejection of cultural, moral, and aesthetic hegemony. Gómez de la Serna deliberately creates a character who lives in a modern world where moral codes have crumbled and where all certainties have been swept away. Gustavo's rejection of logic places him close to surrealism, at odds with a society governed by what André Breton described as 'the reign of logic'.[48] Gustavo shares similarities with Bell's definition of the proto-typical modernist character:

> With modernism there was a shift in emphasis from 'character', which is the unity or moral codes and disciplined purpose, to an emphasis on 'personality', which is the enhancement of self through the compulsive search for individual differentiation. In brief, not work but the 'life-style' became the source of satisfaction and criterion for desirable behaviour in the society.[49]

Throughout the novel Gustavo is looking for individual differentiation which is customarily expressed through his individualistic behaviour, which does not rely on logic or any form of causality. On one occasion he dressed up in tails for no apparent reason: 'Se vistió de frac sin saber para qué. Muchas veces se había vestido de frac y se había tenido que volver a desnudar porque no encontraba donde ir en frac' (p.33). In Galdós' *Fortunata y Jacinta* the use of the frac became symbolic of a homogenised society, where social classes are intermixing creating an amorphous middle class. It might be that Gómez de la Serna in this section of *El incongruente* is deliberately parodying the bourgeois middle classes who blindly adhere to social norms. Gustavo does not blend in to a homogenised society, but provocatively stands out. The events that surround his everyday life are bizarre, such as when Gustavo is visited at home by an art critic, who believes that concealed under the veneer of paint of his grandfather's portrait lies an authentic 'Velázquez' painting. The search for authenticity in a world of make-shift appearances with few bearings to the real world, would seem a strange quest for a character such as Gustavo who appears aloof and unconcerned about life in much of the novel. And yet Gustavo invites the art critic in and watches as he applies a variety of potions on the portrait, with a view to revealing the true original. Gustavo's high hopes are dashed when it becomes evident that there is no Velázquez original beneath the portrait. The art critic duly apologises, but then notices what appears to be a portrait of a woman which, he claims had been painted over a Leonardo da Vinci original. The critic applies the same potions to the second picture whilst Gustavo looks on in anticipation. As the paint is effaced, they both sense a movement in the picture to then see their own faces reflected in what is in fact a mirror. The episode ends with Gustavo chasing the critic out of the house, disillusioned and frustrated with 'aquel señor absurdo que le había suprimido un antepasado' (p.71). Episodes such as this one are portrayed as normal, and Gustavo accepts them without questioning. The unexpected becomes everyday in a world inhabited by eccentric characters who move freely in an unstructured world which is no longer premised on scientific laws, but is instead a product of chance. In a sense it is a dehumanised world, in tune with Ortega y Gasset's views on the direction new writing had taken. Human pain and suffering are absent from the novel, and the reader's interest is engaged by the ingenuity of the author's imagination in full flight, conveying the uncertainties of the modern era with a heavy dose of alleviating humour.

It is by narrating a series of incidents which constitute Gustavo's life that the reader is shown his personality as opposed to his character. This is why Gómez de la Serna's novels (on the whole) frustrate and ultimately fail to engage the reader at any level other than an aesthetic one. It is chance not character which underpins Gustavo's fate. The enigmatic characters who Gustavo comes into contact with drift aimlessly, with no clear history or objective. The characters are defined solely through their actions, and have no sense of past history, and are merely products of the age in which they are living, inhabiting a transient world of ephemeral encounters, where potentially important questions are treated trivially, breaking with traditional values and transgressing the social codes of the day. As Gómez de la Serna states elsewhere: 'No creemos en las cosas lógicas que hay para llenar un vacío, y por eso nos precipitamos a respuestas incongruentes, en palabras sueltas, en frases inauditas con las que aspiramos a conminarle'.[50] *El incongruente* therefore has to be understood as an exercise in avant-garde literature which rests on an irrational interpretation of the world. Ramón, for once, would possibly have agreed with the observation of Pío Baroja when he stated 'En la naturaleza y en la vida hay una cantidad de absurdo imponderable'.[51]

As with many of Gómez de la Serna's works, the edition which I have used for the purposes of analysis differs in various respects to the first edition which appeared in 1922.[52] Any discussion of *El incongruente* should therefore take the first edition into consideration. In addition to minor differences, such as the depiction of a train ticket in the text of the 1922 edition as an example of collage and the importance accorded to visual elements, the differences between the two editions basically concern the number of episodes in each. The 1922 edition is shorter in length, as it does not include the episodes 'Detrás de los decorados de teatro', 'En la playa de los pisapapeles', 'Citación al tribunal', 'A puerta cerrada' and 'Su retrato en el salón'. There is one episode that does not appear in later editions 'Otra mujer de París', towards the end of the novel. Whilst the structure of *El incongruente* is hardly changed by these alterations—they merely confirm its lacunary and improvised nature—there are thematic implications of interest, most notably the inclusion of two episodes which follow in immediate succession of each other entitled 'Citación al tribunal' and 'A puerta cerrada'. In the later edition the first episode relates the disturbing rumour that Gustavo has been accused of child abuse, although he maintains his innocence throughout and believes that he has been blamed for someone else's crime. The second episode is set in the tribunal to which Gustavo is summoned. When asked by the judge whether he accepted the accusations levied against him, Gustavo argues that the facts of the accusation were wrong. The judge then claims that two witnesses saw him, as there was a full moon on the day of his crime. Gustavo takes out a calendar, and assures the judge that there was no full moon on that date, and in any case, he was aboard a ship—presenting the judge with his stamped passport as proof. The judge, confused and annoyed, clears Gustavo of any wrong-doing, and the episode ends with the protagonist leaving the court, puzzled at how his name had come to be included in the prosecutor's file. The importance of these two episodes has to do with the unprecedented depiction of 'Gustavo the accused'. For the first time in the novel Gustavo is depicted as having to answer to someone, whilst in the earlier edition he roamed freely, unaccountable, in gleeful incongruity. Although both these episodes are dealt with humorously, their inclusion undoubtedly alters our perception of Gustavo's world, a world which demands explanations, even though no clear explanation is found.

The promotion of Gustavo's unrestrained self ultimately becomes tedious, repetitive, and fails to grasp the reader's attention in any meaningful way. In this sense it encapsulates something of what the modernist work set out to achieve, whilst simultaneously harbouring the seeds of its decline, breaking all boundaries but ultimately failing to provide an answer to the human condition:

> The impulse of modernism was to leap beyond: beyond nature, beyond culture, beyond tragedy—to explore the *apeiron*, the boundless, driven by the self infinitizing spirit of the radical self. Bourgeois society sundered economics from moral norms to allow the individual to pursue his own self-defined wants, yet at the same time sought to bend the culture to its restricted moral norms. Modernism was the major effort to break away from those restrictions in the name of experience, the aesthetic and the experimental and, in the end, broke all boundaries.[53]

El incongruente consistently questions the dividing line between normality and insanity, between providence and luck, to reveal a character who stands out for his deviation from the norms of the society in which he was living. Gómez de la Serna exploits the humour which arises from the development of such a character, in one of his most avant-garde and unconventional novels of the nineteen-twenties.

'Living matter' and the Transcendence of Things: El secreto del Acueducto *(1922–23)*

Although probably one of the most accomplished of the author's works, *El secreto del Acueducto* is not well known. First published in 1922–1923 by Biblioteca Nueva and then later included in the *Obras selectas* in 1947, it was not until 1986 that it was re-issued in a critical edition. Why it had such a low profile for many years is something of an enigma, as it is one of Ramón's most accessible novels and does not make excessive demands on the reader, despite its poetically-charged prose and heavy reliance on metaphor as a way of abstracting the real world. Although all of the action takes place in the legendary city of Segovia, it has never elicited wide popular interest.

The author's admission in the dedication that he is inspired by 'la elevada grandeza del tema hispano' (p.117), marks a departure from his cosmopolitan and avant-garde (in terms of theme, not narrative devices) novels. Ramón's self-confessed passion for 'el tema hispano' by no means comes as a surprise bearing in mind the themes and settings of some of his other works. Critical attention to date has largely focused on the depiction of Castile within the novel and on Ramon's idiosyncratic writing style, so heavily reliant on metaphor and unusual images for its poetic effect. Most critics [Granjel (1963), Camón Aznar (1972), Rey Briones (1992)] acknowledge the important place Castile occupies in the novel. Granjel points out that more attention is given to the scenery in the novel than to action,[54] whilst Antonio del Rey Briones argues that 'es una novela de pretexto realista, incluso casticista: la vida provinciana en una ciudad de Castilla [...]'.[55] He argues that it is Ramón's first 'mature' novel, citing Guillermo de Torre's assertion that it represents 'Uno de sus libros más logrados'.[56] Camón Aznar not only contends that *El secreto del Acueducto* is 'La novela de Segovia',[57] but also draws attention to the importance of the main character don Pablo, who in his opinion, embodies loneliness. He adds that this story, presents 'una entrañable percepción de Castilla'.[58] Alan Hoyle argues that there is a pattern and order to the novel, in which he detects 'an underlying principle of coherence which unites plot, setting and style, and culminates in the aspect of the work that has so far received least attention, namely, the ending, the 'secret' mentioned in the title'.[59] He goes on to argue that the aqueduct becomes 'The main object of 'perspectival' vision and defamiliarisation through language', stating that 'The historical reality of the aqueduct is distorted by subjective associations with time and mortality'.[60] He persuasively argues that the use of perspective by the author to describe the aqueduct, shows similarities with Ortega y Gasset's theory of perspectivism. Ignacio Soldevila sees *El secreto del Acueducto* merely as an excuse for the author to flaunt his verbose literary style: 'no es sino un pretexto para engarzar ingeniosas y variopintas greguerías en torno a un tema, hasta que se agotan la inspiración, el inspirado y, al cabo de la lectura, sus lectores'.[61] Carolyn Richmond, attaching great importance to the physical location of the novel, matches the places mentioned in the work to real places in and around Segovia.[62]

El secreto del Acueducto is an interesting work at various levels. It poses questions about the complex relationship between fiction and reality, between a novel and autobiography—questions which lie at the heart of Gómez de la Serna's fiction at large. Ramón's own experience of Segovia is central to a better understanding of the novel. He himself states in *Automoribundia* the deep impression engraved on his mind by the Castilian landscape:

> Nada ha ensanchado mi alma como esas visiones de Castilla que el destino de mi padre permitió que observasen mis ojos, emplazándome en sus plazas y plazuelas. (*AM*, p.318)

Such confessions strongly confirm the important contract between Gómez de la Serna and his world, and the mechanisms by which he describes his surroundings oscillate between a sustained description of local architecture and detail, and a poetic re-embellishing and transformation through aesthetic formulations that distort the surrounding landscape. The importance of the Castilian landscape for Ramón is not only interesting because of his childhood memories, but because of its treatment by other authors of the time. Ernesto Giménez Caballero, for example, was eager to present a new vision of Castile by re-invigorating its traditional connotations through a detached and intellectualised vision. In his vanguardist essay 'Paisaje en materia gris', Giménez Caballero argues:

> La nueva poesía que suscita Castilla es toda intelectual. De belleza fría y suprema. Para creer de nuevo en Castilla hay que, previamente, tener fe en la verdad del intelecto desnudo. Hay que amar el paisaje encefálico: de materia gris.[63]

Landscape, according to Giménez Caballero, is not to be presented as an emotional extension of the soul as the Romantics prescribed, nor is it to be used symbolically in the style of the Generation of 98 to question the state of a nation in decline. It is, instead, to be treated as an endlessly fertile source of material for a process of defamiliarisation, providing a plethora of images for the author to play with, to shed the emotionally charged images of the past, expressed in the cliché-ridden language of literary convention, and to write about experience through a renewed and invigorating perception of the world. However, to suggest that Ramón simply defamiliarises the Castilian landscape in *El secreto del Acueducto* would be an over simplification. Numerous passages in *El secreto del Acueducto* approximate *costumbrismo* in the attention accorded to localised detail and tradition. Even the plot, at face value, essentially revolves around the recurrent theme in Spanish literature of the cuckolded husband: a theme as old as literature itself and used by numerous authors, Cervantes' *El celoso extremeño* being a case in point. The combination of these influences make *El secreto del Acueducto* difficult to classify.

Written shortly after the death of Gómez de la Serna's father—an event which undoubtedly contributed to the at times melancholy tone which pervades the novel, and its preoccupation with the passage of time and the process of ageing—*El secreto del Acueducto* centres around the character of don Pablo: a retired middle-aged man living in the city of Segovia. Much of the narrative acquires focus through the character of don Pablo, whose growing fixation with the aqueduct becomes the central preoccupation of the novel. Through Don Pablo's daily visits to the aqueduct Ramón is able to evoke the aqueduct through a mixture of *greguería* and other poetically imaginative treatments.

Contrary to the general belief in Segovia, don Pablo asserts that the architect of the aqueduct was Egyptian rather than Roman (an opinion apparently confirmed, when towards the end of the novel, he claims to have seen a stone of the aqueduct in the form of an Egyptian sarcophagus). Running parallel to don Pablo's bizarre obsession with the aqueduct, is the figure of his niece (Rosario), who lives with him and marries him in chapter sixteen, towards the end of a long and hot summer. But when financial hardship sets in, they find themselves having to take on a lodger (a priest named don Antonio), who has an affair with Rosario. The dynamic of the relationship between the three characters is intensified by don Pablo's obsession with the aqueduct—arguably, Rosario is unfaithful to her uncle because he has neglected her for the aqueduct—highlighting once more the importance of the material world in Gómez de la Serna's fiction.

With the realisation of Rosario's unfaithfulness, don Pablo spends most of his time by the aqueduct, gradually degenerating into a state of madness. The autumnal sky, waning in to the cold winter, is cleverly woven into the narrative, to correspond with don Pablo's changing emotions. The last scene of the novel depicts him wandering under its colossal archways. A mixture of melancholy and sadness at his lonely condition haunts the last pages of the book.

Whilst little attention is given to everyday life in Segovia, the places which appear in the novel do correspond to real places in Segovia. More importantly, however, parts of the surroundings (and in particular the aqueduct) are presented through the eyes and mind of don Pablo, in a way which defies any sense of realism. Despite the fact that the novel is set in a real city, it is not a historical novel, and is built on an aesthetic idea rather than on a social one.

El secreto del Acueducto deals with fairly traditional and universal themes: loneliness, betrayal, love, the effects of landscape on the individual. From the outset of *El secreto del Acueducto*, narrative is replaced by images and poetic description plays a more important role than plot itself. The opening paragraph of any novel is always important for setting the rhythm of the prose. *El secreto del Acueducto* opens with a Biblical metaphor of eating daily bread, which is metonymically used to convey the arrival of dawn: 'Había que comerse el pan grande de un nuevo día' (p.119). In chapter one don Pablo's solitude, compounded with his desire for sensual love is memorably evoked, whilst the important contract which he forms with his surroundings is poetically elicited through images of eating: don Pablo claims that 'El horizonte está exquisito' (p.119) and refers to his first breath of air as 'la primera bocanada de la madrugada' (p.120). Don Pablo is presented as a part of his world, a sentiment which is poetically evoked by the allusion to dawn:

> Era rijoso el amanecer. Lo amaba y lo temía. Le promulgaba hasta el horizonte y después le retraía, le ceñía, le apretaba el cinturón carnal, jugaba con él como un mar de viva resaca. (p.120)

The limited action in the opening chapter allows the pace of the narrative to be dictated by don Pablo's thoughts as he observes his world: 'Donde ponía la vista mucho le duraba el mirar' (p.119). The importance of contemplation ('mucho le duraba el mirar') over action is fundamental to the novel, so it is fitting that the narrator warns the reader of it early on. Chapter one evokes a variety of visual images from the view of the city of Segovia from don Pablo's balcony, to the tower of San Esteban and the surrounding landscape, the convent of the Discalced Carmelites founded by Saint Teresa, and the bees flying in and out of his window. All of these images promote visual contemplation over action, a delaying device which disrupts the flow of narrative.

Much of *El secreto del Acueducto* is taken up with the aqueduct itself, in descriptions which go beyond mere documentation to evoke it through poetic images and metaphors. It is described as a reptile moving its vertebrae, as a giant tortoise in the winter months, as a snow-capped mountain. Its porous stones are compared to 'esponjas del tiempo' (p.164), its structure to that of a giant centipede and to a comb which has combed all the armies which have passed under its archways. It is compared to a crutch for the heavens to rest on, to a calendar with thousands of pages, and in a direct reference to Jorge Manrique's famous elegiac lines, to a 'Puente por cuyos ojos pasa el caudal de las vidas que van a dar en el mar' (p.168). Gómez de la Serna's recreation of the aqueduct through a series of new images, whilst including clear references to Spanish literary tradition, adds to the richness of his prose style.

The importance placed on atmosphere over action is a central feature of *El secreto del Acueducto*. Primarily it is a novel about the power of observation, the power of the imagination to recreate and remould a given landscape. Although there are passages which depict aspects of Segovian daily life, such as the old women who congregate under the aqueduct, or the tourists don Pablo shows around, these elements are by no means essential to the plot, and their presence provides little more than a credible background against which to set the character's rambling thoughts. The passages which are most representative of the novel as a whole are those which poetically evoke aspects of don Pablo's world, as seen in this simple description of a summer night:

> Los ocasos del verano requemaban las piedras que los resistían como carbones extintos que ya pasaron de la edad de arder, pero a los que siempre, como al amianto, les queda porosidad y consistencia para retener el ocaso sin consumirse. (p.190)

Or the description of evening sunlight:

> El sol del atardecer en la provincia es como una filosofía añeja, que se vierte en casa. Ningún dorado antiguo como este dorado. El ocaso sucede lejos y el pobre hidalgo no mira hacia allí porque es una belleza regia y él es pobre y mortal. Prefiere ver el reflejo de ese momento en las cosas y en las casas, viendo cómo es de compasivo y consolador. Todo tiene bajo ese sol como una mirada, como una nostalgia que atrae. (p.217)

Much of the narrative is taken up with descriptive passages such as these, where the natural world is observed and described. Movement and action are minimal, presented subjectively as occurring in the mind of the protagonist. The surrounding world becomes a source of imagery which is at times imbued with human characteristics: 'todo bajo ese sol tiene como una mirada [...]'. In this way, Ramón reminds the reader that the world presented in the novel is one which comes into being in the eye of the beholder. It is a world made up from the various sense-impressions of the main character, combined with the changing effects of light. The timeless presence of the natural surroundings ('belleza regia'), contrasts with the mortality of the onlooker, as he only sees the momentary reflection of things in the here and now. Experience is lifted to a poetic plane, and traditional plot construction is suspended in favour of poetic prose. The descriptive power of Gómez de la Serna enables him to construct a novel without needing to situate his characters in imaginary or cosmopolitan worlds, and the simplicity of its plot coupled with its well-known setting make few interpretative demands on the reader. What Ramón achieves is an unlocking of a poetic dimension, promoting imaginary and artistic sensibilities over reality itself.

Don Pablo, unlike characters typical of the genre of the adventure novel, remains largely on one level throughout the novel. His fate does not rise and fall with the events of each chapter, his trajectory through the novel does not comprise great voyages but is almost exclusively concerned with his trips between his home and the aqueduct. What stands out most clearly is his presence throughout, his vision of the surrounding scenery, his relationship with his niece and his final descent into insanity. However, don Pablo also writes about what he sees. The aqueduct has become an essential part of his existence, a sort of vital organ: he refers to it on one occasion as the 'riñón de su existencia' (p.132). Don Pablo is part of his world, which he forever re-creates and partakes of. As with the prototypical Romantic hero, the surrounding landscape becomes an extension of his soul, and as such, is relentlessly fluctuating and variable. Alongside the poetic descriptions of the aqueduct and city, Gómez de la Serna refers to places which evoke the historic side of Segovia and the real-life characters who live in the city. There are even digressive passages which resemble of a country diary. Ramón's fictional use of the aqueduct is no different to the commonplace practice of using mythology in a modern-day novel. The function of including myths or legends in a particular novel is usually one of reducing the anecdotal content of the work, as the author can assume that the reader is familiar with the story. This enables the author to dwell on presentation rather than on establishing the narrative.

El secreto del Acueducto is both a story about frustrated love in a provincial Spanish city which had not yet succumbed to the throes and excesses of modernisation, and about the important bond between landscape and the individual. Don Pablo, like many of Ramón's characters, displays solipsistic tendencies which not only place his own aesthetic experience at the centre of the novel, but eventually exclude him from any final integration into society. His descent into insanity is caused both by his bizarre dependency on the aqueduct and his neglect of human relationships. In this sense he is centrally placed within Gómez de la Serna's fictional world, in which the main cause of human unhappiness is presented as the difference between hope and reality, between the abstract world of dreams and the everyday.

The importance placed on contemplation over action, the attenuation of narrative, the innovative presentation of aesthetic material achieved without drawing imagery from the modern world but by setting the work within the familiar are *El secreto del Acueducto's* main features. Despite its traditional themes and setting, *El secreto del Acueducto* is arguably one of the most important of the author's works, and one which heralds a new approach to writing without relying on typical avant-garde motifs.

The ending of *El secreto del Acueducto* is somewhat ironic: don Pablo's quest ends abruptly when he shouts the word 'Eureka', claiming to have discovered the secret about the origin of the aqueduct. If most of the novel is concerned with finding the secret to the aqueduct, then its end is brought

about by a random, ill-founded and subjective belief on the part of the main
character don Pablo. At the end of the novel don Pablo descends into insanity
and emerges from the novel as an anti-hero, reminiscent of Don Quixote,
claiming things which are not true. In this sense, the character of don Pablo is
rooted in the Spanish literary tradition. It is significant that he is known as 'el
loco del pueblo' after the children attach a paper shape of a man to his coat-
tails, highlighting that he is someone who does not fit the social norm. His
relationships and friendships are sacrificed for his ideal, and yet his ideal is
flawed and not grounded in the truth. However, Ramón is not interested in
what constitutes the truth, but in a similar vein to Oscar Wilde, believes that
it is the duty of the artist to embellish, transform and depart from the truth, as
a means of experiencing aesthetic pleasure. As Ortega y Gasset argued: 'Los
ojos en vez de absorber las cosas, se convierten en proyectores de paisajes y
faunas íntimas. Antes eran sumideros del mundo real: ahora, surtidores de
irrealidad'.[64]

The Poetics of Modernity: Cinelandia (1923)

Ramón Gómez de la Serna's relatively unknown novel *Cinelandia* (1923) is
the first Spanish novel to focus on the emerging world of the cinema. Set in
Hollywood, *Cinelandia* gives us a glimpse of life in the modern metropolis.
The nature of the city described in the novel is imaginatively recreated and
obviously far removed from the reality of the Spain of that time. It is a novel
that draws on modernity, foregrounding the effects of the modern experience
on the individual.

In keeping with Gómez de la Serna's fiction at large, and with the broad
tenets of modernism, *Cinelandia* is a novel built up from a series of fragments, rather than a carefully constructed over-arching narrative. Gómez de
la Serna is undoubtedly enthused by the new aesthetic possibilities afforded
by modernity, and delights in the poetic transformation of that which is pro-
saic and not generally the locus of poetic expression. Despite Gómez de la
Serna's fascination with modernity, in *Cinelandia* there is also an underlying
sense of despair at the homogenisation of the human form, and the suggestion that human experience is ultimately vacuous. The historian Oswald
Spengler wrote about 'The unanchored late man of the mega polis' who inhabited a world of growing commercialism, pervasive materialism, dis-
sonance and fragmentation. The world depicted in *Cinelandia* is not distant
from that decried by Spengler, capturing the loneliness of modern man who
inhabits a burgeoning city, uprooted and alone. In this sense it is a novel very
much of its time.

Most critics have viewed *Cinelandia* in fairly negative terms. Camón Aznar points to its lack of 'hilo argumental', but argues that Ramón does not need to build on traditional cues of narrative as his style 'se desenfrena y extiende toda su pompa verbal, que hace desfilar ante nosotros con la velocidad y el deslumbramiento de una película'. Antonio del Rey Briones rightly praises *Cinelandia* for constituting 'una de las primeras novelas sobre el mundo del cine, en la que intuye con asombrosa lucidez la significación del fenómeno cinematográfico en el contexto del arte contemporáneo y su repercusión en los comportamientos sociales'. Carolyn Richmond argues that, together with *Seis falsas novelas* and *El novelista*, *Cinelandia* pertains to the author's novels which are inspired 'en una realidad que poco o nada tiene que ver con la física'.[65] This unflattering critical reception is no doubt fuelled by the awkwardness of the novel itself: individual episodes militate against the overall development of the story line, in a deliberate attempt to divest fiction of traditional plot devices. Ramón is a master at ridding literature of sentimentality and emotion, and *Cinelandia* is a particularly good example of these tendencies, depicting a fast-moving world of cinematographic images, inhabited by an itinerant group of characters who are never explored in much depth.

In *Cinelandia* there is no central plot, adding to the disjointedness of its structure, arguably imposed by the author in a deliberate attempt to emulate cinematic techniques. Much of the narrative switches between descriptions of the city itself and depictions of the characters who go there in search of work. Unlike most of the author's works, there is no central protagonist, making it difficult to achieve any clear narrative focus. Visual sensations are brought to the fore, evoking images which range from the comically absurd to the sombre, simultaneously expressing avant-garde playfulness and the transient nature of human life.

Cinelandia begins with the arrival of the elusive Jacobo Estruck to Cinelandia in search of work, and ends with the city being ordered to close down by order of the council of the 'Metropoli', prompted by the violent death of actress Carlota and as a punishment for resembling the Biblical cities of Sodom and Gomorrah. A summary of the plot of *Cinelandia* would do little to help us understand the novel. One of the principal preoccupations of Ramón is to give us a multi-faceted picture of the city and its inhabitants, not a rounded and neat storyline. In a sense, it might be argued that Ramón is responding to a similar stimulus to that which prompted Ezra Pound to write his poem 'Hugh Selwyn Mauberley' (1920), a stanza of which captures the need to provide an image which can convey the modern age:

The age demanded an image
   Of its accelerated grimace,
   Something for the modern stage. [66]

Cinelandia may even have elements of Eliot's 'unreal city' in *The Waste Land*, made up, in the words of the poet himself of a 'heap of broken images'; an idea which Eliot borrowed from Baudelaire's poem 'The Seven Old Men' which reads: Swarming city, city full of dreams, / Where the spectre in full daylight accosts the passer-by'. *Cinelandia* reverberates with images of modernity. These images are not always arranged neatly, which is more difficult to justify in a novel than in poetry. This is why Francisco Umbral has argued that Gómez de la Serna's novels fail because they are born from a poetic idea. In Eliot's *The Waste Land*, the poet's utterance 'I can connect nothing with nothing' comes as a kind of climatic catharsis, a poetic apotheosis unveiling the anguished modern soul confronted with a world which he cannot rationally explain or fully understand. It sums up the confusion which has been so forcefully conveyed in the preceding stanzas of the poem. No such moments of climactic thrill are to be found in *Cinelandia*, although, like Eliot's poem, the glimpse of modern society which Gómez de la Serna provides is ultimately one of pervasive loneliness and disillusion. The human types in *Cinelandia* lack individuality and human depth. The sociologist George Simmel says that:

> The deepest problems of modern life derive from the claim of the individual to preserve the autonomy and individuality of his existence in the face of overwhelming social forces.[67]

In most of Gómez de la Serna's novels the protagonists do retain a strong sense of their own individuality that sets them a part from the majority of the population. Whether we consider don Pablo and his peculiar aesthetic sensibilities in *El secreto del Acueducto* (1922), or Gustavo's surreal incongruity in *El incongruente* (1922) they do not necessarily represent a prototypical blueprint of modern man. But in *Cinelandia*, as we have seen, there is no central protagonist. The shallowness of the characters suggests a world akin to that described much later by the historian Roland Stromberg:

> The individual who feels bewildered and alone in a huge, impersonal world, who has lost the guidance of tradition and religion, and can find no source of values outside of self, who has lost contact with the community—such a person is surely all too typical of modern urbanised and industrialised society […]. (p.226)

These words could as well be describing the characters in *Cinelandia*. The first character the reader is introduced to is deliberately given a name that is difficult to place. Jacobo Estruck is a symbol of the modern cosmo-politan citizen, whose individual character traits and background have been progressively elided. He believes in nothing, it is not clear where he comes from, or what language he speaks, he has no strong ties with the community, he shows no signs of spiritual thirst, no emotions, no highs or lows. Instead, he is assimilated into the artificial and superficial world of Cinelandia. This process of assimilation is captured a little later in the novel by the actress known as 'venus de plata' when she says: "Al entrar en Cinelandia se pierde el nombre y se es bautizado con el nombre cinematográfico, el nombre de las pantallas" (p.10). The monotonous and claustrophobic nature of Cinelandia prompts the actors Max York and Elsa to escape it by driving away to the eponymous 'pueblo de los sombreros viejos'. Elsa sometimes sleeps in a cupboard to escape from the world: 'Dormir en un amario es como dormir fuera del mundo...Estoy cansada ya de la tierra...Por eso me he salido de ella un rato' (p.20). However, this behaviour does not prompt Elsa to engage in ontological or existential questioning. These issues are swept to one side. Instead Elsa dreams that she was in a forest of umbrellas. In Cinelandia death too is covered up and avoided when possible. Corpses are customarily re-moved from the city in milk vans or removal vans to try and disguise the fact that their fellow inhabitants die. If asked about the whereabouts of the re-cently deceased the citizens in Cinelandia will say that he or she had left the city without leaving an address. The inhabitants of Cinelandia will avoid fac-ing up to reality at any cost. The feeling of emptiness in Cinelandia grows as the novel progresses. There is even a sense of repetition, of monotony brought about by mass produced culture. The actress Mary feels that she can no longer love now that she has starred in a thousand films.

The city of Cinelandia is symbolic of modernity driven to an extreme. Any beauty evoked does not offer any glimpse of eternity, but points instead to the transience of the modern world, which will end in a flash like the ex-tinguishing of a cinematographic light. The characters in Cinelandia are aware that they live in a world of artificial nature. When Jacobo re-appears, after a temporary absence later in the story, he is depicted walking with the actress Mary though a false city which had been built for a film and was des-tined to be burnt down:

> Jacobo y Mary siguieron su camino por entre las tiendas con figurines y género, que iban a arder al día siguiente. Todo tenía la tristeza esencial de lo que estaba sentenciado. (p.56)

When Abel encounters the actress Virginia, her words sum up their con-dition:

¿Por qué has venido?... Aquí hay el mismo vacío, por más que la mañana sea una alegre mañana de playa [...] Tenemos violada el alma por los grandes focos. (pp.142, 143)

The character's conversation mirrors their futile condition, either verging on the absurd or reinforcing their lack of hope. In one episode celebrities discuss the connection between razor blades and the cinema,[68] when one of them asks the most searching question of all: "—¿Y no te preocupa el más allá?—preguntó Edma Blake a Elsa".

The answer is revealing of the kind of people they are:

Nada...Unos seres entre la sombra y la realidad como nosotros, no tienen ni que pensar en eso. (p.130)

The lack of belief which is a feature of many of Gómez de la Serna's fictional characters is compensated by relying heavily on the absurd as a means of coping with life. Josué, for instance, described as 'El célebre gracioso de Cinelandia' (p.201) has ducks walking through his hotel room: 'Tiene una granja en la que cultiva patos, innumerables patos, patos que aparecen y se pasean por todas las habitaciones de su hotel, sólo patos' (p.201). Josué talks to the ducks, believing that it will enable him to preserve his youthful spirit. His decision to live alone, it emerges, was taken after a friend had died of laughter watching one of his films. In such ways Ramón combines the tragic with the absurd, creating black humour as a way of coping with death and loneliness. Josué, like many of Gómez de la Serna's characters is essentially an avant-garde creation in his aberrant behaviour and lifestyle.

There are numerous chapters which do not feed directly into the narrative, but focus on an array of individual descriptions of anything from Russian princesses to fox-terriers. There are chapters about the Japanese and the black inhabitants of the city, episodes on blind people, drunks, fat people, and a man with face of clay. In this sense, *Cinelandia* is characteristic of modernist fiction at large in the way in which there is a proliferation of non-events, which serve to reinforce the sense of fragmentation and eclipse of an overall, all-encompassing narrative. A multifaceted picture of a modern cosmopolitan city emerges. Because these episodes are tenuously linked and not developed in much depth, they fail to engage the reader on any human level. There is recognition on the part of the characters that their souls have been conditioned by their contact with Cinelandia. Over dinner one of the characters says:

—Nuestras almas están filtradas...demasiado filtradas.
    —Y nuestra proyección es monótona. Si yo tuviese un hijo le prohibiría ir al cine. (p.250)

Life in Cinelandia is depicted as paradoxical and ephemeral, expressed by the narrator in the closing paragraphs: 'Con esa retentiva de vivir resulta más absurda aún la paradoja del no vivir, del dejar de haber vivido aún en el parpadeo del pasado'. (p.217)

The only consolation offered by Ramón at the end of *Cinelandia* is that of having existed: 'El consuelo está en el hecho innegable de haber estado' (p.218), the very same ethos which lies behind much of the avant-garde itself, in that it values itself purely in the present as a way of challenging preconceived ideas, but not as a lasting legacy. The closing lines of Cinelandia depict a world where the glittering opulence and style of the cinema world has given way to impermeable darkness: 'Y en los vanos percheros de los cinematógrafos que anunciaban películas de la muerta, se colgaban el gabán de la noche.' (p.219)

The world depicted in *Cinelandia* is one which continually fluctuates between reality and fantasy. Its constant shift between avant-garde lightheartedness and a critique of the frivolous superficiality of the cinematographic world, seems to underpin a number of the conflicts in the mind of the novelist himself. Without presenting detailed character analyses Ramón still manages to convey recognisable human traits, but fails to create a novel which engages the reader's interest and sympathies at every level. Instead, it should be understood as a sustained exercise in avant-garde aesthetics, drawing on many of the ideas outlined by Ortega y Gasset in *La deshumanización del arte*. Its deliberate rupture of overall structure places it at the heart of modernist literature, and even foreshadows aspects of postmodernism in its crude incorporation of mass culture and its disbelief in society as a whole. It should be taken as an experimental engagement with the new aesthetic formulations of the times.

The bleak depiction of the human condition in *Cinelandia* by no means comes as a surprise. Ramón's controversial theatre play *Los medios seres*, as he makes clear in his autobiography *Automoribundia*, is preoccupied with a similar theme: 'Quería que se comprendiese con más tolerancia el medio vacío de las vidas gracias a mi anatomía diseccionada a la vista del público.' (*AM*, p.525)

Is *Cinelandia* meant to represent western civilization which is in decline? In *El tema de nuestro tiempo* Ortega y Gasset sees a general malaise in western society which he calls 'desorientación vital', the idea that there are no longer any absolute truths or certainties: 'El hombre de occidente padece una radical desorientación, porque no sabe hacia qué estrellas vivir', a sentiment not dissimilar to that which led Ezra Pound to proclaim 'I want a new civilization'.

Is *Cinelandia* representative of a society where the dividing line between the real and the rational has become increasingly blurred? Miguel de Unamuno in *Del sentimiento trágico de la vida* states:

> Hegel hizo célebre su aforismo de que todo lo racional es real y todo lo real racional; pero somos muchos los que, no convencidos por Hegel, seguimos creyendo que lo real, lo realmente real, es irracional; que la razón construye sobre irracionalidades.[69]

Unamuno goes on to express his despair at the futility of a non-theistic modern western civilization which offers little spiritual comfort:

> Sí, si, lo veo; una enorme actividad social, una poderosa civilización, mucha ciencia, mucho arte, mucha industria, mucha moral, y luego, cuando hayamos llenado el mundo de maravillas industriales, de grandes fábricas, de caminos, de museos, de bibliotecas, caeremos agotados el pie de todo esto, y quedará, para quien? [...] Y sucede que a medida que se cree menos en el alma, es decir, en su inmortalidad consciente, personal y concreta, se exagerará más el valor de la pobre vida pasajera[70].

Oswald Spengler again expresses a similar malaise to that of Unamuno when he states:

> In place of a world, there is a city, a point, in which the whole life of broad regions is collecting while the rest dries up. In place of a type-true people, born of and grown on the soil, there is a new sort of nomad, cohering unstably in fluid masses, the parasitical city dweller, traditionless, utterly matter-of-fact, religionless, clever, unfruitful, deeply contemptuous [...] This is a very great stride towards the inorganic, towards the end.[71]

Cinelandia offers us no explanations, no solutions but a picture of an inorganic modern society which cannot ultimately bring about human well-being. If Gerald Brenan was right when he argued that 'disillusion' was a central theme of Spanish literature which could be traced in almost any generation, then *Cinelandia* is in keeping with the Spanish tradition.

Subverting the Crime Novel: El Chalet de las Rosas

El Chalet de las Rosas (1923)[72] is a bizarre attempt at a crime novel, which centres on the character of 'Don Roberto' who lives in 'Ciudad Lineal' on the outskirts of Madrid. Don Roberto is portrayed as a man of basic and ruthless instincts. Although little is known of his background, the reader is informed that he had previously lived somewhere in the Spanish colonies. Don Roberto suffers from inverted values. Throughout the novel he befriends a number of women and then chillingly murders each one, celebrating remorselessly after each crime, for which no motive is given. He kills out of a combination of boredom and misogyny, and is prepared to lie and deceive in order to cover his tracks. His first victim, his wife Matilde, dies after he stabs her to death and buries her in his back yard, covering her in a corrosive liquid to eliminate all traces of the corpse. He meets his next victim, Dorotea Mayel, on a bench near the Prado museum. After six months, he grows tired of her and poisons her. Don Roberto then meets a different woman by the name of Aurelia, who was standing on a railway platform looking as if she was awaiting someone, prompting Don Roberto to invite her home. Aurelia and Don Roberto collude to claim the inheritance of a previous victim doña Dorotea, which they succeed in doing by falsifying legal papers in Don Roberto's custody. Fearing the authorities, they decide to escape to Paris, in search of anonymity, operating under the false names of Fernando and Ana. In Paris they come into contact with bizarre and secretive characters who live on the margins of society. One such character, a Polish Jew by the name of 'Krotzia', had kidnapped a girl twenty years before, holding her hostage in his own home. The world presented is one of inverted values and cruelty. Out of a combination of boredom and an obsession with death, Don Roberto and his new lover Aurelia open a shop of stuffed animals, believing it would allow them to lead a sheltered existence away from the prying eyes of the authorities. After Aurelia visits a fortune-teller, who predicts that she will be Don Roberto's next victim, she reports him to the authorities and he is consequently extradited to Spain to face trial. In Spain, the authorities order an excavation of his back garden, after which they discover the evidence. In his defence, Don Roberto argues that every back garden is a cemetery waiting to be uncovered. He also claims an act of altruism for having reported the Jewish man Krotzia for holding a woman prisoner for twenty years. The latter, with the curious name of 'Tu', attends Don Roberto's trial in the hope of aiding his acquittal. Instead, justice takes its course and he is sentenced to life imprisonment. The novel ends with Don Roberto in jail, where he writes postcards which serve as a kind of confession. The closing lines of the novel adopt a moralising tone, appealing directly to the reader to leave Don Roberto to die alone in his fear and shame.

Most critics agree that *El chalet de la rosas* is an experiment with the crime genre, which is not repeated in subsequent works.[73] On the one hand, it might be argued that Gómez de la Serna is merely experimenting with the genre of the crime novel: the moralising tone adopted by the narrator at the end of the novel is a common trait of the crime-novel genre. On the other hand, it might be argued that his decision to write about a difficult theme such as the one explored in the novel, is in line with what Guillermo de Torre was referring to when he stated "El espíritu nuevo admite todas las experiencias, aún las más aventuradas".[74]

It is interesting that Gómez de la Serna refuses to be limited by the conventional features of the crime novel, bearing in mind Dennis Porter's
contention that the crime novel genre generally remains within the realist
tradition in that it 'reproduces the authority of the social order', and 'situates
its actions in contemporary social reality', and that the characters are chosen
for 'their easily identifiable human or social types'.[75] In *El Chalet de las
Rosas* Don Roberto does not fall into the category of a 'social type' as such,
nor is there much emphasis on the social milieu within which his crimes are
committed. Don Roberto displays traits found in other Ramonian characters
which identify him with extreme insanity at best and cruelty at worst. After
observing people who appear to be reading crime reports in newspapers
whilst travelling on the trams, Don Roberto believes that their faces display a
delight in crime, and therefore is convinced that his criminal activities are
beneficial to society. Rather than presenting the criminal as essentially evil, it
could be assumed that the public at large and the media are in fact responsible for creating the criminal.

The actual process of detection depicted in *El Chalet de las Rosas* departs from that which usually features in conventional detective fiction. In
traditional crime fiction the central preoccupation of the narrative is with the
'closing of the logico-temporal gap',[76] created by presenting the crime first,
and then the steps leading up to it. Suspense is usually brought about by making the reader piece together the various strands of evidence in order to
establish the exact sequence of events and thus uncover the criminal. However, in *El Chalet de las Rosas* Don Roberto is identified as the criminal at an
early stage so that there is no conventional mystery-sequence to draw the
reader in.

Much of the opening chapters are devoted to the surroundings of Ciudad
Lineal—the landscape serving as a vehicle of expression for the mood-
swings of the protagonist. The setting, rather than the crime itself, is evoked
in detail. Much of the imagery of the opening pages is sombre. The opening
scene of the novel is that of Don Roberto and doña Dorotea walking through
Ciudad Lineal towards the chalet. Ciudad Lineal is described as a 'living
cemetery' with little light. The narrator describes the 'pobres hoteles' with
sick people inside, whom he refers to as 'arruinados de luto' (p.187). Don
Roberto is more interested in the trivial events of everyday life, whilst he
treats death with contempt. He shows no remorse after murdering his wives,
but he is preoccupied about people who dye their hair: 'él pensó en la tristeza
de la vida, que hace que las gentes se tiñan' (p.210). After killing his first
wife, he calmly pours himself a glass of cider. Before killing his second victim (doña Dorotea), he deals himself a hand of cards, which decides her fate:

Se puso a hacer un solitario con la baraja. Dorotea, que le veía con fijeza, no sabía que su Roberto estaba echando su suerte, que el 'as' de copas era 'tengo que buscar algo fulminante que le pare el corazón', y el siete de bastos era: 'cuando se me queje de dolores, le daré tal dosis de cafeína, que creo dará al traste con su corazón.' (p.210)

The use of cards to determine whether he will kill her, not only serves to reinforce Don Roberto's insanity, but underpins the importance of chance and luck. Don Roberto's world is one of gratuitous violence and chance encounters. Although the events of the story are recounted with no emotion or sentimentality, the narrator frequently conveys a feeling of emptiness and discontent on the part of Don Roberto: 'El domingo siguiente dejó grandes huellas en su espíritu. Apareció más vacío que nunca, perfilándose los estores blancos sobre la clara luz de domingo' (p.214). Don Roberto and Aurelia's discontent with their surroundings prompts them to hang panes of green glass from their balcony, in an attempt to change the impression given by the surrounding scenery. On various occasions both Aurelia and Don Roberto stare longingly at a picture on the wall, imagining that they are travelling by train through the scenery depicted in the picture. Throughout the novel there is a strong feeling that the characters want to escape their world. In this sense, they are reminiscent of Elsa in *Cinelandia* who sleeps in a cupboard as a form of escape, and to Gustavo in *El incongruente* who frequently embarks on trips on his motorbike to get away from the city. The desire for escape in *El Chalet de las Rosas* is complemented by the characters' feeling of enclosure, of being trapped.

The oppressive descriptions of Ciudad Lineal, the imprisonment of the kidnapped girl by Krotzia and the hidden existence of Don Roberto and Aurelia in their shop full of stuffed animals all convey a sense of oppression. At the end of the novel it is fitting that Don Roberto is trapped in prison, serving a life sentence for his crimes.

The reader's interest is sustained through the exploration of poetic images rather than any sophisticated plot devices. Even a straightforward image such as that of Don Roberto playing the piano can evoke an ambience of death:

Don Roberto entonces se acercaba al piano y tocaba la polca de los huesos, algo tan destemplado, en cuya música sonaban todas las desafinaciones y, sobre todo, el tono marfileño y huesudo de las teclas. Ante esa música temblaban todas las cosas [...] Emprendía una danza macabra, oscilante de ir a caer, cuando arreciaba la música del piano. (p.226)

By comparing the piano tune to 'la polca de los huesos' and using the adjective 'destemplado', the author conveys a sense of death. Don Roberto plays out of tune, causing surrounding objects in the room to tremble in a macabre dance of death. In this way Gómez de la Serna creates a degree of tension and suspense, even though the reader is aware of who the criminal is, and who his next victim will be.

The use of imagery to create a sense of mystery and suspense, replacing the need for the device of suppressing and revealing information used in conventional detective fiction, is perhaps the most important device for keeping the reader's interest alive. Don Roberto's world is alive with imagery, and the protagonist can feel threatened by a tree in the garden, or by the presence of a dark bird sitting in the branches. On another occasion Don Roberto and Aurelia observe birds in flight from their balcony, the railings of which are described as bars of a prison cell, portending the final dénouement of the plot and contrasting the freedom of the birds with the imprisonment of the characters.[77]

El Chalet de las Rosas is replete with dark and disturbing imagery conveying an ominous sense of crime and transgression. Don Roberto's obsession with death permeates and fashions his surrounding world, the objects in his house, the streets he walks through, even his walking stick: 'Acariciaba la bola de billar del cráneo de la muerte con encanto secreto que le confortaba. Todas las tapias del jardín eran tapias de cementerio' (p.240). The shop of stuffed animals which Aurelia and Don Roberto live in is a product of his morbid fascination with corpses. When Roberto is walking through the various stalls at a fair, his deceptive mind tricks him into thinking that he is looking at the severed head of one of his victims. He seldom walks in full daylight, since the fading light of the evening and encroaching darkness provide better cover for his crimes. The natural world, created in the mind of the protagonist, exists in relation to his particular mind-set. Whereas in many naturalist novels nature is depicted as a powerful external force in the life of an individual, here nature is moulded and tailored to the changing moods of the protagonist:

> Con cada crimen se encalma la naturaleza. El paisaje de Ciudad Lineal se sentía adormecer con el nuevo crimen [...] En todo su nuevo paseo notaba por eso cierto triste bienestar. (p.239)

However, the underlying reason for Don Roberto's criminal mind is not explained or explored. Whether this is deliberate on the part of Gómez de la Serna in an attempt to promote a vision of society where the laws of causality have ceased to exist, is debatable. Although *El Chalet de las Rosas* ends on an arguably moralistic note, the narrator's attitude to the crimes carried out in the novel is ambivalent. The episode when Don Roberto observes the public's appetite for crime in the press, which he takes as a justification for his own criminal acts, would appear to suggest that society creates the criminal. Don Roberto is presented as a deranged individual, out of step with normality and extremely solipsistic. In this sense he is similar to most of Gómez de la Serna's fictional characters. However, whilst the eccentricity and madness of other of Ramón's characters is usually of a benevolent nature, Don Roberto's insanity drives him to extreme cruelty. It is not by chance that Gómez de la Serna's characters (including Don Roberto) are extreme individualists living in a society undergoing rapid change. Their deranged, incongruous and eccentric minds are a product of their interaction with a society with which they cannot integrate. Instead, they wander aimlessly on the periphery, their only consolation derived from ephemeral relationships they establish with women, which in most cases end prematurely and certainly do not bring any fulfilment. The vision Ramón presents of the world is almost Schopenhauerian in the extent to which man is depicted as living in a material world, subservient to blind will. Driven by an egocentric and destructive force he is drawn to females to ensure the continuation of the human race. His only possibility to escape the will is through art, through the contemplation of the heavenly realm where the individual loses his personality as he is no longer of himself. However, in *El Chalet de las Rosas*, Don Roberto, despite his interest in art, turns to crime.

In addition to any personal views of the author regarding detective fiction or the nature of crime, there was in Spain, in general, throughout the nineteen-twenties, a renewed interest in the criminal mind, fuelled in part by Freud's forays into the depths of the subconscious mind, and also evident in the surrealists' obsession with the transgression of social norms. In 1921, the journal *Cosmópolis* published a series of articles by Edmundo González Blanco under the heading of 'La antropología criminal en España',[78] which not only confirms a renewed interest in this subject at that time, but which sets out various theories which seek to explain the nature of the criminal mind. It is highly likely that Ramón had read these articles, as he frequently contributed to the journal and despite occasional differences with the editor, Cansinos Assens, his work was frequently reviewed. In one particular article Edmundo González Blanco argues that nowadays there is more interest in the criminal than in the crime itself. He claims that there are no innate criminals, but that most criminals start out as normal people who later turn to crime. He argues that in certain cases the criminal's sophistication is evidence of a superior intelligence to the average human being, which in his opinion, stems from extreme individualism on the part of the criminal, who is only interested in his personal well-being.

The clear parallels of the issues raised in this article with the treatment of the topic in *El Chalet de las Rosas* reflects the prevalent interest in the criminal mind during the first half of the nineteen-twenties. *El Chalet de las Rosas* is therefore important not only because of its contemporary relevance to this issue, but because once again it attests Ramón's ability to create a novel from practically any theme. Departing from traditional approaches to the crime-genre, he creates his own idiosyncratic criminal who shares many traits with other Ramonian characters, and by means of a bizarre and at times disconcerting plot, weaves a narrative of curious dimensions, relying heavily on imagery drawn from his interest in the aesthetics of the crime-novel.

The Bourgeois Don Juan and the Novel of Diminished Horizons: El Gran Hotel *(1922–23)*

Although *El Gran Hotel* (1922–1923) has much of the cosmopolitan flavour to be found in works such as *El caballero del hongo gris* (1928) or *El incongruente* (1922), it is a very different type of novel. Unlike these two works, its setting hardly moves beyond the confines of the hotel depicted in the title. *El Gran Hotel* is particularly interesting for the way in which space is of central importance to the narrative. Action is minimal, and remains for most of the novel within the confined space of the hotel, save for a few sporadic incursions on the part of characters into the town and surrounding hills. Its heavy reliance on the poetic re-creation of space, as a way of compensating for its simple plot, is reminiscent of other of the Gómez de la Serna's lyrical novels. However, despite the lack of experimentalism in terms of style and technique, the current vogues woven into the fabric of the work (mention of foreign cities, travel, cosmopolitanism, dance and sport), classify it thematically alongside the avant-garde works of the author.

Even a superficial reading makes it apparent that *El Gran Hotel* is an experiment in the genre of the 'cosmopolitan' novel relying on the proliferation of non-events as the main driving force underpinning its narrative. Quevedo, the protagonist, decides to spend his inheritance living a life of leisure and comfort, in the opulent surroundings of a big hotel in the city of Geneva. The space of the hotel is far removed from the toils of everyday existence, and its detachment from social problems provides the perfect opportunity for Ramón to engage in an aesthetic appraisal of life, avoiding any social commentary on society at large.

El Gran Hotel is certainly one of the most traditional of Ramón's novels in terms of plot construction. Little attempt is made to experiment with narrative structure. The decision to set most of the action in the foreign city of

Geneva is a deliberate attempt to avoid any 1898 preoccupation with Spain, although the central character Quevedo, as his name suggests, is evidently Spanish.[79] It is a novel which relies heavily on the cult of the image, at the expense of narrative. Despite Gómez de la Serna's disassociation with the Ultraist movement, there are clear parallels with aspects of their poetics. As critic García de la Concha argues:

> El ultraísmo y creacionismo arrancan del mismo propósito, el rechazo de la poesía mimética realista, comparten idéntica obsesión por el cultivo de la imagen aislada; mostrando una clara seducción por imágenes y léxico ligadas al mundo del cine, del deporte y lo dinámico.[80]

The plot of *El Gran Hotel* centres on the character of Quevedo and his sojourn in the hotel. Much of the narrative is taken up with his thoughts and observations as he sits in the quietness of his own room, or as he meets a variety of itinerant guests. The novel ends with Quevedo finally leaving on a train after having spent all his money. The novel carefully balances the shallow optimism and material comfort of a glamorous life-style, with the monotony of daily living. *El Gran Hotel* is a well constructed novel, albeit slow-moving and digressive at times. The main character is not motivated by ideology or any social motives. His delight in style and beauty, coupled with his desire for a life of leisure are all features reminiscent of 'Wildean' characters. His experiences are frequently described in poetic language. Soon after his arrival there is an arresting image of Quevedo who claims to feel drunk by the brilliance of the light which is flooding into his bedroom. Much of the prose reads like a country diary:

> También en el lago había tormentas. Se anuncian por grandes bandadas de gaviotas, que ensucian el cielo mucho más que los vencejos y las golondrinas. Parecen las aguas del cielo, cuando se cubren de gaviotas, unas aguas en las que se han echado los pedazos de una carta, o unas aguas como las de las artesas cuando se echan los trozos de palo de jabón. (p.77)

Poetic deambulations such as the above have no immediate bearing on the plot development, but instead serve to draw the reader into a world of poetic contemplation. The use of landscape as aesthetic material allows an escape from the confined space of the hotel. According to the critic Victor Fuentes, this kind of lyricism was a current trait in the vanguardist writers at large as a way of creating a poetic world of harmony which rises above that which is mundane and common-place: 'Los autores protagonistas se proyectan en sus creaciones, sobre pasando la realidad que novelan, en el papel del poeta—de aquí el marcado carácter lírico de esta nueva novelística—

como liberadora y creadora, que aspira a establecer un Nuevo orden basado en la armonía y en la gratificación'[81].

In a similar fashion, the descriptions of the views from Quevedo's balcony rely on a heavy dose of lyricism: 'Las noches de su hermoso balcón eran noches de perlas, era como si viajase a bordo de un barco por las aguas dulces del Bósforo' (p.137). The imagery is vivid and enchanting, the pearl-like sky meeting the ocean, whilst he imagines that he is sailing across its tranquil surface. Although the action of the novel rarely goes beyond the four walls of the hotel, some of the most beautiful passages take place in the mind of the protagonist. Unhindered by the constraints of time and space, the reader is able to join him on a lyrical voyage which takes place in his imaginary world, thus opening new spaces in an otherwise confined and somewhat claustrophobic novel.

However, Quevedo's sojourn in the hotel is not presented as fulfilling. He frequently feels lonely, a mood ingeniously conveyed through a treatment of objects: 'Los mismos cigarillos le sabían a palillo de la soledad, tenían ese desabrimento a madera desusada y deshilada' (p.21). On various occasions Quevedo reminisces about previous hotels he had stayed in. The language used to describe them is frequently tinged with melancholy and a sense of foreboding:

> Se acordaba de los hoteles sórdidos de París, con sus cortinas de color alpaca de plata con flores negras, con su aspecto de ir a caer enfermo en ellos, con una conmovedora facha de habitación para almas anónimas y que han de morir pronto. (p.12)

The acquaintances Quevedo strikes-up with the various people who pass through the hotel are of an ephemeral and largely superficial nature. Conversations seldom transcend the banal, in what seems a direct attempt to reject a world premised upon rational foundations. Towards the end of the novel, Quevedo is seen talking with 'Olympia' (one of his latest conquests) who is about to depart by train to the city of Berne. When he asks her what her ambitions are, she answers: "A lo más querría poder fumar en pipa y poder colgar en mi cuarto un reloj cuco" (p.189). On another occasion Quevedo has a conversation with a complete stranger. Not knowing her name, the narrator refers to her as 'la flaca'. They discuss her proud resistance to men's advances, which becomes the subject of their conversation. Then there is a humorous twist when she asks whether Quevedo knew her name. Because Quevedo had seen it in the registry book, he answers with the correct name (Mary Ardennes), which elicits the following response in Mary: "Eso me ha conmovido... Bueno, quédese aquí...ha tomado posesión de su cuarto" (p.33). The reasons behind her decision are absurd and fortuitous. Mary is moved by words and token gestures. What follows is an erotically charged scene of Mary undressing and arranging her clothes and jewellery. The moment when she opens her wardrobe is imaginatively brought to life by the author:

> Se había abierto para él la confidencia de aquel armario, y aquella mujer había dejado que se escapasen, para abrazarle, los perfumes de todos aquellos trajes, los deseosos abrazos de todos aquellos brazos caídos, los perfumes de su cuerpo en otras noches de fiesta, muchos abrazos y propensas de aquellos diferentes días del pasado en que fué como otra mujer. (p.33)

The strength of this passage lies not in any peculiar defamiliarisation of reality, but in describing the effects of the perfume and images of her hanging clothes on the protagonist. Any eroticism stems from the exploration of recondite and intimate spaces such as that of Mary's wardrobe.

It would therefore appear that the strength of this work lies in its bringing together of the ephemeral and superficial (life in the hotel) with a deeper and poetic vision of the world (Quevedo's thoughts on life itself). The opulence of his lifestyle is cut short by his limited fortune. Furthermore, his relationships with other men and women are either ended by their departure or amount to no more than brief encounters. Mary Ardennes, for instance, leaves to live in the mountains shortly after his arrival. She is described as someone who would cast 'su silueta de deportista', and spends much of her time engaged in recreational and social activities such as playing tennis and drinking champagne. She is an embodiment of the typically 1920s woman living a hedonistic life of pleasure-seeking.

The reader is not told much about the other women he meets. Elisa is poetically described as a queen who had emerged from the aquamarine depths of a lake. On another occasion Quevedo attempts to seduce a Yorkshire woman, but is unsuccessful as she already had a boyfriend. Matilde, the Cuban woman is abandoned by Quevedo because she is more interested in sport than catering for the nostalgia she elicited in him. He has a short affair with Renée after watching her play tennis, and then meets another woman called Mercedes, has an affair with a cyclist, falls in love with a Russian countess and spends the remainder of his time with Olympia, who eventually leaves for Berne.

In short, as with much of Gómez de la Serna's fiction, the protagonist does not find any lasting fulfilment in his relationships with women. The successive relationships form part of his short-lived quest for happiness within the hotel. Whilst there is much humour, especially in the dialogues between characters, there are constant references to Quevedo's sad recognition that life in the hotel is ultimately unfulfilling. The light which bathes his world is appropriately described as 'luz de limbo' (p.87), and in a revealing episode he admits "No tengo nada…no creo en nada" (p.114). He talks of the need to save his life from 'una fogosidad demasiado estéril' (p.117), and although he admits to having found a degree of happiness in the hotel, he admits that it is ultimately vacuous: 'Era fuerte la alegría del Gran Hotel, pero estaba como vacía' (p.121). Life is presented as temporary and even unreal: 'Pero todo era provisional. Todo en el mundo estaba lejos del mundo. La vida en el hotel era, después de todo, como una vida en el espejo' (p.169). Towards the end of the novel, when he is about to catch a train out of Switzerland, he senses that once the train leaves his only feeling would be 'aquella sensación de vacío' (p.199).

The vision portrayed of the modern world in *El Gran Hotel* is ambivalent. Despite the glamour of those living in the hotel, far from the sphere of social problems, their life-style is presented as ultimately unfulfilling.

Whilst the plot of *El Gran Hotel* is by no means complex, the way in which the protagonist's emotions and feelings are described make it a work of some literary merit. The interest of the novel lies in its poetic vision of life coupled with a deliberate inclusion of modern-day themes, in an attempt to incorporate the emerging aesthetics of the day.

A further point of interest, pointed out by a number of critics is the reworking of the 'don Juan' character-type in the protagonist Quevedo. The reason for naming the main character 'Quevedo' is not explained. However, if we take Ramón's book entitled *Quevedo* into account a plausible explanation begins to emerge.[82] Gómez de la Serna would naturally hold the father of Spanish satire in very high esteem, and in his book on the poet, he claims that 'Quevedo fue uno de los amadores más célebres que en el mundo ha habido'.[83] Ramón argues that Quevedo, despite his religious beliefs, was a kind of 'don Juan', similar, in this sense, to the protagonist of *El Gran Hotel*. He argues that Quevedo had deliberately never married, citing his *letrilla* 'Dicen que me case / digo que no quiero' (p.183). Furthermore, Ramón is attracted to the figure of Quevedo because of the society in which he was immersed: 'La sociedad aristócrata y señoril que le rodea parece quererle escarmentar por sus amoríos locos y por sus sátiras contumaces'. But the passage which most strongly suggests that the protagonist of *El Gran Hotel* could be inspired on the real-life figure of Quevedo is Ramón's personal account of Quevedo's outlook on life:

> La fatalidad de Quevedo, junto a su dualidad, es que lo menor vence en aparencioso a lo mayor, lo anecdótico a lo profundo, sus breves chabacanerías a sus largas sublimidades, su poca fe en la vida a su gran fe en la muerte […]. (p.183)

The protagonist of *El Gran Hotel* is a mixture of all of these traits. He is both a kind of modern-day 'don Juan', and belongs to the upper-middle classes. His lifestyle in the hotel largely consists in minor anecdotal and banal events rather than deeply entrenched spiritual experiences or life-changing situations. His attitude to life is characterised by a lack of faith in anything. Gómez de la Serna presents the main character of *El Gran Hotel* as a mixture of a modern-day Quevedo, and a turn of the century aesthete who delights in the transitory pleasures contemplating life's beauty. Similar to other of Ramón's characters, Quevedo is finally condemned to solitude, as none of his friendships lead to anything prominent. *El Gran Hotel* has to be understood as an exercise in the genre of the cosmopolitan novel, incorporating typically Spanish literary traits through a lyrical prose which lifts human experience to a level of poetic beauty.

Bucolic Retreat and the Lyrical Novel: La Quinta de Palmyra *(1923)*

Although Ramón Gómez de la Serna is principally associated with bringing the avant-garde to Spain, much of his work evinces a poetic and lyrical style of writing which shares considerable ground with movements such as aestheticism and Hispanoamerican *modernismo*. This hardly comes as a surprise, bearing in mind the protean nature of his literary style. In *La Quinta de Palmyra* (1923) although references to the modern world are by no means excluded, they do not constitute the basic recourse of the narrative. Instead, poetic impressions are foregrounded, reminiscent of Anglo-American aestheticism, or French Parnassianism, in the importance accorded to poetic beauty over and above social concern. In *La Quinta de Palmyra* Gómez de la Serna takes his poetic style to new heights, abstracting the immediate world through a lyrical transformation of reality. The world becomes an aesthetic playground of infinite possibilities where the reader is enmeshed in a flux of poetic images and language. The concept of the lyrical novel dovetails neatly with Ramonian aesthetics at large as it represents a kind of 'anti-novel', whereby narrative is based around a combination of poetic images, which attenuate the importance accorded to plot. Earlier on we have seen how Ramón departs from the idea of the traditional novel by compounding his own idiosyncratic aesthetics with avant-garde experimentalism. In *La Quinta de Palmyra* traditional narrative practice is jettisoned through a lyrical transformation of the world.

In *La Quinta de Palmyra* perception is more important than action, and the characters pursue poetic ideals which are ultimately unattainable. At the heart of aestheticism is the idea that the work of art is a means in itself, rather than a means to an end, and that non-aesthetic judgements—whether they be social, religious, or aesthetic—be considered irrelevant. Art is lifted to a sphere of poetic privilege to rival Nature herself, or in Oscar Wilde's words:

> Art finds her own perfection within, and not outside herself. She is not to be judged by any external standard of resemblance. She is a veil, rather than a mirror. She has flowers that no forests know of, birds that no woodland possesses. She makes and unmakes many worlds, and can draw the moon from heaven with a scarlet thread.[84]

The prioritising of the poetic over social, moral and political concerns is central to many of Ramón's works, enabling him to break with traditional narrative practice. Ralph Freedman argues that the lyrical novel 'assumes a unique form which transcends the causal and temporal movement of narrative within the framework of fiction. It is a hybrid genre that uses the novel to approach the function of the poem',[85] and that the narrative is 'poetically manipulated' by an author whose view is 'crystallised in his protagonists, which transform their perceptions into a network of images' (p.16). Freedman suggests (a suggestion which is very relevant to the narrative techniques deployed by Gómez de la Serna) that the world created by the artist becomes a 'picture, a disposition of images and motifs, of relations which in the ordinary novel are produced by social circumstance, cause and effect, the schemes fashioned by chronology' (p.271). In a similar vein, Leon Edel explains these changes in the novel were brought about by what he calls 'the inward turning', whereby 'rationalism' and 'reason' progressively give way to 'introspection' and 'feeling',[86] resulting in a novel which is 'read not as a time sequence but as a heterogeneous series of perceptions each catching its movement of intensity without reference to what lies on the succeeding pages, but the entire reading of which conveys a poetic synthesis'.[87]

Poetic synthesis, prioritising perception over action, imagery over plot and an attenuation of narrative lie at the heart of what Gómez de la Serna is attempting to achieve in these works. These aesthetic preoccupations undoubtedly sit comfortably with modernism at large in their rejection of realist aesthetics. But it would be simplistic to suggest that a renewed interest in perception and poetic imagery is merely a product of the influence of current trends, with no antecedents in earlier literary paradigms. Much of the practice of poetic embellishment as a means of drawing attention to the importance of artifice could equally be attributed to the Baroque. The critic and historian Orozco Díaz argues that the Baroque is a 'constant' which re-emerges in different epochs, generally characterised by 'una agitación y complicación de las formas y sobrecarga y desbordamiento ornamentales'.[88] Díaz compares the Baroque to an irregular pearl which deviates from the perfection of classicist ideas of beauty, causing a particular work of art to stand out in it strangeness, similar to the use of metaphor deployed by the Generation of 1927, as a way of bringing about visual surprise, through a preference for figurative meaning over real meaning. Clearly, the overlap of poetry and narrative has been a recurrent phenomenon since the emergence of the novel, and is by no means exclusive to Ramón Gómez de la Serna's narrative fiction.

Although *La Quinta de Palmyra* was published the same year as *Cinelandia* (1923), *El chalet de las rosas* (1923) and *El novelista* (1923), its style and tone are extremely different. The poetic descriptions of the sea, the opulent setting of the mansion, the decadent life-style of many of the novel's characters, and the unrelenting insistence on the promotion of beauty are reminiscent of *fin-de-siècle* decadentism. Ramón's experiences of Portugal undoubtedly lie at the heart of the novel, and his account of his departure from Portugal in 1925, recorded in *Automoribundia*, sheds some light on his frame of mind when he moved there to have a break from Madrid. It is to be expected that he writes of Portugal in a positive light, after all, like Spain it was untouched by World War I, and as an outsider living on the relatively wealthy Portuguese coast he may not have been aware of poverty and social deprivation :

> Allí encontré sol y aire de últimos de siglo, un lado del mundo rezagado y cordial, lejos de todo, lejos de Europa y lejos de América, un escondite de gaviotas [...] Aquel Portugal no trastornado ni desvariado por la guerra, ilusionado aún por los sueños antiguos, virgen para el turismo, me entusiasmó y me hizo volver al pasado. (*AM*, p.302)

He later describes Portugal as 'una ventana hacia un sitio con más luz, hacia un más allá más pletórico' (p.303). The expectancy and optimism he openly voices, compounded with the nostalgia he feels for the past ('sol y aire de últimos de siglo'), permeates *La Quinta de Palmyra*. In this novel experience is lifted to a sphere of poetic beauty through a lyrical prowess not to be found in earlier novels. Portugal becomes a kind of Arcadia, enabling him to find serenity and solace in natural surroundings:

> Yo era un estudiante perdido y la literatura sólo era idilio, mirar por las ventanas el campo y el mar. (*AM*, p.303)

In this passage Ramón hints at the simple approach he claims to have adopted when writing *La Quinta de Palmyra*: a strait-forward observation of the surroundings. Unlike *El secreto del Acueducto* or even sections of *El novelista*, Ramón does not describe an emotionally charged setting such as

74 THE DILEMMA OF MODERNITY

Segovia or Castile, steeped in legend and history, but is writing about a new landscape, to which he remains an outsider. It is therefore not surprising that the prose of *La Quinta de Palmyra* is permeated with an exceptional freshness and vitality. All critics agree on the lyrical depth of the work.

Luis Cernuda, for instance, characterised Gómez de la Serna's work as a whole as 'la expresión poética en prosa', arguing that:

En Gómez de la Serna encuentra nuestra lírica el antecedente histórico más importante para ciertas formas de 'lo nuevo', captadas por la visión y expresión.[89]

Darío Villanueva argues that *La Quinta de Palmyra* is essentially in line with Ortega y Gasset's idea of dehumanisation. He sees the novel as an artistic object from which the human dimension has been removed in a direct rejection of realism and naturalism. However, he does not analyse the work in any detail, or attempt to analyse the nature of its prose style. Despite the novel's largely optimistic tone, Camón Aznar highlights its 'melancolía insuperable', whilst Granjel dismissively states:

La novela no es sino la crónica de unas fáciles seducciones en las cuales la peculiar situación de quienes las protagonizan, la ausencia en todos de represiones éticas o frenos sociales, priva a los sucesos de dramatismo y hasta de anécdota.[90]

None of the above critics attempt to place the novel within a meaningful context. The most detailed analysis is that of Carolyn Richmond, who argues that *La Quinta de Palmyra* is 'una transformación del ambiente portugués que conoció Ramón'.[91] Much of her introduction is devoted to matching the places which appear in the novel with real places in Portugal—no doubt a useful exercise in that it reminds us of the complex relationship the author had with his surroundings, and removes any illusions we may have about fictional invention. She then goes on to analyse the thematic content of the work, stressing the importance of the sensual dimension of the novel and the fact that Gómez de la Serna's characters are engaged in a perennial search. She contends that the main theme of the novel is 'La búsqueda del amor de un hombre para compensar la soledad de su mundo' (p.81), the failure of which drives the protagonist to embark on a lesbian relationship. Richmond ends her introductory study—after exploring the novel's links with mythology—by raising the problem of literary creation, arguing that the novel is built on a tension between what she defines as 'lo transitorio' (the love affairs of Palmyra) and 'lo eterno' (the relationship between 'la Quinta' and Palmyra even though the description of the Quinta relies heavily on allusive and ephemeral poetic devices, which would suggest that far from establishing the Quinta as a place of eternal value, they make it little more than a poetic construct). She arrives at two different readings, one of which she defines as 'circular' and the other 'linear'. Borrowing Valéry Larbaud's description of it in 1926, she refers to it as 'cette symphonie Portugaise'.

La Quinta de Palmyra (1923) narrates the story of a woman by the name of 'Palmyra', and her attempts to escape loneliness through a series of short-lived relationships. Palmyra lives in an opulent setting ('la Quinta'), and spends much of her time entertaining guests, or riding on horseback through the grounds of the estate. The reader is not told of how she came by her wealth and possessions and throughout the novel she remains something of an enigmatic character.

When Palmyra is alone she speaks to herself. Her loneliness, however, is not existential but aesthetic. It sparks off beautifully melancholic sensations rather than any deep thoughts. Her relationships mainly come about through fortuitous encounters or through guests who come to stay at 'la quinta'. The first to arrive is Armando, who poses as an aristocrat. As time progresses she realises that his motives are not genuine. She has a total of five lovers before she meets her true love, a woman by the name of Lucinda. The lovers range from Armando, described above, to an American sailor who had jumped ship and turned up on her doorstep. She also has a brief affair with the engineer 'Fausto', but soon gets bored with him because he speaks numbers instead of words. Prior to Lucinda's arrival, she falls in love with the eccentric pianist 'Felix', who believes that in order to play the piano successfully, one should always clean one's teeth. The novel ends with Palmyra's decision to establish a relationship with Lucinda out of a mixture of curiosity and a growing disenchantment with men.

Despite its plot, *La Quinta de Palmyra's* strength lies in its lyricism. The surroundings and the world of Palmyra are elevated to a sphere of aesthetic beauty. It reads as a modern pastoral, a kind of Arcadia, where nature is presented as idealised, a place for escape from city-life. Through a combination of highly stylised language, Ramón conveys a world far removed from the harsh social-reality of the everyday world, with no attempt to evoke a real-life picture of Portuguese society, written when he himself was living on the coast at Estoril.

In addition to the novel's avant-gardist humour and its depiction of characters preoccupied with fashion and opulence in a typically nineteen-twenties style, the processes at work are reminiscent of aspects of *fin-de-siècle* aestheticism in the underlying attention accorded to beauty, and the absence of history or ideology. The world of Palmyra is a source of imagery, the description of which halts the flow of narrative and draws attention to the poetic devices at work.

At the end of the novel the narrator implies that the central theme of the work is the quest to be accepted and understood. The work ends with a resolution: Palmyra finds in Lucinda someone who fully understands her. Thematically, it is similar to many of Ramón's novels in its depiction of a slightly eccentric character in search of companionship, following a fairly straightforward plot which presents the reader with no particular difficulties. Stylistically, the picture is more complex. Interwoven with the lyrical passages describing the scenery are clear avant-garde influences, and an underlying ambivalence which informs both the narrator's and the character's view of modernity. Alongside Palmyra's desire to surround herself with 'dulce paisaje' where she could hear 'la respiración de las cosas que se pierden en el ruido de la ciudad',[92] the modern world is always present. The recurring mention of a train passing, and the descriptions of the scenery which flash past in quick succession alternate with the tranquil pastoral settings of the 'quinta'. When some of the characters visit Palmyra, their conversations mirror the age in which they are living. Don Vasco, a friend of Palmyra states how the electric train will be a part of everyday life, whilst Don Mariano is more interested in the aesthetic effects of the electrical sparks illuminating a dark sky. They also express fear that the electric train might efface the beauty of the countryside: 'El tren eléctrico pasaba por sus imaginaciones como guión que suprimiría el campo...' (p.49), and then randomly go on to discuss the value of spiritism and the scourge of the flu.

Palmyra also shows that she has modern sensibilities. On an outing to the Portuguese coast with a group of tourists she delights in the movement of the car, which is described in a style reminiscent of futurism: '[...] Les lanzaba destellos de todos sus cristales, triángulos de luz, losanjes volanderos' (p.95).

If taken at face value, these descriptions are extremely different in nature to the descriptions of the scenery surrounding the 'quinta', and indicate the various tensions which operate throughout the work. The attitudes to modernity found in the novel are ambivalent: on various occasions Palmyra looks out to sea and observes the transatlantic ships which inspire freedom and travel, whilst in another passage we are told of how a woman had died by jumping from a window onto telegraph wires.

It would be misleading to suggest that the inclusion of motor cars, transatlantic ships and fast-moving electric trains are the only way in which Gómez de la Serna evokes the modern age in which he was living. Both the characters he creates and the way in which they interact with each other embody many contemporary traits in terms of their hedonistic outlook on life, their banal conversations and their preoccupation with modern themes. When a party of visitors converge on Palmyra's Quinta, one of the characters asks:

"¿De qué vamos a hablar?" The answer says much about the kind of people they are:

De nada...de esas cosas que se cazan al vuelo, de lo que si no se hablase de ello la vida sería demasiado imponente... pequeñeces. (p.46)

In a world where conversations largely centre on the trivial and banal, small gestures take on increasing significance. We find out more about a character by them hanging their hat on a hat stand than through their conversations:

Su sombrero de luto, con gran pena, colgado del perchero, ponía de luto toda la casa, por eso no lo quería Palmyra. (p.47)

Palmyra's universe is one which is full of imagery, at times conveying the mood of characters. This enables Ramón to avoid in-depth psychological descriptions. Their speech frequently borders on the absurd, as they seek to express their inner sentiments. On one occasion Palmyra tells don Felix—the eccentric piano player—of how she is feeling:

No tengo tristeza humana esta tarde, pero tengo tristeza—dijo ella.
    —¿Pues entonces, de qué clase es?
    —Tengo la tristeza del primer pino en que comienzan los pinares junto a las playas...
    —Siento no sentirme yo otro pino para poderte consolar. (p.137)

Absurdity prevails over reason, and these lines once again show Ramón's interest in characters whose speech departs from rational and meaningful discourse. What makes this conversation even more remarkable is that it is conducted with such naturalness, as though it formed part of a normal world. Palmyra engages in a similar conversation with Samuel, the American sailor who had appeared at her door. Here she deliberately gives incongruous answers to his inquisitive and bizarre statements:

—Ya ves que estamos sentados, pues recorremos kilómetros y kilómetros sobre el terráqueo que se mueve.
    Ella le contestaba con incongruencia para distraerle:
    —Los pinos hacen el día de un verde escarchado. (p.147)

In *La Quinta de Palmyra*, the natural world is a source of harmony. Whether or not this is deliberately intended by Ramón is unclear. On the various occasions when the characters in the novel encounter each other, their conversations are largely banal, frequently bordering on the incongruous and the absurd. Their inability to interact meaningfully as a group mirrors Ramón's own solipsism and extreme individualism. His characters seldom form part of a particular community, or strive for a social cause. Instead they are social misfits, living on the margins of a society undergoing rapid modernisation. The extreme solitude of their world stems from the conflict between hope and reality, and an inherent ambivalence towards modernity. Ramon's characters are born from a mixture of *fin de siècle* decadentism and avant-garde humour, and therefore can never be fully integrated into society. The characters in *La Quinta de Palmyra* are devoid of any tragic resonance at any level, even human pain and sorrow are played out aesthetically. Despite the numerous instances in the novel when Ramón poetically evokes the modern world, much of the lyricism in *La Quinta de Palmyra* derives from the surrounding scenery, or the palace itself—as seen in the opening paragraph of the novel:

> Era un palacio clarito y triste. En los copones de sus esquinas estaba depositada el agua de las lluvias antiguas como reservorio de las lágrimas del cielo. (p.33)

Natural elements such as the sky and the sea constitute much of the subject matter being described. The open spaces of the sky and sea evoke a sense of optimism and possibility. Nature is never presented as a vehement and threatening force. Instead it is domesticated and humanised: 'las lágrimas del cielo', and serves as a vehicle for aesthetic experience. For Palmyra, the sea not only symbolises freedom, but constitutes a part of her everyday life:

> El mar entró en la habitación como colcha de damasco azul, de las que resbalan voluptuosamente porque cuando se abre la primera ventana frente al mar, el despertar de la vida tiene algo de ola. (p.131)

The natural elements change Palmyra's perception of her surrounding world, elevating everyday scenes to a place of poetic beauty. The colour of a table cloth can be evoked with a reference to snow: 'La nieve del mantel caía sobre la mesa...'(p.55), and drinking wine from a glass becomes a vehicle for aesthetic experience:

> Bebía con delectación su vino predilecto, que veía enrubecido por la luz que caía del sol a través de las nubes. (p.55)

However, it is not only the physical environment of Palmyra that is aestheticised. She too is presented as a poetic idea, her beauty idealised in a fashion reminiscent of the Petrarchan lyrical tradition in the depiction of her luminous gaze and ethereal qualities. Palmyra, despite her incursions into the world of 1920s travel and conversation, is a product of literature. She is not drawn from society, but is modelled on the pastoral: in Spring she is clothed in roses, and in autumn she is dressed in leaves:

> Y en las primaveras se sentía adornada con canesús de rosas y en otoño se sentía vestida con trajes de larga cola, trajes verdes hechos con hojas ensartadas. (p.118)

The fact that much of the narrative of *La Quinta de Palmyra* is devoted to descriptions of her, comes as no surprise. In a similar way to a number of female characters of Gómez de la Serna's (Cristina in *La viuda blanca y negra*, Lucía in *La mujer de ámbar*, Aurelia in *La nardo*), she is described solely in poetic terms. She is said to be filled with 'un silencio ambarino precioso' (p.64), and her skin is so clear that it has 'calidades marinas' (p.134). Descriptions of her are lifted to a poetic plane in order to reinforce her distance from the harsh realities of life. Whether she is lying on the expansive beaches of the Estoril coastline, or playing the harp in the confines of her home, everything she does is lifted to a plane of poetic beauty:

> Palmyra arrastraba hasta el centro de la habitación su arpa y llovía sobre los muebles del gran salón, sobre todo dentro de los espejos, la lluvia del arpa, con sus grandes y atravesadas gotas de lágrimas lentas […] Las manos de Palmyra en las cuerdas doradas eran como pájaros musicales que hiciesen sonar su jaula. (p.67)

The melancholy tones of her music are conveyed by the metaphorical treatment of notes as tears which are falling like rain. The image of her hands as birds, fluttering along the strings which are compared to the bars of a cage, is once again evidence of his poetic sensitivity.

It is not always easy to define Gómez de la Serna's lyricism and where it stems from. Many of the poetic images he creates rely on a fairly straightforward metaphorical mechanisms (many of his *greguerías* function in this way), whilst other images are deliberately influenced by the modern age, such as the following description of steam emanating from a ship's funnel: 'Los vapores blancos parecían aeroplanos lanzados en la imensidad celestial del mar' (p.77). However, towards the end of the novel, when Lucinda has arrived at the 'quinta', Lucinda reads Palmyra extracts from what she claims to be a book which was dedicated by one female lover to another. The passage she reads is analogous in terms of imagery to aspects of *modernismo* in its depiction of white swans as a paragon of elegance and beauty[93]:

> ¡Ah! tu carne, bajo el agua y bajo mi carne, mi carne que busca todo lo que la huye y se la parece...Los cisnes turbados por nuestra rivales blancuras se aproximan y nuestros cuerpos se mezclan al 'duvet' de sus alas. (p.176)

The image of the swan in Rubén Darío's *Prosas profanas* was deployed to represent a pure and perfect form of elegance, gliding along the surface of a lake. Its slender white neck and fine plumage set it above other birds which is why it was adopted as a symbol of *modernista* poetry, which sought distance from the harsh and gritty reality by focusing on pure forms of beauty. Its inclusion in Gómez de la Serna's novel confirms the strong influences of the Hispanic *modernista* writers on his style, and shows—at least at one level—the tensions which operate in his work. The inclusion of this passage within *La Quinta de Palmyra* not only militates against realism, but against the images and motifs of the avant-garde. By foregrounding imagery drawn from *modernismo*, Ramón confirms his debt to this movement and the important role it plays in the novel. Palmyra, despite her cursory incursions into the modern world, has something of the turn-of-the-century heroine in her opulent lifestyle and embellished surroundings. She does not share the pathos of a Romantic heroine, and in any case, her surrounding world lacks the turbulence of a Romantic landscape. Her mannerisms and life-style (her endless quest for pleasure and beauty) are reminiscent of numerous Wildean characters, and the idyllic setting which surrounds her is one which stands out for its beauty. Palmyra represents a *fin-de-siècle* heroine living in a world undergoing rapid modernisation. She inhabits a world which stands out for its idyllic beauty, whilst the encroaching world of modernity moves in. Her ambivalence towards modernity stems from her own questions about a world which is moving on regardless of her sedentary lifestyle in 'la quinta':

¡Qué importa quedarse si todo eso se va! ¡De qué vale que nos creamos inmóviles!, pensaba Palmyra asomada a los cristales y viendo pasar las nubes cinematográficas de aquella tarde. (p.174)

The use of modern imagery in this passage is deliberate. By describing the clouds as 'cinematographic clouds', the author is distancing himself from traditional sky-imagery in order to illustrate the changing nature of Palmyra's world. Palmyra is aware of this change world as she is of the passing clouds over her dwelling. Even the descriptions of her solitude shift between a fairly traditional use of the natural elements, to images taken from the sphere of travel:

Las noches tenían monotonía de travesía. El marino fumaba en su camarote aunque estuviese con Palmyra. El cigarro estaba lleno de nostalgias cubanas. (p.153)

It is the fusion of the modern and the traditional which lies not only at the heart of *La Quinta de Palmyra*, but at the heart of much of Gómez de la Serna's 1920s fiction. In *La Quinta de Palmyra*, however, the balance is more heavily weighted towards aestheticism in its continual emphasis on beauty. However, unlike *El alba*, it is channelled into a narrative which expresses an experience common to most of his fictional characters.

La Quinta de Palmyra is essentially an exercise in poetic prose, an evocation of a modern-day Arcadia, depicting the banal existence of a decadent bourgeoisie, with very little in the way of social criticism on the part of the author. The transatlantic ships, the numerous foreign tourists, the itinerant sailors add a cosmopolitan flavour to this modern-day pastoral. Sharing many common traits with other of the author's works, it certainly stands out as one of his most poetic novels.

Notes

I have borrowed this title from Roger Shattuck's The Banquet Years: The Origin of the Avant-garde in France, 1885–1918 (London: Southern Cape, 1969).

1   Ramón Gómez de la Serna, *La sagrada cripta de Pombo* (Mardid: Visor Libros, 1999) p.12. From now on all citations from *Pombo* will be referred to as *PB*.

2   In most of the literary journals of the nineteen-twenties the theme of travel featured strongly. E.Gómez Carrillo, for example, wrote an extensive article on the fashionableness of travel: 'La psicología del viaje', *Cosmópolis*, 1 (1919) 610–631.

3   Francisco Umbral argues that 'Hay una relación clara entre cosmopolitanismo y vanguardia. A la vanguardia europea y española le mueve una razón romántica, el progreso, y una razón anti-romántica: el internacionalismo. Con la vanguardia mueren los nacionalismos románticos. El vanguardista quiere ser de todas partes', *Ramón y las vanguardias* (Madrid: Espasa-Calpe, 1978) p.123.

4   Antony Leo Geist, cited in: *La poética de la generación del 1927 y las revistas literarias: de la vanguardia al compromiso: 1918–1936* (Barcelona: Guadarrama, 1980) p.61.

5   Christopher Innes, *The Avant-garde Theatre (1892–1992)* (London and New York: Routledge, 1993) p.38.

6   Víctor Fuentes, 'La narrativa española de vanguardia (1923–1931). Un ensayo de interpretación', in *La novela lírica II*, ed. by Darío Villanueva (Madrid: Taurus, 1983) pp.155–163.

7   Victor Fuentes, 7.

8   Guillermo Díaz-Plaja, *Estructura y sentido del novecentismo español* (Madrid: Alianza editorial, 1975) p.202.

9   Fernando Vela, 'La poesía pura', in *Revista de Occidente*, no. 41 (November 1926) 217–240.

10 Wylie Sypher, *Rococo to Cubism in Art and Literature* (New York: Vintage Books, 1960) p.264.

11 Wylie Sypher, p.266

12 This article appeared in the revue *Cosmópolis*, 33 (1921) and can also be found in Paul Ilie's compilation of articles and manifestos: *Documents of the Spanish Avant-garde* (Chapel Hill: University of North Carolina, 1969).

13 Paul Ilie, p.396.

14 G.G. Brown.

15 Guillermo de Torre, 'Problemas teóricos y estética experimental del nuevo liricismo', Cosmópolis 32 (1921) 585–607 (p.594).

16 Luis Fernández Cifuentes, 'Fenomenología de la vanguardia: el caso de la novela', *Anales de la Literatura Española*, no. 9 (1993) pp.45–59 (p.52).

17 I use the word 'renewed' as various forms of literature of the fantastic have obviously co-existed with realist literature at other times and cannot be solely attributed to the nineteen-twenties.

18 Ramón Gómez de la Serna, *El Gran Hotel* [1923] (Barcelona: Al Monigote de papel, 1942). All quotations from now on will be made from this edition.

19 Gómez de la Serna, *Cinelandia* [1923] (Madrid: Valdemar, 1995).

20 Ramón Gómez de la Serna, *El caballero del hongo gris* [1928] (Madrid: Alianza Editorial, 1970). From now on all quotations will be made from this edition.

21 It is interesting that the journal *Cosmópolis* dedicated a monthly article entlitled 'Fisionomía de ciudades', giving an outline of the cultural developments in various European cities after the war, commenting on new theatre productions, books and architecture.

22 Ramón Gómez de la Serna, *El doctor inverosímil* [1921] (Madrid: Destinolibro, 1981). I will be quoting from this edition from now on.

23 Rafael Cansinos Assens, *La novísima literatura*, (Madrid: Paez, 1925) p.372,3.

24 Cited in Rafael Fuertes Mallá, 'Ortega y Gasset en la novela de vanguardia española', Revista de Occidente, no. 96 (May, 1989) 27–56.

25 The newspaper El Sol had a regular column entitled 'Biología y medicina', in which Dr. Marañón offers advice to his readers whilst disclosing the latest advances in medicine. This is not only significant because it confirms the importance of the humorous treatment of medicine to the nineteen-twenties, but because Gómez de la Serna was personally aquainted with Dr. Marañón (see *AM*, p.270). The issue dated 22nd February 1923 (Año VII, no. 1,683) includes a cartoon which tells the story 'Andanzas y desventuras de un microbio', adopting a jocular tone analogous with Ramón's depiction of malady in El doctor inverosímil.

26 Renato Poggioli, *The Theory of The Avant-garde*, trans. by Gerald Fitzgerald (Cambridge, MA: The Belknap Press for Harvard University, 1968) p.111.

27 Poggioli, p.111.

28 It was published in 1921 by Atenea, in Madrid.

29 I will be citing from the Destinolibro edition (Barcelona,1981) as it follows the original text closely.

30 Rodolfo Cardona sees this work as both evidence of 'Ramón's theory of the influence of 'things' in our lives'—many of the character's maladies appear to derive from the presence of specific objects in close proximity—whilst at the same time displaying Freudian revelations before his ideas had been widely accepted and divulged to the public'. (Cardona, 1957, p.125). Antonio del Rey Briones argues that it contains 'la mayoría de los elementos que configuran la narrativa de nuestro autor' (Briones, 1992, p.111) whilst Camón Aznar calls it 'una de las novelas más representativas de Ramón' (Aznar, p.304). Granjel cites Nora's well known view that El doctor inverosímil takes the reader 'por el camino del más absurdo y juguetón humorismo', (Granjel, p.197) whilst Guillermo de Torre, as early as 1921 stated: '*El doctor inverosímil* viene a constituir uno de los más netamente expresivos ejemplos del humorismo acrobático y la sagacidad mental de Ramón Gómez de la Serna'. Guillermo de Torre, 'Cinegrafía: el cinema y la novísima literatura: sus conexiones', *Cosmópolis*, 33 (1921) 97–107.

31 Patricia Waugh, *Metafiction: The Theory and Practice of Self-conscious Fiction* (London and New York: Routledge, 1984) p.10.

32 Waugh, p.10.

33 The Surrealists were also fascinated with gloves and in André Breton's 1924 manifesto gloves are associated with death: 'Surrealism will usher you into death, which is a secret society. It will glove your hand, burying therein the profound M with which the word memory begins' (Breton, p.32).

34 He states: 'En mis ideas médicas se mezclan la realidad y la fantasía' (p.687).

35 Ramón Gómez de la Serna, *Nuevas páginas de mi vida: lo que no dije en Automoribundia*, 2nd edn (Madrid: Alianza Editorial, 1970) p.74.

36 Gómez de la Serna, *El incongruente* [1922] (Barcelona: Ediciones Orbis, 1982).

37 Harrison and Wood op. Cit (p.1118)

38 Ibid

39 Ibid, (p.1119)

40 Ibid, (p.1118)

41 Antonio del Rey Briones states: 'Ramón colabora—junto con Kafka—a instaurar, como alternativa, la novela de situaciones caracterizada por la exposición de sucesos y circunstancias entre los que no deben mediar necesariamente las relaciones causales o las motivaciones lógicas que configuran un proceso'. In 'Ramón y la novela', *Insula*, 502 (1988) 17–18.

42 Many years later Ramón, writing on Dalí, shows his continuing contempt for Sartrean Existentialism: 'El destino del surrealismo era el de empalmarse con otra doctrina más alta y más nueva que no fuese de ningún modo el chabacano y monstruoso existencialismo sartriense'. In *Dalí* (Madrid: Espasa Calpe, 1985) p.95.

43 Op cit David Bell, in Harrison and Wood, (p.1118)

44 Paul Ilie describes *El incongruente* as an 'intellectual fairy-tale'. *The Surrealist Mode in Spanish Literature*. (Ann Arbor: The University of Michigan Press,1968) 152. Agustín Sánchez Vidal in 'Ramón y el surrealismo', suggests that there are considerable similarities between Gómez de la Serna, Buñuel and Dalí: 'Hay en esa actitud algo de preludio de las técnicas preconizadas por Luis Buñuel y Salvador Dalí, los dos creadores a los que cumplió históricamente asentar el surrealismo en España. También en ellos sus respectivas matrices poéticas parten de una ruptura del vehículo que une a los objetos a su entorno habitual para redefinir su identidad en otro contexto mediante un proceso de extrañamiento, proponiendo disociaciones y asociaciones inusitadas, tal como pedía Ramón', *Insula*, 502 (1988) 13–14. Camón Aznar sees it as 'Un anticipo del suprarrealismo' (Aznar, p.316). Rodolfo Cardona claims that it is 'A greater masterpiece of surrealism than Breton's landmark novel *Nadja*', (Cardona, 1957, p.22). Antonio del Rey Briones states: 'Capta admirablemente la obra el espíritu de su época: la derrota de la razón y el desconcierto latente, por lo que su parentesco con el mundo kafkiano resulta innegable [...]'. (Rey Briones, 1992, p.117). Mainer argues that Gustavo, the protagonist of *El incongruente* 'es la encarnación humana más apta para la sobrevivencia física y moral en el difícil y proteico mundo ramoniano'. José Carlos Mainer, Prólogo a *El incongruente*, (Barcelona: Editores Picazo, 1972) pp.11–34 (p.28). Ignacio Soldevila, similar to Rodolfo Cardona's earlier observations, argues that in *El incongruente* the author is 'Un precursor de la vanguardia, y aquí con una actitud postdadaísta, sienta precedentes, se anticipa al *surréalisme* francés, que al año siguiente Breton inaugura con su primer manifiesto'. In 'Del punto al contrapunto: *El incongruente*', Iona Zlotescu (ed). *Ramón Gómez de la Serna: Obras Completas: Novelismo I (El doctor inverosímil y otras novelas 1914–1923)* (Barcelona: Galaxia Gutenberg-Círculo de Loctores, 1997) pp.61–63 (p.61). Hoyle argues that *El incongruente* subjects traditional narrative conventions 'to a form of fragmentation that produces an effect of abstraction and estrangement from familiar reality, and is also a playfully provocative self-projection of the author's personality (not as novelist but as self-caricature)'. Alan Hoyle, 'Ramón Gómez de la Serna: Avant-garde Novelist *Par Excellence*', in *Hacia la novela nueva: Essays on the Spanish Avant-garde Novel*, ed. by Francis Lough (Oxford: Peter Lang, 2001) pp.61–77 (p.69).

45 André Breton, p.14.

46 Discrepancies between the various editions of this novel will be discussed at the end of this section.

47 Gómez de la Serna's own idea of the world is one of incoherence which can only be expressed incoherently: 'Un mundo incoherente no puede tener otra expresión que la de la incoherencia'. Cited in Francisco Rico (ed) *Historia y crítica de la literatura española:*

época contemporánea: 1914–1939, Victor García de la Concha (Barcelona: Ediciones Crítica, 1984) VII, p.208.

48 Breton, p.9.
49 Bell Op cit, (p.1119)
50 Ramón Gómez de la Serna, 'Las palabras y lo indecible', *Revista de Occidente*, no.51 (January,1936) 57–87.
51 Pío Baroja, *La caverna del humorismo* (Madrid: Colección Selecta, 1919) p.200.
52 Ramón Gómez de la Serna, *El incongruente* (Madrid: Los Humoristas-Calpe, 1922).
53 Op cit Bell, (p.1121).
54 Luis Granjel, *Retrato de Ramón* (Madrid: Ediciones Guadarrama, 1963) p.199.
55 Antonio del Rey Briones, *La novela de Ramón Gómez de la Serna* (Madrid: Verbum, 1992) p.115.
56 Briones, p.115.
57 Camón Aznar, *Ramón Gómez de la Serna en sus obras* (Madrid: Espasa Calpe, 1972).
58 Camón Aznar
59 Alan Hoyle, 'Towards an Understanding of *El secreto del Acueducto*', in *Studies on Ramón Gómez de la Serna*, ed. by Nigel Dennis, Ottawa Hispanic Studies 2, (Dovehouse Editions Canada, 1988) 173–198 (p.174).
60 Hoyle, p.174
61 Ignacio Soldevila, 'El sexo y la eternidad de la piedra', *OC*, IX, 1999, pp.55–57 (p.56).
62 See Carolyn Richmond's introduction to her 1986 edition: *El secreto del acueducto* (Madrid: Cátedra, 1986). All quotes will be taken from this edition.
63 Ernesto Giménez Caballero, 'Paisaje en materia gris', in R.Buckley and J. Crispin, *Los vanguardistas españoles: 1925–1935.* (Madrid: Alianza Editorial, 1973) pp.24–27 (p.24).
64 Ortega y Gasset, 'Sobre el punto de vista en las artes.', *Revista de Occidente* (1924) pp.129–160, (p.143).
65 Camón Aznar, *Ramón Gómez de la Serna en sus obras* (1972, p.324). Antonio del Rey Briones (Verbum, 1992). Carolyn Richmond, 'Proyección de lo falso: *Cinelandia*', Zlotescu, 1997, pp.27–31, (p.27).
66 Ezra Pound, 'Hugh Selwyn Mauberley', in *The Norton Anthology of Modern Poetry*, Ed. by Richard Ellmann and Robert O'Clair, 2nd ed (New York: Norton and Company, 1988) p.383.
67 George Simmel, cited in Stromberg p.226.
68 This reference to the razor blade and cinema is reminiscent of the opening scene of Dalí and Buñuel's surrealist film *Un chien andalou* (1928) made several years after the publication of *Cinelandia*. In this sequence a razor blade is depicted cutting the human eye, according to Paul Ilie symbolic of 'human knowledge' being 'obscured' and 'deformed' by 'a technique of deliberate mutilation that appears to be rationally controlled, but which commits an absurd act.' He goes on to suggest that 'This is the work of the razor blade and the new sensibility it brings. It allows the sectioned eye to continue seeing, but the pupil will now register a disjunctive image upon the retina. And this kind or perception is just like the sensory dislocation which we have found to be so common in the surrealist experience'. *The Surrealist Experience in Spanish Literature: An Interpretation of Basic Trends from Post-Romanticism to the Spanish Vanguard* (The University of Michigan Press, 1968) p.178
69 Miguel de Unamuno, *Del sentimiento trágico de la vida* (Madrid: Espasa Calpe, 1976) p.29.
70 Ibid, p.56.

71 Oswald Spengler, cited in Roland N. Stromberg, *An Intellectual History of Modern Europe* (New York: Appleton, 1966) p.124.

72 Ramón Gómez de la Serna, *La Quinta de Palmyra y El Chalet de las Rosas* [1923] (Barcelona: Bruguera, 1968).

73 Camón Aznar characterises *El Chalet de las Rosas* as 'la novela del crimen', arguing that it boasts of 'una prosa muy apretada, y de las más transparentes de Ramón' (Aznar, p.318). Antonio del Rey Briones argues that Gómez de la Serna 'acierta a proyectar su personalidad sobre un tema y un estereotipo narrativo de la época que no volverá a repetir' (Rey Briones, p.120). Ignacio Soldevila on the one hand argues that the author distances himself ironically from the protagonist of *El Chalet de las Rosas*, whilst simultaneously arguing that it reflects 'la creciente misogenía Ramoniana', in 'Bajo la hoja de parra', Suplemento CULTURAS, *Diario 16*, 2 July 1988, p.2.

74 Guillermo de Torre, 'El espíritu nuevo de los poetas', en *Cosmópolis*, 1 (1919) 17–28 (p.22).

75 Dennis Porter, *The Pursuit of Crime: Art and Ideology in Detective Fiction* (New Haven and London: Yale University Press, 1981) p.121.

76 Porter, p.29.

77 Gómez de la Serna's use of imagery instead of intricate plot devices or formal innovations, confirms the view of Camón Aznar, who argues that in traditional literature everything is geared towards the final dénouement of events, whilst Gómez de la Serna does precisely the opposite. 'Los poros, las puertas que se abren al mundo vivo, requiriendo interferencias en el argumento. Por eso su genio auténtico se manifiesta en las greguerías, que son como perlas sin hilo. Todo cortado, con una visión cuántica de la realidad. Con esas interrupciones con que la vida va cerrando los sentimientos y las perspectivas que quieren ser unidas formando bloques emotivos y argumentables, pero que Ramón desgrana en las manos de todos los encuentros y fenómenos causales' (Aznar, p.34).

78 Edmundo González-Blanco, 'La antropología criminal en España', *Cosmópolis*, 26 (1921) 285–399.

79 Despite its lack of experimentalism, some critics have made reference to the collage techniques, and argued that they confirm a cubist influence. However, it is my contention that the use of collage to which they are referring—namely the inclusion of hotel menus and registry forms within the text—are of tangential importance to the novel as a whole. Their only use is that of saving narrative time, as the reader finds out about Quevedo through the information he gives to the receptionist in the form of a hotel registry, rather than being informed by a narrator.

80 Cited in Rico, 1984, (p.211).

81 Cited in Darío Villanueva, 'La estética ramoniana de la novela', *Insula*, 432 (1982) 7.

82 Ramón Gómez de la Serna, *Quevedo* (Madrid:Biblioteca Nueva, 1950).

83 Ramón, *Quevedo*, p.182.

84 Oscar Wilde, 'The Decay of Lying', *Complete Works of Oscar Wilde*. (London and Glasgow: Collins,1966) pp.970–993 (p.982).

85 Ralph Freedman, *The Lyrical Novel: Studies in Herman Hesse, André Gide and Virginia Woolf*, 3rd edn (Princeton: Princeton University Press, 1963) p.1.

86 Leon Edel, *The Modern Psychological Novel* (Gloucester: Peter Smith, 1972) p.27.

87 Edel, p.137.

88 E. Orozco Díaz, 'Introducción al Barroco Literario Español', *Historia de la Literatura Española* (Madrid: Guadiana, 1975) pp.23–177 (p.27–28).

89 Luis Cernuda, *Estudios sobre poesía española contemporánea* (Madrid: Ediciones Gudarrama, 1957) p.168.

90 Luis Granjel, *Retrato de Ramón* (Madrid: Ediciones Guadarrama, 1963) p.201.

91 Carolyn Richmond, 'Una sinfonía portuguesa: estudio crítico de La Quinta de Palmyra', in *La Quinta de Palmyra* (Madrid: Espasa Calpe, 1982) p.42.

92 Although I have made reference to Carolyn Richmond's edition of *La Quinta de Palmyra*, due to the printing errata which have duplicated parts of the text and omitted others, I will be citing from an earlier edition of the work: Ramón Gómez de la Serna, *La Quinta de Palmyra* (Barcelona: Ediciones Bruguera, 1968) p.39.

93 This is reminiscent of Rubén Darío's depiction of swans in *Prosas profanas* (1896–1901): 'Oh cisne! Oh sacro pájaro! Si antes la blanca Helena / del huevo azul de Leda (See also the poem of Darío on Leda) brotó de gracia llena / siendo de la Hermosura la princesa inmortal / bajo tus blancas alas la nueva Poesía / concibe en una gloria de luz y armonía / la Helena eterna y pura que encarna el ideal.' Extract from 'El cisne', *Prosas profanas* (Caracas: Biblioteca Ayacucho, 1977) p.213.

Chapter 3. The Art of Un-Making Novels: *El novelista* (1923)

I am drunk from having swallowed
the entire universe, on the quay
from which I saw the darkness flow,
and the barges sleep.
> Guillaume Apollinaire (1880–1918)

Madrid es no tener nada y tenerlo todo.
> Ramón Gómez de la Serna (1888–1963)

La soledad no se nota si está llena de cosas.
> Ramón Gómez de la Serna

In *El novelista* (1923), normal narrative conventions are subverted through a departure from traditional plot devices, in a deliberate attempt to break with naturalistic organicity. *El novelista* is a novel which is essentially about the process of writing itself, and is therefore central for anyone attempting to come to an understanding of Gómez de la Serna's poetics. The protagonist of *El novelista* is himself a novelist who is writing a varied collection of novels and stories, which when pieced together, form the overall work: *El novelista*.[1] It is arguably Ramón Gómez de la Serna's most ambitious work, in that it attempts to create a literary whole from a mosaic of individual anecdotes and potential novels in the making. Whilst the laying bare of the creative process on the part of Ramón is not a device which is exclusive to this work, Ramón takes the practice of 'novela del novelar' to new lengths, and in the process questions the relationship between fiction and reality. What first strikes the reader about *El novelista* is the breadth of its scope as a novel. It is made up of over forty individual stories and fragments of novels, all tenuously linked through the author-protagonist Andrés Castilla. What emerges is a multifaceted, labyrinthine literary construct set over a variety of cities and locations including Madrid, Paris, London, Lisbon and rural Castile. The surname of the protagonist ('Castilla') is, in my view, highly significant. Both Castile and Madrid feature heavily as the backdrop to much of *El novelista*, which is to be expected given the importance of Madrid to Gómez de la Serna (and by extension, Castile). Regarding the important link between Madrid and Castile, Manuel Lacarta argues that:

Madrid representa, a fuerza de un centrismo político no deseado por los madrileños de siempre, el desorden de Castilla hasta culminar con una autonomía uni-provincial, artificial y desgajada en atención a su peculiar geografía urbana.[2]

Lacarta argues that the Generation of 98 attempted to re-engage with the Castilian landscape with a view to '[...] rescatar una parte significativa y acercarse a todo, vislumbrarlo, al menos, desentrañar Castilla en recuperar—por extensión—España.'[3] *El novelista* offers Gómez de la Serna's particular view of Madrid, Castile and beyond through a multifaceted and multi-angled viewpoint, in keeping with the broad tenets of the modern novel—Frank Kermode has defined the modern novel as 'multidimensional, fragmentary, without the possibility of a narrative end'.[4] What better way to draw attention to man's fragmentary and fleeting perception of the world than through a narrative structure which deliberately rejects the organic structures of 19th century realism and naturalism? Cubism had shown the world that the work of art is more important for the sum of its parts than for the whole; and this is precisely what *El novelista* sets out to do. There is no over-arching narrative underpinning *El novelista*, no sense of final resolution, and only a limited plot progression. As Patricia Waugh suggests, the literature of that time mirrored developments in science, confirming the view of a world made up of small individual parts, and the idea of an organic whole, of an overall structure giving way to an increased awareness of the importance of isolated fragments[5]. Implicit in *El novelista* is the view that 'reality or history are provisional: no longer a world of eternal verities but a series of constructions, artifices, impermanent structures'.[6]

However, the extent to which Ramón consciously adopts a meta-fictional framework for his novel *El novelista* as a direct response to the process of history is unclear. It seems more plausible to attribute the work's formal innovations to the already mentioned parallel developments in the world of avant-garde art and science. With the demise of Newtonian physics and the growing perception that the world was not built upon fixed values, it is understandable that the artist's understanding of the world should undergo considerable change.

El novelista emerges at a time when these changes in the perception of the world were beginning to take hold and artists were beginning to respond to them. Where its narrative structure is concerned, *El novelista* needs to be understood within the context of modernist fiction at large. In addition to linking Ramón with contemporary international literary figures such as Joyce or Woolf in the way in which traditional notions of literature are subjected to questioning, *El novelista* also provides the reader with a blue-print of Ramón's approach to writing. The metafictional thematising of the process of creative writing allows the reader to observe the author at work. However, despite its fragmentary structure and poetic qualities, much of *El novelista* consists of realistic descriptions of real-life characters.[7]

It is worth bearing in mind that cubism not only broke down the unitary viewpoint from which to observe an object, but it also showed that 'all entities or factors in the universe are essentially relevant to each other's existence', as 'every entity involves an infinite array of perspectives'.[8] It is by presenting the reader with 'an array of perspectives', a variety of plots and settings that Gómez de la Serna experiments with generic conventions of the novel.

The depiction of Paris, Madrid, London and Lisbon, or a village in rural Castile in *El novelista* for example, differs from the bizarre and at times surreal settings to be found in novels such as *Cinelandia* (1923) or *El incongruente* (1922). The vision of the world projected by Ramón is one which is largely drawn from his observations of life. Characters are not located in a surrealist dream-world, but in a recognisable and credible environment. This does not limit Ramón's ability to re-create and transform his observations of the world into a poetic construct—the various chapters recounting the story of a row of street lamps is a case in point—but rather suggests that Ramón is primarily interested in questioning the conventions of the novel.

The formal experimentation of *El novelista* through its fragmentary structure, to some extent foreshadows the French writers of the *Nouveau Roman* decades later: namely the way in which the novel not only draws attention to its own artifice, but at the same time flouts the very conventions upon which it is built. It has elements of the post-modern conception of the novel (before such a term came into being), such as a loss of faith in large-scale structures and an increasing preference for syncretism. Such interpretations of Ramón's work are by no means new; critical commentaries have recurrently highlighted the fragmentary nature of his writing. Contemporaries of Ramón, such as Pedro Salinas, argued that 'Para Ramón el trabajo literario es una especie de anticreación; todo debe desajustarse, deshacerse, desmontarse...',[9] whilst Amancio Sabugo Abril considers that Gómez de la Serna's style of writing is in keeping with a modern desire to dismantle prose: 'Intención moderna de descoyuntar la prosa—como en la pintura hará Picasso—reduciéndola al esquema esquelético, deshumanizado, de huesos y nervios'[10]. It is debatable however, whether a fragmentary and disjointed structure should necessarily imply a greater degree of dehumanisation, and the idea that this technique is limited in that it only presents us with what Sabugo terms a 'nervous system', is misleading. It could equally be argued that by breaking away from a unitary viewpoint, and opening up the novel to a multiplicity of different narratives, the author is in fact providing the reader with a fuller, albeit a more complex vision of the world.

Nigel Dennis argues that the fragmentary nature of Gómez de la Serna's writing stems from a desire to reject the legacy of the nineteenth century and the concept of a 'complete, fully-rounded literary artefact'[11]. He takes the view that Gómez de la Serna tended towards a kind of 'deconstruction', whereby there was an 'insistent' move away from 'the wholeness towards the isolated, self-contained fragment'[12]. Thus, Gómez de la Serna deliberately moves away from a 'single, harmonious, intelligible artistic entity', towards a systematic process of rupture 'breaking it down into multiple component parts, each of which is then studied, explained or interpreted separately'[13]. This conclusion is to a large extent largely confirmed by comments made by Ramón himself, when, in the preface to his *Greguerías selectas* (which is not simply referring to *greguerías* but to prose writing in general) he advocates a style of writing which attenuates narrative:

> La prosa debe tener más agujeros que ninguna criba y las ideas también. Nada de hacer construcciones de mazacote, ni de piedra, ni del terrible granito que se usaba antes en toda construcción literaria. Hay que romper las empalizadas espesas.
>
> Todo debe tener en los libros un tono arrancado, desgarrado, truncado, destejido. Hay que hacerlo todo como dejándose caer, como destrenzando todos los tendones y los nervios, como despeñándose. 14

Ramón not only highlights his deliberate departure from traditional approaches to writing, but also intimates that because there is no absolute truth, it is the author's duty to evoke a chaotic and jumbled picture of the world. He openly admits that he prefers his novels to resemble the image of a jungle than that of a carefully cultivated garden.[15]

As a consequence of its fragmented narrative structure the narrative thread of *El novelista* is elusive. Between the opening chapter, where the novelist Andrés Castilla can be seen correcting a draft of one of his novels *La apasionada*, to the final chapter when he moves into a new home where he will spend the rest of his days in a solitary existence surrounded by all his works, the reader encounters a plethora of different stories and diverse episodes, ranging from encounters with various characters to reflections on the actual process of writing. In the closing chapter the novelist has settled into his new home overlooking the sea, the descriptions of which draw the reader into a dreamy world of melancholy lyricism often found in Gómez de la Serna's work. The proximity of the sea sparks off existential questions in the mind of Andrés, whilst at the same time revealing some of the motives behind the writing of such a prolix novel. The closing lines, therefore, are an appropriate place from which to start an analysis, as they contain some of the reasons which prompted Andrés to adopt the style of writing he did, whilst at the same time they convey the author's need to write as a way of making sense of life. Because of the central importance of these lines, they are quoted here in full:

> Los novelistas deben ser muchos, distintos, entrecruzados, pues hay mil aspectos de lo real en sus mareas movidas por lo fantástico que hay que perpetuar. Todas las combinaciones del mundo son necesarias para que éste acabe bien desenlazado, y si inspira a la vida una ley de necesidad, se podría decir que está bien que existan todas las novelas posibles y que alguien tenía que tramar las que aparecieron viables.
>
> Hay que decir todas las frases, hay que fantasear todas las fantasías, hay que apuntar todas las realidades, hay que cruzar cuantas veces se pueda la carta del vano mundo, el mundo que morirá de un apagón.[16]

The idea that it is the duty of the writer to include diverse portraits of the world and bring them together in one novel is the key to understanding *El novelista*. The fact that many of the individual parts which make up *El novelista* are reasonably realistic, is significant in the same way as a cubist picture is. A cubist picture has a strong impact not because it presents the viewer with bizarre imagery, but for its geometric and recognisable shapes which have broken with a unitary view point of the object or panorama being observed. In a similar fashion, *El novelista* is constructed from individual stories which in most cases adhere to a fairly traditional style: it is their arrangement within the novel as a whole, the way in which the episodes do not follow each other in a traditional and linear sequence that gives *El novelista* its particular structure. This system of composition obviously has repercussions on the nature of time in the novel, as linear time is disrupted. The overall structure of *El novelista* appears to be very close to the Russian Formalist idea of plot construction, whereby the artistry of an author is judged by the arrangement of the narrative material. By the time the reader reaches the end of *El novelista*, it is unlikely that he or she will have a clear and fixed idea regarding its narrative. The reader will, however, have witnessed the extent to which the arrangement of aesthetic material within the novel is an important feature of the work as a whole.

It is its apparent deregulation and lack of any clear blueprint, save that expressed in the closing lines of the novel, which makes *El novelista* unique. In the intervening narrative between the first and final chapter (there are forty-seven chapters in the novel), the reader is presented with at least a dozen different drafts of potential novels, ranging from stories set in Madrid or the country-life in a backwater village in Castile, to far-fetched accounts of *El inencontrable* and *Las siamesas*. Scattered between these profuse attempts at narrative drafts, are episodes which deal with the actual process of writing itself. The line between fiction and reality becomes increasingly blurred through a deliberate ambivalence created by Andrés Castilla, the protagonist and author within the novel, who never makes it clear as to whether his characters are purely fictional or not. The interaction of fictional characters with their author is a phenomenon which came to be associated with Pirandello's play *Sei personaggi in cerca d'autore*, even though there is strong evidence to suggest that Ramón's theatre, written several years before his narrative fiction, promotes a pre-Pirandellian use of characters. Gómez de la Serna's *El teatro en soledad* appeared in 1911, almost a decade earlier than Pirandello's play.[17]

It is precisely the convergence of many different influences which make *El novelista* such a heterogeneous novel. Within a fairly innovative framework, there are clear influences of realism, *costumbrismo*, aestheticism, fairy-tale fantasy, and even some instances of what could be called magical realism. Written a year after Joyce's *Ulysses*, it might be best understood as part of a wider international trend of innovative approaches to writing. However, it would be wrong to draw too many parallels between this novel of Gómez de la Serna and the modernist style of the Anglo-Irish tradition. One of the noteworthy aspects of *El novelista* is the traditional style of its individual components, and, as opposed to Joyce or Virginia Woolf, there is no use of techniques such as the stream of consciousness or interior monologue. Instead, what makes his work distinctive is his own idiosyncratic vision of the world, broken down through his deconstructive and *greguería*-infused prose.

It has already been argued that in Gómez de la Serna's fiction there is a tension between a desire to 'aestheticise' on one hand, and a penchant for avant-gardist experimentation on the other. The fusion of these two tendencies, which despite being in direct opposition, converge in his fiction. *El novelista* embodies a fusion of styles, which draw on a mixture of realism and aestheticism.

The realist and *costumbrista* element is arguably the strongest and appears most consistently throughout the novel as a whole. The sub-novels (a term chosen for the multiple fragments of novels which make up *El novelista*) such as *La criada*, *Todos*, *Libídine*, *Al balcón*, *Pueblo de Adobes*, *El barrio de Doña Benita* and *Novela de la calle del Arbol*, draw, as their titles suggest, on a fairly straight-forward observation and representation of the surrounding world. All of these stories have realistic settings, with credible plots and life-like characters. The settings pertain to a visible and generally conventional world, whilst there are barely any distortions imposed by an undue attention to the psychological spaces of the mind. Many of the characters are portrayed in a behaviourist fashion, seldom allowing the reader to gain access to their minds, but only observe their actions and conduct.

In *La novela de la calle del árbol* for example, the imagery presented is drawn from the real world of streets and balconies in the city of Madrid. There is no inclusion of bizarre and esoteric images. Andrés himself informs the reader that this novel is 'un juego de balcones, de historias, de público de las tiendas, de transeúntes' (p.39). Clearly preoccupied with the passage of time, he admits to writing this novel in order to document a contemporary street scene, aware that life would change in years to come. The mood transmitted is understandably nostalgic, evoking a picturesque world of reassuringly normal occurrences: women shaking cloths out the window, and children playing in the street. There is scarcely any attempt to explore the individual characters in any depth, the author appears to be much more interested in portraying a general vision of the inhabitants in this tree-lined street, akin to what Camilo José Cela was to achieve many years later with his characters in *La colmena*, where the reader is invited to contemplate the lives of over a hundred characters in a Madrid café.

El barrio de Doña Benita, which Andrés starts in the second chapter of *El novelista* also draws on a *costumbrista* and realist tradition in terms of style. The plot, on the other hand is somewhat far-fetched and bizarre. Set in a Madrid neighbourhood, the recently widowed Doña Benita decides to build a neighbourhood on a rubbish heap. Her reasons for doing so are not entirely clear, although the impression is given that she was attempting to avoid loneliness in the wake of her husband's death. The characters who live in this town are also drawn directly from life: rag-and-bone men, retired colonels and night-watchmen, an ex-governor of the Philippine Islands, a woman called 'doña Fanny', and Rafael, the young explorer who frequents a local café. Much of the narrative consists of descriptions of the actual surroundings. The neighbourhood in *El barrio de doña Benita* is said to have been constructed on the past:

> [...] edificado más que sobre tierra, sobre un falso montículo hecho de lo que tiró todo el pasado a la que entonces fue la sima más lejana de las afueras. Sobre el más ancho vertedero estaba construido aquel caserío, de una realidad desesperada, cruda, atroz, sobre la que lucía como una luna muy transparente y de óvalo muy pequeño, el rostro de la hija del trapero. (p.19)

The detailed surroundings are easily visualised in the reader's mind, and the observations in *El barrio de doña Benita* are clearly drawn from the author's experience of provincial Spanish rural life.

Rafael arrives in the neighbourhood with no particular plans save that of becoming integrated into the normal pattern of life. His marriage to Rosario (daughter of one of the rag-and-bone men), is, in part, an attempt to be accepted into the close-knit community. Much of the narrative is caught up

with the description of the neighbourhood and its surroundings. Rafael is introduced to Fernando, Rosario's brother. Rafael, jealous of the attention
Fernando receives from Rosario, kills him, an act which marks the end of the
novel. This short novel unfolds at different stages and in different sections of
El novelista. Interspersed with chapters are accounts of Andrés (the novelist)
meeting with a personified 'inspiration', and a novel about a street lamp.
This disjointed approach breaks with narrative continuity. Similar to *El barrio de doña Benita; Pueblo de adobes*, *Al balcón*, and *Las criadas* all draw
on a realist tradition of portraying real-life characters and settings. In *Las
criadas*, Andrés Castilla shows compassion for the plight of servant-girls
who work in opulent homes around the city, pondering on the unfairness of
their plight compared to the freedom enjoyed by passers by. The plot of this
short piece is simple and yet moving. Andrés Castilla informs the reader of
how he will go about writing it: 'Bastaba con que su protagonista pasase por
muchas casas y viese la tragedia de las otras compañeras y sufriera su propia
tragedia' (p.49). This apparent compassion for women also contrasts with the
usual sense of threat and fear which women in Gómez de la Serna's works at
times elicit. As Hoyle suggests, despite the roles played by many women in
his works, Ramón was a keen supporter of egalitarian feminism, and his
long-standing relationship with the suffragist Carmen de Burgos bears this
out.[18] In *Las criadas*, the female characters are not depicted as objects of the
author's desire, but elicit the readers sympathy in an unprecedented way for
Ramón. The admission of Andrés Castilla that he will write *Las criadas* after
observing their plight suggests a traditional approach to writing where narrative is born from an author's observation of the surrounding world.

The desire on the part of Ramón to root his narrative in the real world is
central to understanding *El novelista*. Current critical opinion would confirm
this view. In the most recent study on *El novelista*, Hoyle argues that it 'projects the private experiments of the avant-garde writer into a public realm of
the realist novel'.[19] *Pueblo de Adobes*—one of the longer novels within *El
novelista*—is a good example of this style, taking the reader into a rural
backwater somewhere in the heartland of Castile. Andrés embarks on a trip
to the country in an attempt to rid himself of his growing scepticism. He
informs the reader of his decision to write a novel along the following lines:
'debía vivir un pueblo castellano, macizo, enterizo, con escalofrío de siglos,
los pasados y los futuros, en crespo entrechoque' (p.128). Whilst the narrative is laced with *costumbrista*-like passages, this sub-novel is interesting
because there are instances which prefigure magical realism, and the presence of characters such as the giant, bring about a sense of the fantastic.

Pueblo de adobes centres primarily on the noble figure of 'don Daniel'
and his wife 'Prepedigna'. Together with two other local people, don Daniel

is the proprietor of a village well. The surroundings are evoked in a relatively conventional style, but don Daniel's well is described in a poetic and imaginative style more typical of many of Ramón's works:

> El pozo de don Daniel tenía una ventana a otro cielo en su fondo y como en una aspiración que naciese del infierno mil manos ansiosas, escarbajeantes, arañadoras, querían libertar a las almas caídas, trepando por el enladrillado desigual que lo revestía. (p.130)

Don Daniel's well acquires mythical status for many of the villagers, as its water is believed to be purer than that of the other wells. People travel from far away to drink from it. Don Daniel is portrayed as a respected and wise man, who draws his wisdom from his well, which he always visits when he has to make an important decision:

> Insistía en sus pensamientos el pozo como una fuente de sabiduría, y cuando tenía que resolver algo grande y trascendental, recurría a él, lo abría como un libro y sacaba un cubo de agua, que se contentaba con ver babear y chirbatear fuera del cubo, como agua inquieta que sintiese el deslumbramiento de la luz y el temblor del mundo. Al mirarse en las aguas de su cubo, encontraba el fondo de espejo más verdadero que se conoce, y veía su cabeza como degollada por la verdad... (p.131)

The magical properties of the well lift *Pueblo de adobes* out of the realm of traditional realism, infusing the story with an element of fantasy. The growing fascination with the well prompts 'Juan el pocero' to convince don Daniel to clean it out, although the latter is reluctant to disturb whatever lies at the bottom. When one day don Daniel finds that he cannot pull the bucket up as usual, he enlists the help of others. After a considerable exertion of energy, they pull up what appears to be the corpses of two soldiers from a Napoleonic regiment, who had been thrown down the well during the war of Spanish Independence. The soldiers are still holding their guns in a crouching position. This causes don Daniel's well to be talked about even more. The fusion of a realistic setting with aspects of magical realism[20] clearly adds to the varied nature of this work as a whole, and the difficulty in placing it under strict category. *Pueblo de adobes* continues with an interjection on the part of the novelist Andrés, who admits to writing a novel that would appear to be 'amasada más que escrita', and 'contemplada más que relatada' (p.139). There is an episode which depicts the fascination of five village boys with the pigeon huts strewn across the harsh table-land which surrounds their village. There is an account of the wintry months in the village, and of don Daniel's spacious barns of grain, the contents of which he generously distributes to the poor and needy. There is an account of men who had wandered the flat plateau-land of Castile in search of bread, who become direct benefi-

ciaries of don Daniel's hospitality. Don Daniel gradually shows signs of ageing, and falls victim to various ailments. After a brief intervening passage in
which Andrés is criticised by an anonymous interlocutor for not giving his
characters enough psychological depth, and for writing a hybrid kind of literature, Andrés continues to write *Pueblo de adobes* introducing new
characters which he asserts to be typical of any Castilian village: that of a
madman, a giant and a dwarf. These characters imbue the story with fairy-
tale-like qualities, and after various possible endings of this novel are discussed with a character, Andrés moves on to another story, leaving *Pueblo de
adobes* unfinished and open-ended.

   Whilst much of *El novelista's* style draws on traditional approaches to
writing, there is a constant fusion of fantasy and aestheticism. The novel
subverts a traditional conception of the novel, through an inclusion of the sort
of device which has subsequently been attributed to postmodernism: a continuous presence of metafictional references, a noticeable 'defocalisation'
which prevents a reader from identifying with a character by not allowing the
reader to spend enough time with the character, to name only a few of the
devices at work. Each one of these techniques militates against a closed concept of the novel, presenting instead an open-ended work where the onus is
on the reader to impose some form of order on a disparate and tenuous narrative structure.

   In *Exaltación del farol*, Ramón poetically recreates a street where the
street lamps converse with each other. The street lamps are compared to
mandolins and guitars, which disperse the melancholy of night: 'Se podría
decir que tocan las guitarras o mandolinas de su luz, despejando de
tristonerías la noche' (p.69). In a similar way to the aesthetic depiction of
dawn in *El alba*, written whilst he was living in Paris, the passage on street
lamps in *El novelista* draws attention to the aesthetic dimension of objects,
questioning the hierarchy of established order by making objects more important than the fictional characters of the novel. The story of the street
lamps is interrupted by various other chapters and continued later on in the
novel, when Andrés is visiting London. One street-lamp in particular catches
his attention, and in a similar style to that of a child's fairy-tale, he describes
its glowing cheeks and the conversations it has with other street-lamps. Their
conversations resonate with a sense of nostalgia and the awareness that a new
kind of light will soon be invented which will replace the flickering gas-light.
The fascination with street lamps and the blurring effects of gas lamps and
fog is reminiscent of Oscar Wilde's description of them in his essay 'The
Decay of Lying'.[21] It might also be argued that Unamuno's *Niebla* (1914),
and Gómez de la Serna's *Novelas de la nebulosa*, partake of a common
Wildean influence in the importance attached to the blurring effects of mist.

Wilde's insistence that it was the artist's duty to move away from the mundane depiction of everyday life through a poetic embellishment which lifts things to a place of aesthetic importance is reminiscent of Gómez de la Serna's style. Furthermore, the idea of mist or fog is like a curtain which, like art itself, should come between reality and the artist, obscuring the obvious and making the process of straight-forward description difficult. To illustrate this point Oscar Wilde argued that art should be a veil, rather than a mirror: 'Art finds her own perfection within, and not outside of herself. She is not to be judged by any external standard or resemblance. She is a veil, rather than a mirror'.[22] Ramón was clearly acquainted with the works of Oscar Wilde. His brother had translated *A Picture of Dorian Gray* into Spanish, and Ramón himself had written a portrait of Wilde, which although focused largely on the anecdotal, and by no means attempted to provide an analysis of Wilde's works, nevertheless confirms the importance of Wilde to Ramón. In the same portrait Ramón reminds the reader that as early as 1909 he had published translations of Wilde's work carried out by his university friend Ricardo Baeza.[23]

Towards the end of *El novelista* in the chapter *Las siamesas* Andrés Castilla writes about two sisters who are literally joined at the hip. Barred from a normal life-style due to their deformity, one of the sisters Dorotea feels attracted to a man. One night she awakens to find her sister dead, and calls for the doctor. The doctor separates them, resulting in Dorotea's death. Although the dénouement of this bizarre story verges on the tragic, there is a heavy dosage of alleviating humour. Whilst at school the sisters had made a deal that one of them would not be held accountable for the other one's sins, to alleviate embarrassment at the confession box. In his biographical sketch of Oscar Wilde, Gómez de la Serna makes reference to a short story of Wilde's entitled: *Los nuevos hermanos siameses*[24]. The plot is very similar to that of Gómez de la Serna's *Las siamesas*. A woman gives birth to twins who are joined at the side, and the doctor predicts that they will not live for very long. However, a man arrives on the scene who believes that there is a chance that they will survive, as long as they learn to hate each other. He then teaches them hatred and jealousy, so that their hearts will eventually grow apart becoming two hearts, so that they can then each go their own way. The plot is interesting as it extols evil as necessary to human evolution. In a similar way to Baudelaire, who in *Les Fleurs du mal* makes direct reference to the Edenic myth of the tree and the forbidden fruit, arguing that knowledge is attained through transgression. It is evident that this notion would appeal to both Wilde and Gómez de la Serna alike, since they were both interested in upsetting the norm, and challenged a complacent acceptance of traditional values.

The break with novelistic conventions in *El novelista* is achieved at two levels: on a formal and structural level, and through a narrative style which draws on a multitude of genres ranging from realism and aestheticism, to magical realism. If all of these influences combine to make *El novelista* Gómez de la Serna's most complex work, they can be also seen in his shorter fiction. However, because of the limitations of the short story, it is more usual for the author to build a short story around one tendency alone, rather than creating a syncretic narrative similar to that of *El novelista*. Revelation rather than resolution is characteristic of a story, whereas resolution is characteristic of a novel. It might be argued that in *El novelista* Gómez de la Serna turns the traditional function of the novel on its head. On the one hand, the myriad plots and sections of novels which constitute the fabric of the novel defy any sense of resolution (many of the novels end tentatively). On the other hand, it is clear that none of the independent stories within *El novelista* conform to the generic specifications of the short story: they are merely sections of novels. A short story and a short novel are by no means the same thing. The techniques employed for each respectively are quite different. In *El novelista* Gómez de la Serna writes a novel about novel-writing, but denies the reader any sense of resolution.

El novelista cannot be properly understood without making reference to the concept of simultaneism as in essence it encapsulates what *El novelista* is all about: namely the heterogeneous depiction of events simultaneously. Roger Shattuck defines simultaneism a concept which is central to the avant-garde enterprise as it allows for contradictory concepts to be held together: 'Simultaneism soon reached the point of assuming a significant relation between all coincidental happenings, objective and subjective, even when the relation was not immediately clear'. He goes on to argue that simultaneism '[...] seizes a new kind of coherence, a new unity of experience [...]' whereby 'unity becomes not a progression but intensification by standing still, a continuous present in which everything is taken together and always'.[25] Simultaneism is both central to *El novelista* and Gómez de la Serna's literary enterprise as a whole, and is central to understanding his poetics. Simultaneism, in Shattuck's view:

> Maintained an immediacy of relationships between conscious and subconscious thought. It encompassed surprise, humour, ambiguity, and the unfettered association of dream. Cohering without transition it gave the illusion of great speed though always standing still. Speed represented its potential inclusiveness, its freedom from taboos of logic and polite style. Stillness represented its unity, its continuous present, its sole permanence: whereas automatic writing strove to divulge the subconscious mind by grasping everything that approaches its surface, simul-

taineism strove to reveal the entire universe in its potential unity at a moment of time.[26]

El novelista presents the whole of Gómez de la Serna's universe in a microcosm simultaneously, thus breaking with the sequential order and outmoded patterns of the naturalist work. María Fernández Utrera argues that *El novelista* is a prototypical avant-garde novel as it is in her own words 'complete' and 'total' in that it apprehends reality in all its dimensions, not dissimilar to Gómez de la Serna's well-known comparison of his prose-writing to a sponge. Utrera states:

> [...] podemos argumentar que la problemática de una gran parte de la novela y el arte de vanguardia española gira en torno al intento de creación de la obra de arte total: la obra pánica, integral, de cuyos parámetros no queda nada excluido, y que aprehenda la realidad en sus tres dimensiones, con todas sus perfiles.[27]

Fragments and Vignettes: A Brief Overview of Ramón Gómez de la Serna's most Significant Short Stories

In his much cited essay 'Novelismo', Gómez de la Serna states that those who write short stories lean out 'a ventanas distintas, a amores variados, a viajes todo lo diferentes que necesitan ser en la vida moderna'[28]. Apart from this vague statement, there is little written about his views on the genre of the short story. This is somewhat surprising, given the large number he wrote. What is more, nothing Gómez de la Serna states in these lines is exclusively applicable to his short stories, but would be true of his longer fiction also. It would therefore be foolish to take Ramón's statement about the short story genre as a reliable blueprint, and better to look at the short stories themselves in order to come to an understanding of the place they occupy within his work as a whole. Bearing in mind the fragmentary structure of *El novelista*, and Ramón's tendency to construct a narrative out of a single impression or a particular object, it comes as no surprise that he wrote numerous short stories, as the genre of the short story, with its tendency to capture one aspect or one impression of reality, is a fictional mode well suited to Gómez de la Serna's style of writing. The *greguería* is a highly useful device in itself, as it enables experience and perception to be succinctly conveyed within the limited space available for short story writing, where lengthy descriptions are not always feasible.

Much has been written on the technique of the short story. What all critics agree on is that the short story begins near to the end, that it generally omits long scenic descriptions. The world it presents is usually of an ephemeral nature, which is presented rather than analysed. The brevity of the short-story demands an aesthetic rather than a mimetic treatment of the world, and therefore tends to avoid realism. Whereas a novel usually develops a theme, a short-story merely shows it. Short stories focus on culminations rather than on developments, and the characters are frequently products of lyrical intuitions.[29] Charles May argues that the short story only 'makes use of those details which are necessary for the purposes of the story, and its progress seems to be directed toward a single goal'.[30] Friedman argues that 'the novel advances and develops its theme, while the story just shows it'.[31] As we will see, these definitions do not always hold true in Gómez de la Serna's work, but are helpful as a way of differentiating the two genres of writing. In-depth character analysis for example, has always been considered a trait of novel characters. However, the lack of character psychology is a trait of both Ramón's short and longer fiction.

Most of the stories to be discussed in this chapter were written between 1917 and 1936, and were largely grouped together in three volumes: *El dueño del átomo*,[32] *La malicia de las acacias*,[33] and *Seis falsas novelas*.[34] A substantial number of them were published in *Revista de Occidente* during the twenties and early thirties, some of which re-appeared in the three compilations already mentioned. Each book-title bears the name of one of the short stories which it contains, with the exception of *Seis falsas novelas*. Even a superficial reading of these stories shows that they were grouped together somewhat haphazardly, and there is no central theme (perhaps with the exception of *Seis falsas novelas*) around which each compilation is assembled. In each of these three volumes there are stories which bear a resemblance to stories in other volumes, and it would therefore be inappropriate to understand them as three coherent compilations, each with a unifying theme or style. There is no evidence to suggest that the decision to group these stories under three headings stemmed from a thematic or aesthetic preoccupation. For example, *La malicia de las acacias*, both a short story and a title of one of the compilations, bears much more resemblance to the story *El olor a las mimosas*, which appears in the *El dueño del átomo* collection, than it does to most of the stories which appear alongside it. Even *Seis falsas novelas*, which, according to Iona Zlotescu, can only be understood as a whole,[35] are disparate and exhibit different aesthetic and thematic preoccupations. *María Yarsilovna (falsa novela rusa)* (1923), for example, is an aesthetic parody of the great Russian novels, whilst *El hijo del millonario (falsa novela norteamericana)* (1927) is a damning critique of excessive materialism and greed in a technologically advanced society, which bears more resemblance to certain aspects of the novel *Cinelandia*, than it does to the other stories alongside which it was published..

Many of the stories focus on human relationships, set against a poetically charged world, some of which are relatively traditional in style and content, although there are often incursions into worlds of strange and at times absurd properties. Others simply evoke the modern world by focussing on typically avant-garde and contemporary themes, such as that of medicine in *El gran griposo* (1927), that of science as seen in *El dueño del átomo* (1926), a magic and quirky world depicted in *La capa de don Dámaso* (1924), the reversal of normal hierarchies as seen in *La mujer vestida de hombre (falsa novela alemana)* (1925) and the preoccupation with form and shapes, as seen in *La casa triangular* (1925). In the following pages I intend to highlight some of the main characteristics of the most important and representative stories written during this time dealing with representative stories from each compilation in order of publication.

La malicia de las acacias (1923), both a short story and the title of one of the volumes of short stories, is set in the Madrid neighbourhood of 'barrio de mediodía' during the months of Spring. In the early pages of the story, the author depicts a world which is bathed in the optimism of spring, where the drowsy scent of flowers fill the air with promise and love: 'Las acacias llovían perfume sobre ellos, que en su embriaguez apoyaban el hombro del uno en el otro'.[36] The main character Fernando frequents a garden of flowers with the hope of meeting a partner. His dream comes true when he meets Flora. The traditional clichés of spring, love and the symbolic use of flowers are re-worked within this short story, drawing on traditional literary tropes such as the 'locus amoenus' garden of love, as a means of asserting the importance of locale. Set against a pervading world of youth and love, is a world of more sombre qualities. There is talk of a typhus epidemic sweeping through the streets of Madrid, and the happiness of Fernando and Flora is threatened by the possibility of death and disease closing in around them: 'Con gran incertidumbre se despedían frente a aquellas noches exuberantes, en que la vida se les prometía muy feliz mientras la muerte acechaba' (p.16).

Although Fernando and Flora are aware of death, they choose to take refuge in their idyllic world of flowers. When they hear that a friend of theirs had died of typhus, they avoid the funeral, retreating instead to a park, where they can walk amongst the comforting shade of the trees. Their world is one of short-lived sensations which partially obscure their vision of harsh reality. The flowers serve to reinforce the idea of short-lived beauty, which is subject to the changing forces of brooding nature. Asserting their right to happiness in a world of transitory beauty and ongoing suffering, they attempt to evade the painful side of existence for a world of natural beauty. The transience of their world is evoked with the changing seasons and the variegated light. When September arrives, their desire to continue living in their world of flowers causes them to frequent a greenhouse, aptly described as a 'biombo laberíntico de tiempo hipócrita, que dejaba intersticios para que alguien pudiese ver lo que nadie veía' (p.21). The end of spring and the summer takes its toll. Despite their efforts to live as though September had not arrived, their lives become increasingly dreary and monotonous. The open spaces of the park soon give way to the sombre enclosed space of their home. They lose their first child through a miscarriage. Their existence becomes increasingly steeped in the monotonous routine of daily life, and the light which bathes their world is monochromatic. The colourful descriptions of the flowers have ceased: 'Eran dos vidas que no podían remontarse, dos vidas cogidas en el cepo de lo cotidiano' (p.36). Their world of idealised love lived out amongst the flowers has now withered into the past, and it soon emerges that Flora has had another miscarriage. The story ends with the burial of their second child.

The imagery of the flowers in this story represents the fleeting beauty of the world which is ultimately short-lived. What started out as a sentimental romance ends with a bleak depiction of family ruin caused by thwarted dreams and personal tragedy. The highly stylised prose intensifies the feeling of decline from the blissful atmosphere of the opening pages, to the sombre mood at the end of the story.

In 1918 the journal *Grecia* published a story by an unknown author by the name of José Mar, with a similar title to Ramón's: 'La venganza de las flores'. The story tells of how a so called Fernando reminisces about his first love Violeta, who had died. Fernando would frequent her tombstone, adorning it with flowers during the bleak winter months. One day, on the way to the graveyard, he encounters his new girlfriend Elvira. Pretending that the flowers were in fact for her, he gives them to her. Later that night he has a disturbing dream, where the flowers in his room take on the form of an octopus, and strangle Elvira. When morning arrives, Fernando asks a servant to send for Elvira, but it soon emerges that she has died that night. According to the doctor she had choked in her sleep due to asphyxiation, which he explained because of the numerous plants and flowers in her bedroom. The extent to which Ramón is influenced by this story or not, is difficult to say, although both Ramón and José Mar use the motif of flowers, turning the traditional symbolism of flowers on its head in a style reminiscent of Baudelaire's *Les Fleurs du mal*.

In *La tormenta* (1921)[37] it is a storm which plays an important role in terms of the effect it has on the protagonist 'Rubén', and because it serves as a means of lifting the prose into a realm of unconventional poetic imagery:

Como un buche de agua contenido en la boca, como un estornudo, difícil de evitar, la tormenta contenía las grandes bolsas de agua que hinchaban los carrillos del cielo. (p.116)

External factors such as the weather, are shown to play an important role in the lives of the characters. In *La tormenta* Rubén and Elvira's feelings towards each other are heightened by the storm: 'Sentíamos, allí acurrucados, el incienso que levanta la tormenta del campo, y caería sobre nosotros el exquisito olor de la húmeda paja de nuestra cabaña' (p.101). Admittedly the youthful lovers are prompted to wait for a severe storm, which they hoped would fuel their passion. The ending of this short story is ambiguous—the final passages describing Rubén's melancholy mood. As a story, it relies heavily on poetic descriptions of the storm, but fails in terms of narrative. Similar to other works, the author is clearly preoccupied by man's place in nature, and the effects the latter has on the individual. Experience and perception are played out through a renewed focus on the natural world.

A story where the relationship between art and life is clearly portrayed, is in the highly poetic account of a young man by the name of Esteban who falls in love with a girl who is reading a book in the Luxembourg Park in Paris. Aptly titled *Aquella novela* (1924), much of the narrative describes Esteban as he walks through this park in the heart of Paris, thinking about the woman he saw there with a yellow book. The yellow book serves as a vehicle for Esteban's imagination. After befriending the woman, who is called 'Matilde', he leaves her when he realises that the only reason she was with him was because he resembled a character in the novel she was reading. Gómez de la Serna presents as the main cause of human unhappiness the persistent conflict between hope and reality. Esteban, unable to savour a lasting friendship, is ultimately left to face the future alone.

In a similar fashion, in *El miedo al mar* (1921)[38] Ramón uses the sea as a background against which to set the plot. It recounts the story of a young engineer (Prudencio) who had been living for two years on a solitary beach. He is from Madrid, and never fully adjusts to living on the coast. Similar to many of Gómez de la Serna's characters, Prudencio is affected by seasonal change. With the arrival of October he feels a strange mood coming over him, and dresses up in riding boots even though he does not own a horse, and shoots into the air claiming that he is killing stars. Despite the apparent absurdity of his behaviour, serious issues are given some treatment: walking along the beach causes him to reflect on the expansive nature of the sea, and the smallness of everything else in comparison. Life is depicted as being empty, and Prudencio lacks direction and motivation: 'Estaba ahí otra vez el gran vacío del invierno y la burla continua del mar, al que no le importaba un bledo nada' (p.144). Prudencio is a modern-day Robinson Crusoe figure, living a life of solitude, surrounded by the constant presence of the sea around him. At times he talks to the sea, and it soon emerges that he fears it more than death itself. He shares his fears with a friend by the name of Sagrario. She however, is of differing opinion and loves the sea, comparing it to a book with many stories to tell. Sagrario and Asunción (a mutual friend of Prudencio and Sagrario's), call for a doctor when they fear that Prudencio may be ill. The doctor's diagnosis is based around the colour of Prudencio's hands, which if of a pinkish hue, is a signal to him that the sea is calling him back. However, it is Asunción who turns out to have pinkish hands, and Sagrario becomes increasingly worried that she would one day throw herself into the sea. One October evening Sagrario sets out to the coast in search of Asunción, fearing the worst, only to find her by the shore. Relieved, she embraces her. Prudencio arrives at the scene, and decides to move back inland. Asunción and Sagrario decide to remain by the sea, claiming that:

> El mar es un poco nuestro divino esposo, el que nos mece y nos aduerme...Antes de dormirnos, cuando estamos allí lejos, en la tierra sorda, tenemos que leer algo...Aquí es él el que nos lee en alta voz y eso basta para dormirse en un sueño reparador. (p.171)

Prudencio decides to move inland. Once again, themes such as the power of nature over the individual, loneliness and frustrated friendships, are played out against the sea which becomes a vehicle for aesthetic experience. The characters are not rooted in any particular socio-historic setting, but are depicted as eccentric individuals living outside the boundaries of conventional society.

El dueño del átomo (1926), is noteworthy in that it raises the issue of splitting the atom before it was achieved by scientists. The plot centres on the eccentric scientist don Alfredo, whose quest is to split the atom. He believes that when he does so, he will become 'el dueño del átomo', which will make him extremely rich. By uncovering the secrets of the atom, don Alfredo believes that he will be in a position to better understand the human race, since, according to him 'somos átomos y vamos a formar una molécula, nuestros núcleos se mantendrán juntos a pesar de la repulsión mutua inevitable'.[39] The ideas discussed by the characters don Alfredo, his wife Angela, and the old school friend Práxedes, are far-fetched to say the least. They discuss experiments, which if successful, will usher in a world where death will no longer exert control on the individual.

On Saturday nights don Alfredo gathers with three friends, Práxedes, Antón the oceanographer and Silvio, an acolyte of don Alfredo's. Together they discuss the possible consequences of splitting the atom. Práxedes' attempts to move don Alfredo away from the subject as he believes that his obsession is unhealthy, end in failure. Alfredo is adamant that the atom is 'la única realidad del mundo' and in his defence humorously says to Práxedes: 'Tú no eres más que un átomo hinchado' (p.64). They speculate about the possible effects of their experiments on future wars with prophetic accuracy:

> En una batalla en que se disparasen medios microátomos se vería desaparecer el enemigo, como borrado por un efecto de espejismo y no habría que recoger ni cadáveres ni impedimenta...Todo disuelto y corroído en lo invisible. (p.72)

After further discussions with an electron expert Bhov, don Alfredo finally manages to split the atom. Together with Angela and Práxedes, they disappear into nothingness with a bang.

Whilst on a formal level there is little innovation to be found in this short work, its subject matter is interesting, not least because Ramón's interest in atoms and particles is part of a wider interest in science of that time. As early as 1901 Planck had suggested that energy could be radiated in discrete units or quanta, leading to Heisenberg's theory of quantum mechanics in 1927. The ending of *El dueño del átomo* is significant in that it suggests that the characters have become involved in an aspect of the world that is beyond their control and understanding. Their world is not depicted as a world of Newtonian certainties, but as an unpredictable world where anything can happen, in line with the theory of quantum mechanics which argues that quarks and atomic particles do not obey Newton's laws of gravity, but are driven by unpredictability. If for little else, *El dueño del átomo* is interesting for its references to contemporary science.

El olor a las mimosas (1922), which is included in the *El dueño del átomo* collection, is similar in many ways (not least in its title) to *La malicia de las acacias*. Written in the first person, *El olor a las mimosas* recounts the memories of a young engineer who had gone in search of a city which was still set in the age of steam. Much of the narrative centres on lyrical descriptions of the sea and hills, which he can see from his hotel room. In the hotel he befriends two women: Paz and Adelaida. Their friendship is poetically set against a background of mimosa flowers. While there are many descriptions which focus on the flowers, some of the conversations between Adelaida and the engineer convey a sense of sadness. The hotels are described as having a 'sad gaze', whilst those who live there are said to be suffering from tuberculosis. The plot of this story is simple, as the intention of the author is to create a poetic work, albeit one which is not devoid of pain. Adelaida and the engineer initiate a relationship, and it soon emerges that Adelaida had been given a small hotel for when she got married.

Much of the narrative describes their walks through the forest, reminisc-
ing about past days when the afternoon was scented with flowers:

> El recuerdo de toda mi vida lo resumen las mimosas... Mis mejores tardes estuvieron
> llenas de perfume de las mimosas... Mi bautizo en el goce de la vida, cuando pensé
> por primera vez que podrías tú llegar fue sentada bajo la voluptuosidad de las
> mimosas... (p.208)

However, similar to the events in *La malicia de las acacias*, the changing
seasons take their toll. When the summer wanes into the greyness of September, the flowers start to fall from the trees and Adelaida begins to pale. The
skies become increasingly grey and autumnal, and the protagonist comes to
the realisation that if the grey skies had not arrived, and the flowers had not
faded, then he might have had a more lasting relationship with Adelaida. The
last pages of the book show the young engineer packing his suitcase and
leaving on a train, on a cold and overcast day.

These two stories are interesting because they depart from the avant-
garde preoccupation seen in other of the short stories by this author. The
plots are simple and credible, the characters are largely normal, and the
world depicted is not strange. The central presence of beauty (embodied in
the flowers and the changing seasons), attests to Gómez de la Serna's interest
in a kind of literature which delights in the poeticization of the world. I have
intimated earlier at possible influences from Oscar Wilde. In many of
Wilde's essays, stories and novels, considerable importance is placed on
flowers as a means of drawing the reader in to a world of beauty, as is the
case in *El olor a las mimosas*. *The Picture of Dorian Gray* for instance,
opens with well known words: 'The studio was filled with the rich odour of
roses, and when the light summer wind stirred amidst the trees of the garden,
there came through the open door the heavy scent of lilac, or the more deli-
cate perfume of the pink-flowering thorn'.[40] In addition to the imagery of the
flowers, and its parallels with trends in the literary paradigm of aestheticism,
El olor a las mimosas and *La malicia de las acacias*, suggests that there is a
clear causal link between the characters and the changing seasons. In both
stories characters are directly affected by the arrival of autumn. In many instances the colour of the sky determines the mood and dictates the degree of
happiness in the relationships forged between characters. This is interesting
because it presents the reader with a very different world to that presented in
his more avant-garde works, where the laws of causality have been progressively weakened (*Cinelandia* and *El incongruente* for example), and is more
reminiscent of naturalism where man is portrayed as being locked in to the
cycle of nature.

La casa triangular (1925) is another example of Ramón's short stories which is significant for the importance placed on a physical space, which determines the main character's day to day existence. This story recounts the story of an eccentric character 'Adolfo Sureda', whose obsession with abstract concepts leads him to enlist the help of an architect to build a house in the shape of a triangle. Adolfo values ideas and concepts very highly indeed: 'Tenía personalidad y lo había sacrificado todo a un ideal' (p.50).[41] The importance placed on geometrical patterns concepts and ideas is reminiscent of cubism, although, it is also typical of Gómez de la Serna's ability to take a simple concept and build a narrative around it, a process clearly at work in many of his *greguerías*.

Adolfo, soon to be married, purchases oddly shaped furniture to match the style of his new house. People's opinions of the house differ: one person remarks that it is a good idea, as post will never get lost and visitors will always arrive there as it would stand out from the other surrounding buildings. However, the mother of his new wife (Remedios), cries when she leaves her daughter there on the night of her wedding, upset by the strangeness of the home. The days ahead are mostly happy: 'parecían volver a la inocencia de los juegos de construcción, cuando con aquellas primeras cajas de cubismo triste encontraban arquitecturas alegres' (p.51). However, the triangular shape of their house soon starts to affect their lives. They begin to receive strange letters from a bizarre sect by the name of 'Triángulo de Fuego', who want to make Adolfo their president, and when Remedios gives birth, it is to three children. They aptly name the three 'Augusto', 'Benito', and 'César', the initials of each deliberately spelling out A,B,C, to resemble the designation of the apexes of a triangle in geometry. When the children grow up and go to school, they are the subject of much curiosity and are asked whether they have a three-armed cook.

One day Adolfo is visited by a white-bearded man who claims to be a geometrician. He tells Adolfo that the reason why his life is affected by the triangular house is because he does not understand geometry. Adolfo accepts the geometrician's tutelage, and as a result grows increasingly confident about his surroundings. Trigonometry equations actually appear within the text itself. A considerable degree of humour is employed, especially when recounting Remedios's reaction to the newly acquired craze of her husband: 'Remedios, ante aquellas elucubraciones del geómetra y su esposo, se aburría triangularmente' (p.58). Adolfo soon becomes obsessed with his home and the mathematical equations, and spends time everyday with the geometrician. He deduces that Remedios had been having an affair with a cousin by the name of 'Enrique', prompting Remedios to take the children to go and live with her mother, and Adolfo to move away to a small hotel after putting the house up for sale, realising that their lives have been drastically altered by the triangular shape of the house.

In addition to its cubist properties, *La casa triangular* bears resemblance to much of Ramón's fiction in its depiction of a slightly deranged character who lives for a bizarre and far-fetched obsession. Imaginatively written, it clearly belongs to the innovative and avant-garde works of the author.

La capa de don Dámaso (1924), also deserves a mention here, as it not only focuses on a character who has a strange obsession with his cloak, but also highlights the importance Ramón places on objects, a trait which is apparent in all of his novels. This story narrates the events in the life of 'don Dámaso' who owns a cloak which brings him exceedingly good fortune. This story exemplifies how apparently trivial objects occupy a more important position in Ramón's fiction than serious matters. Don Dámaso's obsession with the cloak is humorous and deliberately facetious. He wraps himself in it whenever he needs to make an important decision, he attempts to cure a girl by extending it over her, but she unfortunately dies, although the cloak adequately acts as a kind of mourning shroud for the recently deceased girl. Needing to pay his keep, don Dámaso reluctantly pawns the cloak, and as a consequence loses all hope in life. The closing lines of the story centre on don Dámaso leaving on a train to a village, in search of an old overcoat he had left there years earlier.

The plot is well suited to the format of a short story, as most of the focus is on an object rather than on don Dámaso, whilst the humorous tone maintained throughout confirms its status as one of Ramón's avant-garde short-stories.

The commercial world figures elsewhere in Gómez de la Serna's novels and short stories. It is possible that Ramón was influenced by the urban expansion and commercial development undertaken throughout Spain during the nineteen-twenties. Although the title of *El hombre de la galería* (1926) suggests a commercial setting of a shopping-mall, this story is more concerned with exploring the importance of space, rather than the nature of commercialism itself. Set in Naples, the story starts by comparing two shopping malls: that of Príncipe de Nápoles and that of Humberto Primero. The former is described as quiet and melancholy, whilst the second is buzzing with people, ingeniously described as a kind of train station platform with no train. The story centres around the mysterious and curious character of don Giovanni, who, bewitched by the Príncipe de Nápoles shopping centre, spends most of the story walking through it and describing the shops and people who converge there. At first it is unclear as to why he frequents the place, and people begin to speculate as to his reasons for being there. Some think that he may have suffered misfortunes in his personal life, others believe he is avoiding someone. It is later revealed that he owned land which he rented out, and lived in the 'Galería' as he wanted to lead an anonymous and isolated existence. He befriends a woman who works in one of the shops there, who admits that she too likes the gallery because 'aquí se puede pensar con sosiego y ver llegar el futuro'.[42] However, any dreams of a common future are dashed when she says that if she did ever marry him, she would want to leave the gallery 'para huir a espacios más abiertos' (p.309). To maintain his anonymity he befriends a blind man, but soon feels that he is being followed. He cunningly places a piece of cork on the end of his walking stick and wears rubber-soled shoes so as to enable him to walk around in silence. He even rids himself of his tie-pin in case it acts as a kind of magnet which the blind man can detect. The story ends abruptly, when one day whilst walking through the gallery a chandelier falls from the ceiling, killing him instantly.

Despite the simplicity of plot, this story is interesting, as much of its appeal relies on the description of the shopping-mall in poetic terms. The mall is imaginatively described as a cathedral for those who do not believe in anything, denouncing the perils of excessive materialism. Much of the story describes the surroundings in succinct, visual and colourful images, painting an effective picture whilst remaining sufficiently economical to enable this story to comply with the specifications of a short-story. Through a description of objects in a shop window, the author is also able to reflect on the passage of time. In this it bears some resemblance to the much earlier work *El Rastro*, where the author's fascination with material objects and the recondite streets of Madrid is forcefully felt. But more than merely a story about a lonely figure, compulsively frequenting a shopping-mall, *El hombre de la galería* depicts the faceless mass of everyday citizens living in cities which are undergoing a process of modernisation. It evokes the loneliness of the individual attempting to find his niche in society, a quality clearly seen in one of the passages describing don Giovanni's thoughts: 'Lo más importante en la vida es encontrar el sitio en que ocultar nuestra propia descomposición' (p.304). The importance of contemplation over action draws attention away from the plot, to the actual devices at work. The fusion of a chaplinesque figure set against the background of a modern setting, whilst evoking timeless preoccupations such as loneliness, identity, and the passage of time, are effectively brought together within the limited narrative dimensions the author has to reckon with in order to remain within the confines of the short story mode.

Unorthodox character-types feature in both *El defensor del cementerio* (1927) and *El hombre de los pies grandes* (1922). The former tells the story of a man by the name of 'don Amadeo' who attempts to save a cemetery from falling into decay after it was taken over by new owners, although it fails to engage the reader at any level and once again merely draws attention to a character with a bizarre quest which he is ready to defend with his life. The latter describes a peculiar character, who feels different to everyone else because of a physical trait (his big feet) despite people telling him that his feet will bring him luck and success. It reads as a parody of the American dream, in that physical appearance is a determining factor to a character's success or failure. However, Federico's apparent success ends in disaster when he incurs a debt in proportion to the size of his feet.

Both these stories deal with characters who are located on the margins of society, and who are defined exclusively by outward factors, such as a physical peculiarity or a strange situation. This makes it difficult for the reader to identify with them, or feel any empathy. Furthermore, there are no dramatic heights and depths in the lives of these characters, and a deliberate lack of emotion and pathos. Ramón depicts individuals as a product of chance and fortuity, inhabiting a world where sense and rationality have been severely attenuated.

María Yarsilovna (falsa novela rusa) (1923), is an attempt to parody the genre of the Russian nineteenth-century novel. In the opening prologue, the author admits to writing 'la última novela rusa inédita del pasado como homenaje a las novelas fallecidas' (p.183)[43]. But unlike the typical nineteenth-century Russian novel, this story is fast moving, with very little narrative delay, confirming its parodic intent. *María Yarsilovna (falsa novela rusa)* (1923), no doubt offers a stylish escapism into the world of Russian upper-class society. There are hardly any descriptions of the outside world. Instead, the author focuses on fleeting characters who are described with the haste of a brush-stroke: 'una mujer vestida de rojo', 'un señor que parecía atentado de carretera'. Most of the characters exist purely as a background, in an clear attempt to recreate the atmosphere of a crowded high-class parlour.

The story begins with the arrival of a gentleman known as 'el extranjero' to the village of 'Prisviana' in the region of 'Crospa'. After a couple of days in the village hotel, he finds a house to live in. Whilst walking down his street he spots 'María Yarsilovna' through a window, and immediately falls in love. Determined to meet her, he strolls up and down the outside of the house, owned by 'el Gran Fédor', looking in through the window. He is eventually invited in, where he makes the acquaintance of those who converge there. María stands out from the rest, and duly receives most of the narrative attention. Much of the narrative is caught up with describing her beauty, which is brought to life through a heavy reliance on poetic imagery. The plot is simple, as Ramón's main concern appears to be an aesthetic treatment of the main character.

The stuffy atmosphere of the house, evoked by including a lengthy list of esoteric Russian names, whom the reader knows nothing about; contrasts with the occasional descriptions of the view of the street. Ramón uses light impressionistically, and plays with visual contrasts in an effective way which enables him to create lucid images within the limited space of the short-story mode. The boisterous atmosphere of the house contrasts with the peaceful description of the street outside, which is covered in snow. A coal truck passes through the street, dropping lumps of coal, which are compared to deep black holes: 'Dirigió una mirada a la calle. Fuera, todo tenía la sordera de la nieve. Un carro de carbón, muy negro, pasaba sembrando carbones negros sobre la sábana blanca; carbones que semejaban agujeros que diesen a lo profundo' (p.188). María's main attraction is her beauty, although some suspect that she had committed a crime:

> Todos notaban la gran belleza de María Yarsilovna, pero se daban cuenta de algo extraño que había en ella, una especie de apariencia de mujer que ha cometido un crimen y aún no ha podido enterrar el último pedazo de su víctima. (p.191)

The ambiguity surrounding her past adds to her mysterious appeal.

The plot digresses, focusing on the crowds who converge on María's house. She is described as holding some secret, and her resplendent face emits a curious white light:

> El extranjero miraba a María Yarsilovna, siguiendo siempre el secreto de aquel ultimátum de su blancura, de aquella luz de la nada que había en su rostro y que era como una vívida nieve de tocador que le daba un aire delirante. (p.197)

By the end of the story the narrator's voice is vibrant with characteristic lyricism in a story where action has been kept to a minimum. Such developments are assisted by a recurrent interplay of contrasts and an important use of light, underlying the important visual qualities of the story. At the end of the story, the reader knows little more about each character than at the beginning of the story. The ending is bizarre and enigmatic. María is heard shouting out for help, and a priest is sent for because they suspect that she may be dying. After she is absolved by the priest, the rest of the characters merely retreat into the background, and the foreigner leaves, disappointed that he had not forged a deeper friendship with her.

There are no dramatic heights or depths achieved with the rise or fall of characters, neither is the plot neatly drawn to a close. The world depicted is one of surface-deep appearances: María's character is never explored, instead the reader is given an aesthetic description of her appearance, much of the setting of the story takes place in Fédor's front room, the changing light and brush-stroke descriptions of characters forming the main crux of the story. The society described, although set in turn of the century Russia, could be that of any bourgeois society. By setting the story outside of Spain, the author is flaunting his ability to create fiction which directly responds to the growing interest in cosmopolitan themes, prevalent at that time.

Gómez de la Serna's considerable lyrical gift can be seen in *Los dos marineros (falsa novela china)* (1925), which imaginatively recounts a story of love and loss, set against the background of the sea, which elicits feelings of nostalgia and desire in the characters. The curious aspect of this story is that it is set in China. *Los dos marineros (falsa novela china)* (1925), similar to *María Yarsilovna*, essentially stands out for its poetic nature. The opening pages show 'Niquita' looking out to sea. When asked why she looks out to sea, she answers: 'Porque mueve mejor mi corazón...Junto al mar se es como los molinos junto a los saltos de agua...Las aspas de mi imaginación dan vueltas veloces' [44]. Thus, from the start of the story her vivid imagination is brought to the fore, and much of the reader's impression of her is built from an insight into the way in which she sees her surrounding world. When asked what the sea gives her, she says that it brings her necklaces of pearls. However, the reader is soon told that the main reason for her interest in the sea is because her lover Yama, a sailor, had departed.

Niquita's main inspiration derives from the observation of beauty, and spends much of her time lost in her own thoughts and dreams. The opening pages of the story portray a dreamy world set alongside the expansive sea. Most of the action takes place in the mind of Niquita as she attempts to come to terms with Yama's absence. When he eventually returns, Niquita tells him that she had been sleeping an extra hour each day so that she could spend a whole fifteen nights with him, without sleeping. Together, they live out their passion against the undulating background of the sea. However, Niquita becomes suspicious of Yama's integrity when he ominously decides to return to his ship six days before its actual departure. Without him noticing, she follows him back to the port with an escort by the name of 'Fu-San'. Descriptions of the forest at night, the stormy sky, the bird calls and the trees, add to the lyrical style of the story as a whole. The port is described as a sordid place of drunken debauchery. She imagines the worst and returns to her house by the sea. Disenchanted with her sailor-lover, she still looks out to sea as a means of consoling her confused mind. She retires to a life of contemplation, and is visited by butterflies and beautiful insects. She feels that Yama has been corrupted by the life-style of the ports, and turns her attention to a man by the name of 'Nachari' who lives in the forest. The scenery is depicted with expected lyricism:

El bosque lucía una expectación inusitada sobre el lago. El espíritu de la tierra había venido a beber en sus aguas y se abrazaba en ellas. Los árboles más próximos sufrían el reuma de sus raíces. El espejismo religioso del cielo se lucía en su plazoleta central, porque los lagos son las profundas aras del agua. (p.331)

Much of the narrative centres on the surroundings, coupled with passages about Chinese sea-gods, which bring about a sense of the fantastic. In the final episode of this story, the night is described as having dressed in a blue Kimono. Whilst they lie naked with each other, Yama arrives with a sword, and attempts to kill Niquita out of jealousy, but Nachauri kills Yama, and the story ends.

Despite its exotic setting, *Los dos falsos marineros* deals with the familiar themes of troubled human relationships, with the transience of beauty and the impossibility of achieving complete happiness. Despite the incongruity of the main character, and the imaginative descriptions and droll analogies throughout the story, human jealousy is the theme which dominates in the closing pages of the story. It does not matter how Ramón dresses his characters up: in the end they are shown to have some human traits, undergoing universal problems which transcend time and place.

Similarly, *La fúnebre (falsa novela tártara)* (1925), presents a world where normal values have been turned on their head. But rather than focusing on one character who is out of step with the majority, the whole community are engaged in a kind of behaviour which strays from the normal. 'La Tartaria', as the country is known, is depicted with both colour and imagination, depicted as a topsy-turvy world of reversed values. However, this is not due to malice, but rather to confusion:

Los tártaros confunden sus almas porque creen no poderse conocer. Ni su lengua ni su alma son claras, y por eso tienen prontos en que el ser más bueno mata a su madre, y el ser más malo se sacrifica como un verdadero santo. (p.75)

Most of the action takes place in the village of 'Kikir', where the whole village plays the flute. Sometimes the villagers organise concerts, and the entire audience joins in with their flutes. A businessman who put up a notice prohibiting flute playing, was killed by a villager who stabbed him with a flute. However, the plot concerns itself mostly with a woman called 'La Astrakipik', meaning 'La Fúnebre': a title she was given because she had killed seven husbands after which she married the brave 'Baraba'. The plot alternates between 'La fúnebre', and the strange events in the village, one of which involves the village chief summoning the village people to the main square by blowing into a shell, concerned that there was an imbalance between the deaths and those born in the village. Aware that there is a culture of death, he urges his subjects to eat cubes of sugar, which he metes out in the hope that they will develop sweeter attitudes towards life.

Meanwhile, 'La fúnebre' continues to delight in her exploits, hiring a golden throne upon which she places her dead husband for all to see. A frenzied dance ensues, but is abruptly brought to a halt when a man wielding a knife by the name of 'Tubal', orders everyone to leave as he wants to dance with 'La fúnebre' alone. Tubal angers 'La fúnebre' when he actually stabs the corpse of her late husband, and then challenges her to marry him.

When they marry, Tubal carries on living through hunting, and chews wood in the belief that it has magical properties which will enable him to become more gentle. The village-people expect Tubal to be the next victim, and believe that a man by the name of 'Mascafou' who symbolically lives in 'el barrio de los parricidas' (p.83) will be the one to replace him. But Tubal is angered by this, and one day chops off 'La fúnebre's' head with his sword. He defends his actions by saying that she would feel no pain as it would not have time to go to her head. He then moves to 'el barrio de los parricidas' where he laughs at 'Muscafou', for believing that he is safe from death.

It is difficult to understand the author's motives for writing a story such as this one, save for the obvious desire to experiment with unexpected and different aesthetic material. The fact that this story is set in an imaginary eastern country is of interest, and could be seen as part of a wide-spread interest in cultures which had not been corrupted by western values. However, if this is the case, the vision presented here is hardly an alternative solution to the culture of the day. Gómez de la Serna passes no judgement, but humorously plays with imaginary and far-fetched ideas, to create a world which has no referential bearings with the world around him. Despite the setting of *La fúnebre,* it might be argued that Gómez de la Serna attempts to convey through parody themes which are central to his fiction at large, namely the extreme effects of human feelings driven to absurd limits.

La mujer vestida de hombre (falsa novela alemana) (1925) recounts the life of Marien, who from childhood manifests sexual ambiguity. Constrained by the need to write within the framework of a short story, Gómez de la Serna takes the reader from her childhood to the age of twenty-two in little more than a page. Wandering through the streets of Berlin, which are lined with shops and advertising bill-boards, Marien expresses her fear of being no more than a commodity or product, a fear which is reiterated throughout the story. As she walks the streets of Berlin she feels as though society is attempting to mould her into something she does not want to be: 'sintiendo que les tatuaban el alma como con sellos de caucho los letreros comerciales' (p.132). At times the descriptions are almost Orwellian, in their depiction of a mechanised and impersonal world. Groups of three walking down the street are depicted as being devoid of personality, merely products of their time: 'Pasaban numerosos grupos de tres caballeros, todos con serios bastones, que en el fondo eran [máquinas] temibles con alma de caucho' (p.132). However, her behaviour stems from a keen interest in modern-day fashion and fads, rather than with any attempt to make a political point. Marien is portrayed as a free-thinking and anarchic liberal, who refuses to accept the traditional role placed on women by society, and decides to revolt against it. In a deliberate attempt to upset prevailing hierarchies, she cross-dresses, attracting admirers through her ambiguous apparel. She smokes a pipe and keeps company with quirky figures such as 'Sophien', 'Rudolf' and 'Otto', whom she meets in the seedy 'Rupestre' bar, described as a kind of cave where lovers can engage in licentious activities. Otto is attracted to her, and dreams of being able to free her of her ambivalence and return her to a state of unambiguous womanhood. Their relationship is cleverly played out through witty and incongruous conversations, in which a pot of tea can become the vehicle through which Otto expresses his admiration: 'usted preparando el te, es como una hada preparando una infusión mágica' (p.127), or when she states: 'juego al tennis con todas las miradas', drawing on sporting imagery as a means to describe her playful gaze.

The settings in this story alternate between the various bars, cabarets, streets of Berlin, and a film studio towards the end of the story, where Marien ends up living in a bizarre world between fiction and reality. Some of the descriptions of Berlin effectively evoke the commercial and financial side of the city, whilst conveying its greyness:

> En esas tardes de otoño, la gran ciudad se volvía más casillero y clasificador ideal, adoptando los revocos un gesto de impasividad extranjera, hasta para los mismos indígenas. Berlín olía a impermeable y sabía a paraguas de un modo latente y especial, porque no llovía, ni había llovido, ni iba a llover. El plato del día era chanclos a la *financière*. (p.132)

At the same time, in the passage where Marien describes her friendship with Rudolf, the imagery of cigarette ends and ash is used poetically to evoke a strong bond between them:

> En el cenicero estudiantil del cuarto de Rudolf se reunían las cenizas de los cigarros de entrambos, como en una urna común que había reunido sus horas. Ella, al limpiarlo como para despejar la casa de una pesadilla de colillas, se quedaba mirando aquellas cenizas reunidas, como si ése fuera el símbolo de la amistad perfecta. (pp.121–122)

Marien's provocative dress-code soon makes her a well-known figure in the city, attracting the attention of a doctor by the name of Werted, who is fascinated by her. She agrees to meeting with him in his practice, where there are marble statues of Venus. He asks her a string of absurd questions: whether she gets nervous when she drinks a glass of water, or what sensation she feels in her brain when she puts on a pair of shoes or gets onto a tram. She emerges even more sure of herself, and convinced that she can defy science and medicine. Realising that he cannot persuade her to adopt a more traditional life-style, Otto starts to behave strangely, wearing a false moustache which makes him, in the narrator's opinion, resembles a kind of flower bouquet. His intention to woo her through extravagant behaviour fails. She becomes even more distant and accepts an offer to star in film. The film studio is a bizarre building, described as a mixture between a synagogue, an execution room, a theatre, and a bathroom. Here she spends the rest of her days, walking through the artificial gardens of the studio, afraid to go back to life.

This story is interesting not only because it portrays an aberrant character who breaks with convention, but also because it depicts a world of growing commercialism and fashion: two major trends in the nineteen-twenties. At the same time, it questions whether there is a clear dividing line between reality and art, clearly seen in her decision to live in a false cinematic world of artistic creation. In this sense it is similar to *Cinelandia* (1923), and serves as further evidence of Wilde's influence on the author in the dialogue which is established between art and life.

El hijo del millonario (falsa novela norteamericana) (1927) tells the story of an American juggernaut figure, by the name of David Karvaler, son of a millionaire who owns an explosives factory. Obsessed with speed, fast cars and machinery, David is portrayed as a ruthless character, devoid of any human values or morals. He runs people over in his car for the fun of it, then, after taking his victims to hospital, offers to give $10,000 to anyone willing to slash open their stomach. There is a clear intention on the part of Ramón to parody the American-dream blueprint of society, based solely upon material wealth. The description of David's car attests a desire to exaggerate and emphasise the ridiculous:

> Se reunía en aquel automóvil los rincones más perfectos de las cosas modernas: del cuarto de baño, de la peluquería, del despacho, del director de banco, del coche para el jefe de la nación en el tren de lujo, del aeroplano, del ángulo de bar. (p.151)

The plot is far-fetched, set in a world where money has effaced all values, and where human beings are merely exploiters of their fellow men. One of Karvaler's ventures is to found a museum for the collection of women's ears. This episode is narrated with a degree of alleviating humour: an insurance company is set up especially for ears, and numerous jokes about ears appear in the newspapers. He even manages to obtain the ear of a famous opera singer 'Hilda Bons'. He owns a broadcasting studio, from which he emits loud noises to disturb other radio broadcasters. Karvaler's behaviour is both gratuitous and cruel. He burns down his factory, which results in the death of two thousand workers. The fusion of acts of cruelty on the one hand, with absurd and humorous gestures on the other, forms the basis of this short story. In a similar way to the novel *Cinelandia* (1923), there is a clear sense that Ramón is critical of the ruthless pursuit of wealth and of capitalism, although at the same time, intent on presenting the reader with unexpected situations, so as to satirise typically bourgeois taste, and ally himself with an experimental kind of literature.

The skyline of the city described could be that of any modern city, with tall opulent buildings and commercial boulevards. Amongst the conglomeration of buildings, there is said to be no room left for the human soul: 'Todo tenía perdido el alma en tan gran aglomeración' (p.146). The many references to emptiness and the depiction of the city's citizens as 'blind' evokes a sombre vision of a hollow society.

Clearly, the author is fearful of the inhumanity brought about by modernity. Some of the imagery used is ingenious, such as the description of food: 'La comida resultó como siempre, ligera como de quienes han ido mordiendo hojas por el jardín' (p.148). The descriptions of Karvaler's car, the machinery in his factory and the frenzied world around him, suggest a clear desire to endow the story with a futuristic lyricism, dislodging any human dimension and thus bringing it in line with the Ortegian idea of 'dehumanised art'.

The law finally catches up with David, and he is put on trial. Despite the attempts of the lawyer on his behalf to save him, David is sentenced to the electric chair. The final scene is a description of David attempting to put on his monocle, an exercise which in the end proves futile. The reasoning behind the lawyer's defence is absurd, arguing that David is not evil 'sino un impulsivo fatalizado y sin poderse defender de sus impulsos en una proporción de debilidad tan elevada como elevados son los halagos de sus millones' (p.161).

Another feature of Ramón's avant-garde short stories is that of imbuing fictional characters with a degree of aberrant behaviour, so that they frequently transgress the generally accepted parameters of social behaviour, stemming from the avant-gardist irreverent attitude. In *La mujer vestida de hombre (falsa novela alemana)* (1927) and *La fúnebre (falsa novela tártara)* (1925), this would seem to be the case, although there is no time to explore them at this stage.

Notes

1   El novelista is made up of the following stories and chapters: 'Corrige las pruebas de La apasionada', 'El barrio de Doña Benita', 'El crítico y la inspiración', 'El protagonista de La resina', 'La novela de la calle del árbol', 'En la jaula de la calle', 'Otra tarde otro día', 'El usurero sarcástico', 'Conocimiento de la novela', 'En busca de personajes', 'Exaltación del farol', 'Los días trastornados', 'Polémica del hombre de la mañana con el hombre de la noche', 'Fin de La criada', 'El frío y La moribunda', 'El enemigo de las novelas', 'Otro capítulo final', 'Vuelta a la nebulosa', 'La visita de la admiradora', 'Comienza Pueblo de Adobes', 'En el pueblo seco', 'Adobe tras adobe', 'Libídine', 'Bajo las imprecaciones', 'Perseverancia', 'Nueva liberación', 'Al balcón', 'Viaje a Londres', 'El farol rojo', 'En la casa de Remy Valey', 'Rasgando originales', 'Fiebre de novelador', 'En la ciudad novelística', 'la ciudad de los personajes de novela', 'Por las calles intrincadas', 'Días de lluvia', 'En vísperas del embarque', 'Las siamesas', 'En la pura teratología', 'La nueva fantasma', 'Tras la mujer dudosa', 'Enredos', 'Nuevos avatares', 'Detrás del parapeto', 'El empujón libertador', 'Las obras completas', 'En el retiro'.

2   Manuel Lacarta, *Madrid y sus literaturas de la Generación del 98 a la posguerra* (Madrid: El Avapiés, 1986) p.21–22.

3   Ibid, p.29

4   Frank Kermode, *A Sense of an Ending* (London: Oxford University Press, 1968) p.127.

5   Amancio Sabugo Abril contends that literature develops what he calls an 'atomic' approach: 'La literatura se vuelve más atómica por la misma razón por la que toda la curiosidad de la vida científica palpita alrededor del átomo, abandonadas más amplias abstracciones buscando el secreto de la creación en el mismo átomo'. Cited in 'Ramón o la nueva literatura', Cuadernos Hispanoamericanos, 461 (1988) 7–27 (p.21).

6   Patricia Waugh, *Metafiction: The Theory and Practice of Self-Conscious Fiction* (London and New York: Routledge, 1984) p.7.

7   The metafictional approach used by Ramón in *El novelista* is by no means a new literary device. Unamuno had already experimented with this almost a decade earlier in his novel *Niebla*. José Enrique Serrano has argued that Ramón was influenced by Unamuno's 1914 novel, and considers it essential to a fuller understanding of *El novelista*. See 'The Theory of the Novel in Ramón Gómez de la Serna's *El novelista*', in *The Spanish avant-garde*, ed. By Derek Harris (Manchester: Manchester University Press, 1995).

8   A. N. Whitehead, cited in Sypher Wylie *Rococo to Cubism in Art and Literature* (New York: Vintage Books, 1960) p.272.

9   Cited in the appendix of Ramón Gómez de la Serna's *Automoribundia*, p.784.

10 Amancio Sabugo Abril, 'Ramón o la nueva literatura', *Cuadernos Hispanoamericanos*, 461 (1988) 7–27 (p.20).

11 Nigel Dennis (ed) Studies on Ramón Gómez de la Serna. *Ottawa Hispanic Studies 2* (Canada: Dovehouse Editions, 1988) p.14.

12 Dennis, p.14.

13 Dennis, p.14.

14 Ramón Gómez de la Serna, *Greguerías selectas* (Madrid: Saturnino Calleja, 1919) pp.5–6.

15 He states: 'Adquiere así (el libro) un aspecto selvático y salvaje que prefiero a que tenga un aspecto de jardín' (Ramón, 1919, p.6).

16 Ramón Gómez de la Serna, *El novelista* [1923] (Madrid: Espasa Calpe, 1973) p.287. All subsequent references to the novel will be made from this edition.

17 In her book *The Pirandellian Mode in Spanish Literature from Cervantes to Sastre*,
    Wilma Newberry dedicates a chapter to Ramón Gómez de la Serna, where she argues that
    in Gómez de la Serna's *El teatro en soledad* there is a 'striking' resemblance to Piran-
    dello's later work. She argues that El teatro en soledad 'is a very important document in
    the history of pre-Pirandellism in Spain'. She states: 'Like Sei personaggi, *El teatro en
    soledad* is a play which serves to dissect the theatre and the techniques employed to de-
    stroy theatrical illusion by showing people and elements which should remain behind the
    scenes. There are several levels of reality: in fact, in the list of characters the participants
    are separated into two groups in both plays: characters and actors. In addition, the author
    and the spectators, who were to become so important in Pirandello's theatre-within-the-
    theatre trilogy, are discussed. The characters are even more important in Ramón's play
    than in Pirandello's, since the stage belongs to them completely during most of the play.
    The actors and characters do not occupy the stage simultaneously as they do in Piran-
    dello's play, and the actors are unaware that the characters exist: however, the characters
    have a critical attitude toward the actors very similar to that shown in *Sei personaggi'*. She
    goes on to argue that both Pirandello and Ramón were directly influenced by cubist aes-
    thetics, which also supports the contention that there are clear influences of cubism in *El
    novelista*. The citations from the chapter of Wilma Newberry's book are from *Contempo-
    rary Literary Criticism: Excerpts from Criticism of the Works of Today's Novelists, Poets,
    Playwrights, and Other Creative Writers*, ed. by Dedria Bryfonski (Michigan: Gale Re-
    search Company, 1978) IX, pp.237,38.
18 For a full account of this, and an insightful understanding of Gómez de la Serna's ambiva-
    lent political stance see Alan Hoyle, 'The Politics of a Hatless Revolutionary', in *Studies
    in modern Literature and Art presented to Helen F. Grant, ed. by Nigel Glendinning* (Lon-
    don: Tamesis, 1972) pp.79–96.
19 Alan Hoyle, 'Ramón Gómez de la Serna: Avant-Garde novelist Par Excellence', in *Hacia
    la novela nueva: Essays on the Spanish Avant-Garde Novel*, ed.by Francis Lough (Oxford:
    Peter Lang, 2001) pp.61–77 (p.68).
20 Further on in the novel there is a passage which points to a magical world which con-
    verges with the everyday. It depicts Andrés walking through 'la realidad supuesta como
    por una novela de magia en que hablan los cuadros y un plumero se convierte en un ramo
    de flores, hasta con la gola de los grandes ramos'. (p.109)
21 In 'The Decay of Lying' , Wilde masquerading under the persona of 'Vivian', argues that
    Nature follows art rather than art following nature, he supports his view with the following
    argument: 'Where, if not from the Impressionists, do we get those wonderful brown fogs
    which come creeping down our streets, blurring the gas-lamps and changing the houses
    into monstrous shadows? To whom, if not to them and their master, do we owe the lovely
    silver mists that brood over our river, and turn to faint forms of fading grace curved bridge
    and swaying barge? The extraordinary change that has taken place in the climate of Lon-
    don during the last ten years is entirely due to a particular school of Art. You smile.
    Consider the matter from a scientific or metaphysical point of view, and you will find that
    I am right. For what is Nature? Nature is no great mother who has borne us. She is our
    creation. It is in our brain that she quickens to life. Things are because we see them, and
    what we see and how we see it depends on the Arts which have influenced us. To look at a
    thing is very different from seeing a thing. One does not see anything until one sees its
    beauty. Then, and then only, does it come into existence. At present, people see fogs, not
    because there are fogs, but because poets and painters have taught us the mysterious love-
    liness of such effects. There may have been fogs for centuries in London. I dare say there

were. But no one saw them, and so we do not know anything about them. They did not exist until art had invented them. Now, it must be admitted, fogs are carried to excess. They have become the mere mannerism of a clique, and the exaggerated realism of their method gives dull people bronchitis. Where the cultured catch an effect, the uncultured catch a cold'. Oscar Wilde, 'The Decay of Lying' in *Complete Works of Oscar Wilde*, New edn 1966 (London and Glasgow: Collins, 1966) p.986.

22 Ibid, p.982)

23 Ramón Gómez de la Serna, *Nuevos retratos*, p.361.

24 See Ramón Gómez de la Serna, 'Oscar Wilde', in *Nuevos retratos contemporáneos y otros retratos* (Madrid: Aguilar Mayor, 1990) p.383.

25 Roger Shattuck, *The Banquet Years: The Origin of the Avant-garde in France, 1885–1918* (London: Southern Cape, 1969) p.346.

26 Ibid, p.349,50.

27 María Fernández Utrera, *Visiones de Estereoscopio: paradigma de hibridación en el arte y la narrativa de vanguardia española*, North Carolina Studies in the Romance Languages and Literatura, no 272. Unviversity of North Carolina Press, Chapel Hill, 2001.

28 Ramón Gómez de la Sena, Ismos (1930) (Madrid: Guadarrama, 1975) p.351.

29 See Valerie Shaw, *The Short Story: A Critical Introduction.* (New York: Longman, 1983). See also Charles E. May (ed) Short Story Theories (1976) which brings together a variety of critical opinions on the matter. See also Edith Wharton, *The Writing of Fiction* (New York: Octagon Books, 1973).

30 See Charles May, p.64.

31 Norman Friedman, 'Recent Short Story Theories: Problems in Definition', in Short Story in *Theory at a Crossroads*, ed. by Susan Loaffer and Eilyn Clarey (Boston: Luisiana State University Press, 1989) p.72.

32 Ramón Gómez de la Serna, *El dueño del átomo* (1928); which contains the following, some of which also appeared in Revista de Occidente: *El dueño del átomo* (1926), *El olor a las mimosas* (1922), *La casa triangular* (1925), *La capa de don Dámaso* (1924), *El gran griposo* (1927), *El ruso* (1913), *El hombre de la galería* (1926), *La saturada* (1923), *La hija del verano* (1922), *El hombre de los pies grandes* (1922).

33 Ramón Gómez de la Serna, *La malicia de las acacias* (Valencia: Ediciones Sempere, 1924), containing: *La malicia de las acacias* (1923), *Los gemelos y el guante* (1923), *El joven de las sobremesas* (1923), *La tormenta* (1921), *La gallipava* (1921), *El miedo al mar* (1921), *De otra raza* (1924), *La gangosa* (1922), *Aquella novela* (1924).

34 Ramón Gómez de la Serna, *Seis falsas novelas*, ed. by Iona Zlotescu (Madrid: Mondadori, 1989), containing: *María Yarsilovna (falsa novela rusa)* (1923), *Los dos marineros (falsa novela china)* (1923), *La fúnebre (falsa novela tártara)* (1925), *La virgen pintada de rojo (falsa novela negra)* (1925), *La mujer vestida de hombre (falsa novela alemana)* (1925), *El hijo del millonario* (falsa novela norteamericana) (1927).

35 In her introduction to her edition, she states: 'Si no hubiera reunido las Falsas novelas en un volumen único, la significación de las mismas habría quedado difuminada y cada una de ellas, como un texto aislado, sin redondez y sin la pujanza del volumen en su conjunto'. *Seis falsas novelas*, (Madrid: Mondadori, 1989) p.6.

36 Ramón Gómez de la Serna, *La malicia de las acacias* [1923] (Valencia: Sempere, 1924) p.12.

37 This story can be found in *La malicia de las acacias* collection.

38 This story can be found in *La malicia de las acacias* collection.

39 Ramón Gómez de la Serna, *El dueño del átomo*, in *Revista de Occidente*, no.14 (April 1926) 59–84.

40 Oscar Wilde, p.18.

41 Gómez de la Serna, *El dueño del átomo* collection of short stories, pp.48–59.

42 Ramón Gómez de la Serna, *El hombre de la galería*, in *Revista de Occidente*, no. 13 (August, 1926) 299–316.

43 Ramón Gómez de la Serna, *María Yarsilovna (falsa novela rusa)* (1923) *Revista de Occidente,*, no.1 (Julio, 1923) 183–201. All quotations will be made from this edition.

44 Ramón Gómez de la Serna, Obras selectas (Madrid: Editorial Plenitud, 1947) p.319.

Chapter 4. The Banquet Years II
(1924–1929)

Existence and the world are
eternally justified solely as an
aesthetic phenomenon.

    Friedrich Nietzsche (1844–1900)

En la noche, como los pájaros en sus jaulas, podemos en aqueste ambiente esponjar
nuestro plumaje, regodearnos de nuestra vida sin grandes conflictos, de nuestra gran
resignación de vivir y de morir.

    Ramón Gómez de la Serna (1888–1963).

Parody and Influence in La mujer de ámbar *(1927)*

Although nobody doubts the importance of Ramón Gómez de la Serna's
work to the avant-garde enterprise of the 1920s, his experimental approach to
writing does not obviate the need to trace traditional literary influences in his
work.

As its title suggests, *La mujer de ámbar* (1927) is a highly lyrical novel
where interest is largely sustained through an aesthetic rather than a social
understanding of the world, in keeping with the author's narrative fiction at
large. Similar to many of Ramón's novels, *La mujer de ámbar* recounts the
attempts of a solipsistic character (Lorenzo) to find companionship during a
sojourn in the city of Naples. Similar to many of Ramón's characters, the
protagonist of *La mujer de ámbar* is driven by a desire which is ultimately
not attained, although the erotic pursuit of the ideal woman occupies much of
the narrative. The city of Naples is depicted as being still very much rooted
in the past—the recurrent reference to the volcano Mount Vesuvius acting as
a constant reminder to the reader—but also for its appeal to the modern-day
tourist. At surface level *La mujer de ámbar* shares many thematic and stylistic similarities with many of the author's works: the perennial quest for
human companionship, a fascination with the material world, the fortuitous
comings and goings of characters which are seldom explored in any depth,
and a heavily charged poetic prose. However, despite many similarities with
Ramón's other works, there are strong textual markers which suggest that the
author is in fact deliberately parodying and re-working what has been considered the most important Italian novel of all times: Alessandro Manzoni's *I
promessi sposi*. This aspect of the novel has been overlooked until now by

critics, but in my view has far-reaching implications not only for our under-standing of the novel itself, but for the author's contract with other literary paradigms outside the immediate sphere of the avant-garde. The fact that Ramón chooses *I promessi sposi*, is important, primarily, because of its status in the Italian literary canon. By re-working what is considered by many to be the most important Italian novel of all time, with the deliberate irreverence typical of an avant-garde writer, he is arguably asserting his freedom as a literary innovator and shedding light on his complex dialogue with past liter-ary traditions.

La mujer de ámbar (1927), written at the height of Ramón's literary ca-reer, has commonly been understood as simply another example of the author's ability to play with language and imagery in a trivial fashion, symp-tomatic of avant-garde aesthetics at large. Camón Aznar reductively refers to it as 'Un canto a Napoles'.[1] Anthony Percival argues that:

> Gómez de la Serna's literary method consists in recreating through language raw sensations, spontaneous perceptions in which the imagination and emotion go largely unchecked by understanding: objects as they are nakedly apprehended are the primary materials for Ramon's art. Language is used aesthetically, playfully, to offer escape from workday contexts, released from the confines of convention.[2]

Although the depiction of Naples in *La mujer de ámbar* stands out for its poetic prose, its intertextual affinity with *I promessi sposi*, not commented on until now, offers a new and innovative reading of the text.

The fact that Ramón lived in Naples between the years of 1925 and 1926 must not be over looked. Both for the setting of the novel and the author's contact with the literary world of the day, it is of clear importance. To any author, geographic location is of central importance, no matter what degree of self-imposed ideas about the purity of art an author may profess to have. Ultimately, it is extremely difficult to distance oneself from the influence of physical surroundings, despite any illusions we might have about fiction. Moreover, anyone who has approached Ramón's work will no doubt have noted the importance accorded to cities. It is no coincidence that his last novel *Piso bajo* (1961) is set in Madrid, and in the prologue the author inti-mates at the importance of physical surroundings to the creative process:

> He querido, además, hacer la novela del piso bajo, de esos pisos bajos madrileños que tienen intimidad con el que pasa, que sostienen un diálogo directo con la calle [...] Sólo en Madrid viven alegremente su modestia y la de la ciudad, sabiéndose en contacto con su tiempo de siglos, pues en el mismo momento vive el pasado, el presente y el futuro.[3]

It therefore comes a no surprise that the city of Naples is central to *La mujer de ámbar*, the presence of the volcano closely linked to the aesthetic depiction of events and themes within the novel.

La mujer de ámbar tells the story of the enigmatic character Lorenzo, a Spaniard living in Naples and his doomed quest for companionship. As with many of Ramón's itinerant characters, little is known of Lorenzo's background or how he had arrived in the city. Instead, much of the narrative evokes the brooding mood of the protagonist as he wanders the streets of Naples in search of the ideal woman. When he meets the ethereal Lucía, he believes he has found the key to lasting happiness. Idealised and mystified from the start through an unrestrained and exuberant lyricism, Lucía is referred to as 'La mujer de ámbar' due to the pale orange tone and complexion of her skin which evokes the amber-coloured lava flowing down from Mount Vesuvius. The poetic language deployed to describe her lifts Lucía out of a human plane, and it soon becomes clear that she represents an unattainable ideal, and as such is ultimately beyond his reach. Through Lucía, Lorenzo meets her brother Raffaele, who introduces Lorenzo to the Neapolitan underworld. If Lucía represents an erotic-religious ideal, Raffaele represents the sensual earthly plane of unrestrained desire. He introduces Lorenzo to the elusive 'casa misteriosa', a kind of brothel where he meets the prostitutes Nazarena, Rosario and Ada. Lorenzo's quest for love oscillates between the divine and the earthly, neither of which is shown to be lasting. Despite his own confession towards the beginning of the novel that he had gone to Naples to restore his spirit and rid himself of apathy, he ultimately finds no consolation in human relationships or in religion.

The novel ends abruptly with Lucía's suicide on the eve of her wedding, prompted by her family's disapproval of their relationship, due to a deep-rooted hatred of Spaniards stemming from the death of a relative at the hands of a Spanish soldier. One must also bear in mind the more general apprehension and distrust of the Spanish in much of southern Italy due to Spanish rule in that region from 1559 to 1713. At surface level, Ramón's plot shares common ground with many of his earlier works, where narrative is based around a series of erotic adventures. It would, of course, be wrong to assume that this is purely a Ramonian trait, as it is in keeping with the Spanish literary tradition at large: as early as *El libro del buen amor* (1330–1343) the pursuit of erotic experience has been a central theme and in this sense Ramón is no exception. But Lorenzo's quest for love is not driven by romantic desire or passion, his character lacks the traditional attributes usually associated with the romantic hero such as pathos or long-suffering. The lack of emotion, moral and religious convictions of Lorenzo, suggests a very modern outlook on life, and the lack of pathos suggests a blind acceptance of events against which the protagonist is not prepared to fight. It is therefore appropriate that Lorenzo simply leaves Naples after Lucía's death, endowed with the blank indifference and aloofness typical of a modern-day hero.

Despite these modern-day traits, the author does little to allay the reader's suspicions that he is influenced by Manzoni's text, and deliberately re-works aspects of its plot: not only do his main characters share the same names as those of Manzoni's novel (Lorenzo and Lucía in *La mujer de ámbar*, Renzo and Lucia in *I promessi sposi*), but the title of Manzoni's novel is obliquely referred to towards the end of *La mujer de ámbar*, when the characters enter a restaurant which is suggestively called 'I promessi sposi':

> Lorenzo señaló de pronto el título de una de aquellas cantinas que se ofrecían con mantel y flores: 'I PROMESSI SPOSI', ponía la cartelera. Los dos a una penetraron en aquella sacristía sonriente. Sobre aquellos manteles blancos se verificaba la falsa ceremonia de la promisión. Tuvieron delante la larga espera del primer plato contenimiento de altar y embarazo del último exámen de conciencia, reclinados sobre la baranda sagrada. La llegada del primer plato los sacó de la suspensión. Sacerdotes de servilleta estolar eran aquellos camareros de I Promessi Sposi, y el de su turno iba casándoles según les iba sirviendo, aunque el principal momento de aquel desposorio preliminar fue cuando les entregó la quesera portátil en que estaba la pulverización amarilla de queso parmesano y la cucharita de hueso con que celebrar la liturgia.—¿Más?—le preguntó él sirviéndola con exceso aquel simbolismo celular en que se representaba por el mismo queso la unión de la misma sangre. La promisión había quedado más consagrada por aquella comida que por las amonestaciones ya declaradas. Salieron al campo con el sentimiento de haber asistido a una ceremonia más de la unión indisoluble.[4]

The name of the restaurant is not only significant for its ironic commentary on Lorenzo and Lucía's personal situation (their friendship and plans for marriage are opposed throughout by Lucía's mother), but more importantly for its implicit parody of Manzoni's novel. Ramón reduces, arguably one of the most revered Italian novels of all times to a tacky restaurant setting, to a kind of cheap tourist cafe, where the sacrosanct act of marriage is humorously and ingeniously reduced to a meal, the sprinkling of parmesan cheese ironically used to symbolise a liturgical rite. Eating provocatively replaces the act of marriage, in a deliberate attempt to subvert traditional values in a playful and avant-garde fashion. Ramón's reference to Manzoni should be understood as an ironic comment on the spiritual dimension to Manzoni's novel. The deeply entrenched religious convictions of Manzoni's characters contrast with the modern day aloofness of Ramón's, whose most spiritual experience takes place in a modern restaurant setting. In one sense it might be argued that Ramón sits comfortably alongside other contemporary authors who deliberately set out to parody literary works of canonical status, such as

Jardiel Poncela, with his avant-garde parody of the Don Juan myth *¿Hubo una vez 11.000 vírgenes?*, or even Joyce, and his re-working of the Homeric myth in *Ulysses*. *La mujer de ámbar* is, in this sense, at home within the context of modernist fiction at large.

Understanding La mujer de ámbar as a parodic re-working of Manzoni's novel challenges conventional wisdom on the subject. Rafael Sánchez Maza, a contemporary of Ramón's, argued that Ramón went to Italy to influence rather than be influenced:

> El viaje de Italia, que desde el Siglo de Oro hasta el Romanticismo constituye una tradición itineraria de las letras españolas, Ramón inaugura una época nueva. Los mayores viajeros nuestros del siglo XVI—Garcilaso, Cervantes, Velázquez— venían a Italia a ser influidos. Ramón es el primero—no sé si pasará por la mente de Castelar esta ilusión—que viene decididamente a influir y que ha influido ya poderosamente.[5]

Although there is no doubt that Ramón's idiosyncratic way of envisioning life through a poetic and humorous deconstruction of the world caused him to stand out as an author, it is nonetheless significant that critics have largely overlooked the extent to which he too was permeable to the literary influences of the day. Because Ramón has been famed for having created his own vanguard movement ('Ramonismo'), there has been a danger of taking this to an extreme, and artificially isolating him as a literary figure from mainstream European literature. In *La mujer de ámbar*, the author himself clearly implodes this myth, providing the reader with unambiguous clues regarding his dialogue with Manzoni's text. The critic Cardona readily accepts Ramón's deeply entrenched 'españolismo', despite his association with the avant-garde, stating:

> There is something in Ramón that distinguishes him from other 'modern' writers; there is something in him that rises above all his ultraist, cubist, dadaist, and surrealist tendencies. His work has its own peculiar physiognomy, a differentiating element that seems only natural in a thoroughly Spanish writer such as Ramón Gómez de la Serna.[6]

In addition to Ramón's implicit parody of Manzoni's novel, he is, at the same time, clearly influenced by many of its themes. Even with a superficial reading of *La mujer de ámbar*, the thematic resemblances to Manzoni's *I promessi sposi* cannot be over-looked, even though both texts are evidently different in style. Both works rely on a heavily charged atmosphere of death and religion, the idealisation of the female character (Lucía in both novels), and an important role accorded to history and landscape. I will deal with each of these individually, as they are essential to our understanding of *La mujer de ámbar*, and the author's dialogue with Manzoni's novel. I will attempt to argue that *La mujer de ámbar* arises as both a response to the time in which it was written (its parodic qualities), but in the process allows itself to be influenced by Manzoni's landmark novel. Harold Bloom's contention that '[...] we never read a poet as a poet, but only read one poet in another poet, or even into another poet'[7], highlights the importance of being sensitive to literary influence. Only through an awareness of *I promessi sposi* can we fully appreciate what Ramón sets out to achieve in *La mujer de ámbar*.

As the titles of both novels evoke the female character in each work, it seems appropriate to start by analyzing their significance. Lucía in *I promessi sposi* and the female character by the same name in *La mujer de ámbar* are invested with ethereal and divine characteristics, which sets them on a different plane to their earthly and humanly limited lovers (Renzo and Lorenzo in each novel respectively). The cult of the beloved which is generated by both male characters, coupled with the idealization of the female character who is placed on a pedestal, is a kind of modern-day notion of courtly love. Both male characters are fuelled by the need for love, which becomes the central driving force. Ramón's Lucía is a modern-day version of Manzoni's Lucía: like many of his characters she is an aesthetic creation, and as such lacks human depth (very much in line with Ortegian philosophy contained in *La deshumanización del arte*). Despite her ethereal complexion, she does not undergo any spiritual experience, nor does she display any outward religious convictions or beliefs. Whilst Manzoni's Lucía embodies an unattainable ideal: her unshakeable faith, her long-suffering and unrelenting devotion to Renzo, Ramón's Lucía is solely idealised through her beauty: the tone of her skin and incandescence of her gaze deemed far more important than her human characteristics. If Manzoni's heroine is drawn from a theistic idea, Ramón's is largely aesthetic. Her visual characteristics are central to the novel as a whole, as its title suggests, and numerous pages are devoted to describing the amber glow. This is seldom carried out in a sombre reverential fashion, but Ramón often incorporates an alleviating dose of humour, which serves to contrast the sharpened aesthetic awareness of Lorenzo, with the aloof passivity of Lucía. This can be seen when Lorenzo poetically and humorously suggests to Lucía that her amber coloured complexion had been acquired because she had been buried in lava; a claim she seriously challenges, answering 'hay cosas que no se olvidan' (p.83). In other passages she is compared to a soul in purgatory, the incandescence of her amber glow evoking suffering:

Avanzó hacia la cueva de las ánimas, y cada vez encontraba más parecido entre Lucía y el ánima. El color sudor de fuego del ánima escalada y dorada al horno le aclaraba profundamente aquella cosa sufriente que tenía Lucía. (p.77)

Lucía is created in the mind of Lorenzo, she is a product of his idealised erotic-religious fantasies. But her association with purgatory is not only significant on an aesthetic level within *La mujer de ámbar*, but is strong evidence of the two-way process established between *La mujer de ámbar* and *I promessi sposi* of parody and influence. Don Abbondio, in *I promessi sposi*, is acutely aware of the significance of figures and shapes, and frequently claims to see images of souls in purgatory, in this sense reminiscent of Lorenzo in La mujer de ámbar. At the beginning of I promessi sposi, the reader is given a lucid description of a wall which runs along one of the paths Don Abbondio frequently took on his way home:

The inner walls of the two paths, instead of joining up at the angle, ended in a shrine, on which were painted long, snaky shapes with pointed ends, supposed, in the mind of the artist and to the eyes of the inhabitants, to represent flames; alternating with the flames were other shapes defying description, and these were meant to be souls in purgatory; souls and flames were painted in brick-colour on a greyish background, with the palter flaked off here and there.[8]

I muri interni delle due viottole, invece di riunirsi ad angolo, terminavano in un tabernacolo, sul quale eran dipinte certe figure lunghe, serpeggianti, che finivano in punta, e che, nell'intenzione dell'artista, e agli occhi degli abitanti del vicinato, volevan dir fiamme; e, alternate con le fiamme, cert'altre figure da non potersi descrivere, che volevan dir anime del purgatorio: anime e fiamme a color di mattone, su un fondo bigiognolo, con qualche scalcinatura qua e là.[9]

In Manzoni's novel, the references to suffering and purgatory dovetail with the overall theme of the novel, as suffering and the trials of life are brought about by Providence to test the individual. In *I promessi sposi* Renzo is the one who endures and goes through a process of growth through experience. Lucía remains what she always was, whilst he develops and changes. From being an impulsive immature adolescent he achieves manhood through travail. On the other hand, the association of Lucía with religious imagery in *La mujer de ámbar*, stands out as the author is not interested in the promotion of a religious idea. Whilst Renzo in *I pomessi sposi* is vested with traditional Christian values of growth though travail, Lorenzo in *La mujer de ámbar* remains on the same level throughout, if anything he gravitates towards a blank indifference towards the end of the novel.

Renzo and Lucía's eventual union is brought about by an underlying belief in destiny, stemming from their religious beliefs, whilst the characters in *La mujer de ámbar* live for the fleeting sensations of the day, which inevitably come to an end when Lucía finally jumps to her death. The ending of Manzoni's novel, on the other hand, shows the character reunited with his lost one. The trauma of loss and suffering has reached its end, and the characters have now attained a heavenly realm, rewarded by their earthly suffering and endurance.

The unchallenged promotion of religious ideals in Manzoni's novel is to be expected. Divine providence in *I promessi sposi* gives way to fate and chance in *La mujer de ámbar*, in keeping with a more modern and secular vision of a world where God no longer exists. Paradoxically, Ramón's narrative is more in line with the generic conventions of the love story: Shakespeare's *Romeo and Juliet*, or Fernando Roja's *La celestina* (in which, as the reader will recall, Melibea jumps to her death). The ending of *La mujer de ámbar* evokes a world of self-perpetuating emptiness. The solemn tone of the final scene of *La mujer de ámbar* is far removed from the playful and poetic descriptions of the city of Naples in preceding pages, but is by no means elegiac. The lack of religious convictions of the main characters throughout the story is sustained until the end. Lorenzo is not re-united with Lucía through death, but simply leaves the city. His reaction to Lucía's death is striking for both its aloofness and lack of emotion. He makes no attempt to explain the events from a religious or metaphysical point of view. The cold reaction of Lorenzo is typical of Ramón's characters who seldom believe in anything, but live for the transient beauty of the day which often includes some kind of erotic adventure. Lorenzo's blank acceptance of events suggests a certain inevitability, an ultimate lack of belief in the ability to change anything. Ramón's secular vision of the world directly and deliberately contravenes the theistic world of Manzoni.

The Manzonian influence on *La mujer de ámbar* operates at several levels. The historical tension between Spain and Italy is strongly conveyed in both novels: in Manzoni's novel it is the Spanish born oligarch 'Don Rodrigo' who opposes Renzo and Lucía's wedding, whilst in *La mujer de ámbar* Lorenzo and Lucía's friendship is condemned from the start simply because he is Spanish. The importance of landscape (lake 'Como' in Manzoni's novel and the volcano in Ramón's novel) is central to both novels, conveying a sense of continuity and durability, which contrasts with the ephemeral nature of human life, and descriptions of sickness, disease and dark enclosed spaces alternate with passages which extol divine and idealised notions of beauty.

I will now deal with each of these issues in turn. In *La mujer de ámbar*, different to earlier vanguardist novels such as *El incongruente* (1922) and *Cinelandia* (1923), there is an underlying preoccupation with the past, and its ongoing legacy to the present. This is unprecedented for Ramón, and it is likely that it either stems from the Manzonian influence or from the nostalgia

Ramón might have been feeling bearing in mind the strong Spanish architectural influences on the southern Italy. Whilst there are passages in *La mujer de ámbar* which evoke a cosmopolitan feel to the city: the maritime boulevards and flocks of tourists; the recurrent references to 'el eco español' and the voices of Spanish soldiers crying out from the city squares which Lorenzo claims he can hear, evoke a retrospective and nostalgic tone reminiscent of the 1898 Generation, shedding the emotional detachment to be found in his vanguardist novels.[10] History weighs heavily on Lorenzo, after all, he is essentially rejected by Lucía's family for being Spanish. It therefore comes as no surprise that Lorenzo is obsessed with shaking off the past. Lucía is from a traditional family of social standing (the 'Símili' family) and openly admits that she will not be able to love him because of his past. Lorenzo, the modern-day hero, rejects this on the grounds that the past should be left behind, although he is compelled to apologise to Lucía's godmother on behalf of his ancestors. The past soon becomes an obsession for Lorenzo, which is shown in even the trivial things in life: Giuseppina the cleaning lady does not like cleaning because she feels she is removing the past from around her, but Lorenzo insists on everything being clean. Lorenzo's past, although a serious issue which eventually comes between himself and Lucía, is dealt with here with alleviating humour. It is significant that *I promessi sposi* is set during the years of 1628 and 1631, at a time when southern Italy and the region of Lombardy were under Spanish rule.

Whilst Manzoni, true to the realist tradition, incorporates historical fact into the overall narrative as a way of grounding his characters in an authentic historical time and place, Ramón's motives are more ambivalent. It goes without saying that Ramón is interested in the aesthetic exploration of history as a means of adding another dimension to the work as a whole, and refrains from explicit social commentary, but at the same time suggests his permeability and capacity to be influenced by the Italian author. It is therefore not surprising that landscape is also of central importance to both authors. If lake Como acts as a kind of frame to *I promessi sposi*, appearing at the beginning and the end of the novel, and is the place to which Renzo and Lucía return after their eventual betrothal, the volcano in *La mujer de ámbar* (Mount Vesuvius) not only binds the characters in a tacit relationship with their surroundings, but vividly embodies the central theme of the novel: Lorenzo's passion for Lucía, suggestively evoked by the allusions to lava. The physical setting of the novel is not merely used as a corollary for the aesthetic and psychological ramblings of the central protagonist, so often the case in earlier novels such as *El secreto del Acueducto* (1922) set in the city of Segovia or *La Quinta de Palmyra* (1923) set in Estoril on the Portuguese coast, but is thus used to help the reader visualise the central themes of the novel. For Ramón landscape is both rooted in geography and the hazy boundaries of the human soul itself. The descriptions of Mount Vesuvius in *La mujer de ámbar* are therefore not important for their realistic verisimilitude, but are evidence of the author's ability to transform the material world into a poetic construct: the aqueduct in *El secreto del Acueducto* (1922), the surroundings of Estoril in *La Quinta de Palmyra* (1923), Paris in *El alba* (1921) and indeed many of his *greguerías*, which establish unconventional affinities between a plethora of objects. The use of landscape in *La mujer de ámbar* is therefore two-fold: on the one hand it binds Lucía to her surroundings (she is 'La mujer de ámbar'), whilst allowing the author to engage in the evocation of sensory experience through a lyrical transformation of the physical world.

A similar phenomenon can be observed in Ramón's references to the plague and to the 'lazaroni' (centres for leprous patients) echo those in Manzoni's novel. In *I promessi sposi* it is in the 'lazaretto' where Lucía and Renzo re-encounter each other, after Renzo has survived the plague in Milán during their separation. In Manzoni's work the characters are directly affected by suffering, whereas in *La mujer de ámbar* the characters contemplate it from a distance. Ramón's 'lazarroni' are merely used for background description, and do not tie in with the overall workings of plot. Whilst Manzoni's treatment of sickness and suffering are religiously charged, in *La mujer de ámbar* they are taken to their ultimate poetic consequence in an attempt to move away from the dominant forms of realism and naturalism, and to build a novel which owes its existence as much to the poetic imagination of the author, as to its strong textual links to the Italian literary text. In Ramón's narrative fiction, plot and story are usually attenuated and compensated for by a poetic and lyrical transformation of the surrounding world. His novels are permeated by a certain mood, a particular way of seeing things, which enables him to engage the interest of the reader without relying on carefully plotted narratives. The mood he creates is usually centred around the main character, even though he seldom provides his characters with a deep rooted character psychology.

The distinct texture of each work, despite any similarities in theme or characters, undoubtedly stems from the fact that Ramón is essentially a modernist writer, if we understand modernism as a crisis in the novel resulting from a lack of confidence in reality as such; and therefore does not engage with reality with the tools of a nineteenth-century novelist. This to some extent, accounts for the stylistic differences between Manzoni's novel and his own. Manzoni's heavy reliance on action is in stark contrast to Ramón's depiction of the character's thoughts. The nineteenth century preoccupation with action gives way to a greater emphasis on the psychological spaces of the mind in the twentieth century novel, and although Ramón does not deploy techniques such as of stream of consciousness or interior monologue used by Joyce or Woolf, he projects the characters thoughts on the surrounding world, which in turn becomes a vehicle of expression for the character himself. The surrounding world is thus important for what it expresses, rather than for any realistic verisimilitude. The simple image of sheets hanging out of the window is used to express sadness: 'El blancor de las colchas y embozos tenía tristeza de humanidad aglomerada, y eran huellas que entristecen el alma' (p.21). Similarly, the image of clothes becomes impregnated with Lorenzo's melancholy, bringing sensory perception to the fore in an attempt to render a lyrical vision of the world: '[...] Semejaban aquellas ropas tristonas, llorosas, enjugatorias de todad la ciudad' (p.36).

At the same time, *La mujer de ámbar* is indebted to aestheticism in its unrelenting lyricism and the power it accords to language. This enables the author to lift Lucía out of the plane of the everyday, to a place where she gains poetic status: 'En aquella ribera, Lucía era más encantadora, pero se veía cómo su carne era carne de otros tiempos, ambarinada por la influencia ambarina del aire añejo y del reluz de mar' (p.62, 3). And further on: 'El color sudor de fuego del ánima escalada y dorada al horno le aclaraba profundamente aquella cosa sufriente que tenía Lucía' (p.77). Her radiance and idealised beauty embody the aesthetic and erotic ideal she represents, which ultimately sets her beyond Lorenzo's reach.

La mujer de ámbar is interesting because it fuses the idealised religious and erotic fantasies of the character Lorenzo with the author's own experience of life—his sojourn in Naples, his obsessive jealousy and aestheticization of women—with motifs and themes of Manzoni's novel. Stylistically, *La mujer de ámbar* is very typical of much of the author's 1920s works, which balance a modernistic type of narrative with an exploration of the author's own personal experience of life. Its highly charged prose draws on a lyrical interpretation of reality. In *La mujer de ámbar* the author does not relinquish feelings of nostalgia for the past, but shows strong ties with previous literary paradigms. His work contains a new kind of prose, in which symbolism is replaced by a new exploration of imagery as a way of re-interpreting the world. Whilst not engaging completely with avant-garde aesthetics, he retains a central characteristic of much of his work in his depiction of a character in search of companionship in a changing world which ultimately passes him by.

La mujer de ámbar is not simply an experiment at writing a novel in a new geographic location, but is a deliberate attempt to re-work aspects of Manzoni's plot in a 1920s setting. Its literary strength stems from Ramón's ability to make the borrowed characters his own. He endows Lorenzo with

the character-traits to be found in many of his fictional characters: the misan-
thropic solipsist, whose lack of faith in society as a whole causes him to take
refuge in an aesthetic world which oscillates between the oneiric and the real.
Like many of Ramón's inscrutable characters, Lorenzo's quest for human
love is ultimately unfulfilled, mirroring in many ways the authors ideas about
life itself and definitively rejecting the meaning to be found in Manzoni's
novel. It is in this way that Ramón is able to stand as one of the standard
bearers of the Spanish avant-garde, without neglecting his strong roots in the
European literary tradition.

Parody, the Picaresque and the Modern-day Man of Commerce: El caballero del hongo gris (1928)

El caballero del hongo gris (1928)[11] is particularly interesting for its fusion
of themes typical of the twenties (cosmopolitanism, sport, travel) with a traditional picaresque-like plot. The main character fights for survival and
social betterment through a mixture of wit and trickery, whilst enjoying a
measure of good fortune. Nevertheless, a hasty equation with the picaresque
would undoubtedly constitute an oversimplification.

The effectiveness of El caballero del hongo gris as a novel is debatable.
Although it has a definite structure which is easily discernible by the reader,
the pacy rhythm of the narrative, its profuse inclusion of current trends and
its portrayal of city-life contrast with more contemplative works such as El
secreto del Acueducto (1922) or La quinta de Palmyra (1923). El caballero
del hongo gris follows the blueprint of the adventure novel in that the story
takes place in a variety of countries, and the hero is driven by a desire to be
involved in action.

El caballero del hongo gris is set in a number of European cities (Barcelona, Rome, London, Lisbon, Marseilles), revealing a keen interest of the
author for a cosmopolitan setting. The constant switching of locale undoubtedly affects the treatment of time in the novel. The pace and rhythm of El
caballero del hongo gris is very different from Gómez de la Serna's more
lyrical novels, where the progression of plot is constantly halted by a poetic
rendering of the world. At the same time, the main character of El caballero
del hongo gris, Leonardo, is typically Ramonian in that he lives in a changing world, and stands out because of his peculiar and highly idiosyncratic
behaviour.

The main thrust of the novel is to expose the dangers of the unrestrained
pursuit of wealth.[12] El caballero del hongo gris undoubtedly calls into question the effects of power and money, revealing the shallowness of a society

bent solely on material existence in the wake of rapid market expansion. It is not a coincidence that this novel was written in 1928, at the height of Primo de Rivera's dictatorship which had embarked on a process of rapid, although superficial, modernisation. Great building projects were undertaken to give an appearance of progress, despite the shaky foundations of the economy. In addition to *El caballero del hongo gris's* depiction of society's thirst for capital, it highlights the typically nineteen-twenties preoccupation with fashion, as outlined by Hoyle. The title of the novel accords particular importance to a bowler hat, attesting the growing importance of fashion at large.[13] It is interesting that the hat gives the character a sense of belonging to a particular social group. This is analogous to the penurious knight in *Lazarillo de Tormes* who dresses in finery in order to attain a degree of social standing, despite the hunger he undergoes behind closed doors. The traditional preoccupation with the theme of 'honra', is therefore, to some extent, re-enacted in the character of Leonardo (the protagonist of *El caballero del hongo gris*).

El caballero del hongo gris can be understood as a re-working of the picaresque novel in nineteen-twenties Spain. Even a superficial reading makes the similarity with the picaresque apparent. If the picaresque genre generally relates the story of a character who is born into a humble background and attempts to survive through a mixture of dishonesty and trickery, living by his wits and seeking an easy advantage whilst evading responsibility at any cost (as with Pablo in Quevedo's *El buscón*, or Lázaro in *Lazarillo de Tormes*), then Leonardo in *El caballero del hongo gris* is a modern day *pícaro*. It is also significant that Quevedo's *Buscón* describes Pablo's dreams of becoming a 'caballero', and in Gómez de la Serna's novel Leonardo is known as 'el *caballero* del hongo gris'. Significant in this respect, is Quevedo's well known 'letrilla': 'Poderoso *caballero* es don dinero', a truism which is satirically born out in *El caballero del hongo gris* in which Leonardo is able to purchase anything he wants, from a false identity to a dissected hippopotamus which he imports from India.

The picaresque convention of a hero who perennially shifts between fortune and misfortune, coupled with chance encounters and unrelenting action, is also closely observed in *El caballero del hongo gris*. Its structure resembles the episodic nature of a quintessentially picaresque-plot. The influence of tradition on Ramón's work should come as no surprise. Ramón's cultivation of *españolismo* is well documented.[14] The re-working of the picaresque genre in *El caballero del hongo gris* must be understood in the broader context of the time, when it was commonplace for writers to adapt both myth and legend into modern novels. Jardiel Poncela's re-working of the don Juan legend in *¿Hubo alguna vez 11.000 vírgenes?* immediately comes to mind, whilst other well-known works such as Joyce's *Ulysses* and Pérez de Ayala's *Novelas poemáticas* are also worth mentioning. The re-working of myth and legend must be understood as a means of drawing attention away from the importance of plot and suspense, and a means of highlighting the writing itself.

El caballero del hongo gris starts in a similar fashion to Quevedo's *El buscón*. Leonardo, the protagonist, is born into a family of humble means. He is respected because of his physically imposing appearance—the importance placed on his physical presence is reminiscent of aspects of the American Dream. Like Pablos and Lazarillo, Leonardo leaves home after stealing from his mother and moves to Barcelona where he comes into contact with the big sprawling boulevards and recondite cabarets. At this stage it is unclear what are his means of subsistence. The importance accorded to his physical presence outweighs that of character psychology. In the early stages of the novel Leonardo purchases a mirror to look at himself, as he believes that any power of persuasion depends not on words, but on looks. Leonardo lives in a world where external appearances count, and where instant impressions and decisions have replaced contemplation and thought. In this sense there is a clear resemblance to the picaresque genre. Both Lazarillo and Pablos are constantly in action, and seldom give time to careful thought and contemplation. Unlike other of Ramón's characters, Leonardo is depicted as a character who is not interested in the contemplation of life, or in viewing the world through poetic eyes. Instead he is presented as an individual taken over by action and fuelled by the sole ambition to make money.

In *El buscón*, Pablos buys a horse in the hope that he will be accepted by the nobility, whilst in *El caballero del hongo gris* Leonardo buys a bowler hat in an attempt to gain acceptance among the Parisian business world. The old themes of wealth, respectability and class are re-worked within a modern framework. However, whilst Gómez de la Serna is primarily interested in the aesthetics of the modern day picaresque, Quevedo wrote from the perspective of a member of the upper class, concerned about those attempting social betterment.[15]

Whilst in Barcelona, Leonardo befriends a woman by the name of Aurora who has been widowed by her husband's sudden suicide. His relationship with her is short-lived due to his insensitivity towards her bereavement and his insatiable appetite for women. When she reports him for 'una simple falsificación' which is not explained in any detail, Leonardo leaves for Paris. The reason Leonardo gives for his departure is both curious and unprecedented as far as Gómez de la Serna's novels are concerned, particularly for its overt disaffection with Spanish society. He leaves Spain because 'comprendía que en España todas las cosas se lían y se arraigan con demasiada violencia, amarrando por todos lados al que quiere vivir' (p.17). As with much of Gómez de la Serna's fiction, the character of Leonardo is explored in little depth. More importance is given to his bowler hat, an article which has an effect on others as well as himself:

> Su hongo gris completaba tanto su figura, que había en el ambiente un deseo de que encarnase en estatua con el hongo gris, y las calles se ponían tristes al quedarse sin aquel caballero. (p.31)

Leonardo is a character shaped by his surrounding world, and by dreams of success. He drinks whisky and his speech is littered with foreign words such as *cricket*, *charleston*, and *barman*. Unlike Pablos or Lazarillo, he fails to gain the sympathy of the reader because he lacks human depth. If Pablos and Lazarillo are characters drawn directly from life at a time when pícaros were commonplace, then Leonardo is the dehumanised man of the nineteen-twenties, where money and greed have taken over. It is plausible that Gómez de la Serna deliberately withholds sympathetic traits from his main character in an attempt to reveal the dangers which can result from the unregulated pursuit of material wealth. On one occasion one of the characters states: 'El cheque me encanta...es la única carta de amor y de amistad verdadera' (p.43). Society is depicted as vacuous, its only preoccupation being the pursuit of financial success. In his quest to obtain money Leonardo is prepared to trick, deceive and evade all forms of responsibility. Even the settings in which we find him consist exclusively of banks and opulent homes of the wealthy. However, Leonardo does express concern that money corrupts the soul: 'Esos cheques por los que vendemos el alma'.

However, not all of the characters in *El caballero del hongo gris* are content with the materialistic society to which they pertain, and on various occasions express a desire to transcend its shallowness and corruption. The character Nela feels sad, for instance, because she realises that despite the superficial splendour and opulence of her world, money cannot open up a 'window of light':

> Nela tenía más tristeza que nunca bajo aquella lluvia de esplendeces, pues ningún billete le abría la ventana de luz que deseaba ver abierta alguna vez. (p.113)

In *El caballero del hongo gris*, Gómez de la Serna presents as the cause of unhappiness the perennial conflict between human emotion and materialism, in a society undergoing the strains of change. Language from the world of sport and music is deployed to evoke a feeling of modernity. Dialogue within the novel is full of images drawn from the modern world used by the characters to convey their feelings. On one occasion, when talking to Leonardo, Nela exclaims: '¡Tanto me han abrazado que me he quedado sin mí misma! Ahora me siento tan ligera como lo que puede volar sobre mares infinitos'. Leonardo replies using imagery of an aircraft: '¡Qué modo de hablar, pareces una aviadora!' (p.116). He then goes on to say 'Nos dejáis tan pulidas de caricias que somos bañistas de la muerte', using sporting imagery to describe his outlook. By using sporting terms and references to techno-logical advance Ramón conveys the characters' feelings objectively, as the words they utter are not associated with an emotional past. This is in keeping with Ortega's theories on a dehumanised art which rejects the sphere of hu-man emotion. Conversations therefore do not transcend the plane of superficiality. The recurrent references to jazz music serve the same purpose, as the author sees jazz as a medium which avoids any deep introspection, preferring instead the superficial: 'El intento del jazz es de sacar el mundo a la superficie. Las otras músicas tienen un sentido más recóndito, más subterráneo y más religioso, un sentido introspectivo y letal'.[16] In addition to sport and jazz, speed is used to evoke a sense of modernity. Speed is treated futuristically, a feature which is evident in other works such as *El incongru-ente* and *Cinelandia*. Following Nela's death (she eventually commits suicide out of growing frustration), Valentín (Leonardo's right-hand man) flees from Lisbon, fearing that the authorities will find a stash of stolen money. The plot then gives way to a succession of images related to the effects of speed. He argues that speed creates a different morality, as well as effacing all traces of conventions:

> La velocidad ha creado otra moral [...] La velocidad borra los gestos antiguos y da el cinismo de ver venir lo que los demás ven...la velocidad cohesiona el mundo. (p.122)

In a later episode Leonardo declines a proposal of marriage on the basis that: 'Yo no puedo darte la velocidad que tú necesitas, vete con otro que crea más en la velocidad de lo que yo creo' (p.168). Speed is linked to youth, to cars, to a new generation which feels empowered: 'Un hombre atestado de automóvil es capaz de todo' (p.127). Speed is therefore important because it presents a new vision of the world, but it does not solve problems or provide any answers. It is important because it replaces a peaceful contemplation of the world with an energetic and revolutionising vision. Ramón uses it to show that he is capable of adapting to new aesthetic tendencies at the cutting-edge of the time in which he was writing, whilst combining them with the traditional Spanish literary genre of the picaresque.

El caballero del hongo gris's resemblance to the picaresque is not only thematic, but extends to the episodic narrative structure. Following the episode in Lisbon, Leonardo leaves once again for Geneva, under a false identity (he calls himself 'Rafael' and poses as a Venezuelan). He soon moves on to the city of Marseilles where he founds a society for chimpanzees. The only reason which he gives for embarking on such a bizarre enterprise is that these animals will save the world from decadence: 'Francia iba a ser la exportadora de los animales que habían de salvar el mundo de su decadencia' (p.147).

Leonardo gradually comes to the realisation that he is losing faith in everything except his grey bowler-hat: 'Perdía la fe en muchas cosas, hay que creer en algo, y por eso yo creo en el hongo gris' (p.151). The hat brings him good fortune and financial success, and provides him with the only meaning in an otherwise empty world of financial enterprises and ephemeral relationships. However, it does not save him in his most dangerous hour. The novel ends with Leonardo's death, after he had challenged a look-alike to a duel on the grounds that the world was not large enough to hold two identical individuals each with a grey hat. Confident of his luck and good fortune to the very end, Leonardo dies from a bullet wound. The last scene is that of his side-kick Valentín running to catch a train in order to escape from the place of his death.

The ending is indeed more sombre than that of *El Lazarillo* or *El buscón*. In the latter, Pablos leaves for Latin America in search of a better fortune, whilst Lazarillo ends up in the unenviable role of town-crier, having been cuckolded by his wife. However, the death of Leonardo hardly comes as a surprise to the reader who is acquainted with Gómez de la Serna's fiction, which frequently ends with the death of a prominent character, or their degeneration into a state of madness and senility. The ending displays Ramón's ambivalence towards modernity as a whole. Whilst he is interested in experimenting with the aesthetics of modernity, he conveys a deep-rooted distrust of its effects on the integrity of the individual. The modern-day hero in the character of Leonardo is parodied, and presented at best as a likeable buffoon.

As a novel, *El caballero del hongo gris* maybe lacks the poetic and lyrical depth of other works, which Ramón frequently relies on instead of intriguing plots. The humour resulting from the outlandish endeavours of Leonardo to secure wealth go some of the way to compensate for the lack of character-psychology, whilst presenting a playful attitude to life, in keeping with the avant-garde novel at large. It cannot be considered as one of Ramón's masterpieces, but deserves to be mentioned in relation to his avant-garde works.

Notes

1   Camón Aznar status: 'Era indispensable en la literatura de Ramón el libro dedicado a Nápoles', in *Ramón Gómez de la Serna en sus obras* (Madrid: Espasa Calpe, 1972) p.348.
2   Anthony Percival, 'Ramón Gómez de la Serna's La mujer de ámbar: ¿La novela libre?', Nigel Dennos (ed.) *Studies in Ramón Gómez de la Serna*, (Ottawa: Dovehouse Editions, 1988) pp.199–208 (p.202).
3   Ramón Gómez de la Serna, *Piso bajo* (Madrid: Espasa Calpe, 1961) p.8–9.
4   Ramón Gómez de la Serna, *La mujer de ámbar*, 8a edición (Madrid: Espasa Calpe, 1981) p.144–145.
5   Rafael Sánchez Mazas, 'Ramón en las Hespérides', in Ramón Gómez de la Serna, *Automoribundia* (Madrid: Ediciones Guadarrama, 1974) p.454–457.
6   Rodolfo Cardona, Ramón: *A Study of Ramón Gómez de la Serna and His Works* (New York: Eliseo Torres and Sons, 1957) p.49.
7   Harold Bloom, *The Anxiety of Influence: A Theory of Poetry* (Oxford: University Press, 1973) p.94.
8   Alessandro Manzoni, *I promessi sposi*, trans by Archibald Coquhoun (London: The Reprint Society, 1952) p.3.
9   Alessandro Manzoni, *I promessi sposi*, Introduzione e note di Vittorio Spinazzola (Roma: Garzanti Edotore, 1966).
10 In both *Cinelandia* (1923) and *El incongruente* (1922) the cities are aesthetic creations which border on the surreal and the fantastic.
11 Ramón Gómez de la Serna, *El caballero del hongo gris* [1928] (Madrid: Alianza Editorial, 1970).
12 Antonio del Rey Briones argues that in this novel the author conveys his contempt for capitalism and the effects of greed: 'En diversos momentos de la novela podemos encontrar una crítica directa de los fundamentos arbitrarios de la sociedad capitalista, especialmente en lo que se refiere a la corrupción que engendra la ambición desmedida de riquezas y el poder omnímodo del dinero'. (Rey Briones, 1992, p.143). Camón Aznar calls it 'la novela del dinero' and argues that the main character 'protagoniza muchos aspectos de la vida moderna', (Aznar, p.352) Alan Hoyle refers to *El caballero del hongo gris* as a 'farcical satire on the swindles of banking and commerce'. Alan Hoyle, 'The Politics of a Hatless Revolutionary', in *Studies in Modern Literature and Art presented to Helen F. Grant*, ed. by Nigel Glendinning (London: Tamesis, 1972) pp.79–96 (p.92).
13 Hoyle convincingly links the importance associated with the hat to a short story by the same author entitled *Aventuras y desgracias de un sinsombrerista*, published in *Revista de Occidente* at the later date of 1932. Hoyle argues that 'hatlessness' represents an 'open-minded, irrational, political neutrality', and a 'freedom from grim sectarianism [...]'. In his view, the hat represents an allegiance to a particular ideology or creed: in this novel, to the world of business and commerce.
14 Rodolfo Cardona dedicates an entire chapter to Ramón's *españolismo*, arguing that: 'There is something in Ramón that distinguishes him from these other modern writers; there is something in him that rises above all his ultraist, cubist, dadaist, and surrealist tendencies. His work has its own peculiar physiognomy, a differentiating element that seems only natural in a thoroughly Spanish writer such as Ramón Gómez de la Serna.' For among the most outstanding and obvious characteristics of his works one finds his españolismo. (Cardona, 1957, p.49).

15 See R.O. Jones, *A Literary History Of Spain: The Golden Age* (London: Ernest Benn Limited, 1971) p.135.

16 Ramón Gómez de la Serna, *Ismos* (1930), (Madrid: Ediciones Guadarrama, 1975), p.181.

Chapter 5. Towards a Modernist Aesthetics (1930–1936)

There is one fact which, whether for
good or for ill, is of utmost importance
in the public life of Europe at
the present moment. This fact is the accession
of the masses to complete social power.

> Ortega y Gasset (1883–1963) in *The Revolt of the Masses* 1930

Nous voulons voyager sans vapeur et sans voile.

> Baudelaire (1821–1867)

The irrationality of a thing is no argument
against its existence, rather a condition of it.

> Frederich Nietzsche (1844–1900)

Things fall apart, the centre will not hold.

> William Butler Yeats (1865–1939)

The world is trying the experiment of attempting to form a civilised but non-Christian mentality. The experiment will fail.

> T.S. Eliot (1885–1965).

It is widely perceived in Spanish literature—and European literature at large—that the 1930s mark a departure from the experimental techniques of the 1920s to a more socially realistic approach to writing. With the Wall Street Crash in 1929 and the ensuing economic crisis on a global scale, accompanied by the rise of Fascism in Germany, Italy and Spain, it is generally assumed that the author increasingly felt a heightened sense of social responsibility which was at best expressed through a return to artistic verisimilitude and the depiction of the struggles and plight of the working man. It is assumed that during the decade of the 1930s the artist descended from his so called 'ivory tower' to engage with social issues, abandoning avant-garde playfulness. For many, the avant-garde had been deemed to have run its course. It had become an outmoded fashion not suited to express a world undergoing economic ruin. There is certainly ample evidence to support this view. In Spain authors such as Joaquín Arderius, Díaz Fernández, Cesar Arconada gave shape to the so-called 'novela de avanzada', which attempted to 're-humanise' literature through a depiction of realistic events and characters. Rather than harnessing experimental innovations to bring about a critique of society, there is a widespread return to the techniques of realism and social documentation. However, the picture is always more complex than that which literary historians have made us believe, for it is during this time that Ramón Gómez de la Serna writes one of his most accomplished (and possibly one of his most experimental) novels, *¡Rebeca!* (1936). *¡Rebeca!* Constitutes a radically new form of prose from the dominant modes of nineteenth century realism and naturalism, and a completely different approach to the kind of social-realism that was making its name in 1930s Spain under the guise of the 'novela de avanzada'.[1] At a time when authors at large felt compelled to revert to a more socially driven literature Gómez de la Serna continues to champion the avant-garde. In fact, *¡Rebeca!* goes beyond the experimentation of the 1920s. It is a more complex and challenging work which should place it at the centre of the European modernist novel. David Lodge's definition of modernism is a useful one to bear in mind before analysing *¡Rebeca!* In some depth:

> modernist fiction, then, is experimental or innovatory in form, displaying marked deviations from pre-existing modes of discourse, literary and non-literary. Modernist fiction is concerned with consciousness, and also with subconscious and unconscious workings of the human mind. Hence the structure of external 'objective' events essential to traditional narrative art is diminished in scope and scale, or presented very selectively and obliquely, or is almost completely dissolved, in order to make room for introspection, analysis, reflection and reverie. A modernist novel has no real 'beginning', since it plunges us into a flowering stream of experience with which we gradually familiarise ourselves by a process of influence and association; and its ending is usually 'open' or ambiguous, leaving the reader in doubt as to the final destiny of characters. To compensate for the diminution of narrative structure and unity, alternative methods of aesthetic ordering become more prominent such as allusion to or imitation of literary models or mythical archetypes, and the repetition with variation of motifs, images, symbols and a technique variously described as 'rhythm', 'leitmotif' and 'spectral form'. Modernist fiction eschews the straight chronological ordering of its material, and the use of a reliable, omniscient and intrusive narrator. It employs, instead, either a single, limited point of view, or a method of multiple points of view, all more or less limited and fallible: and it tends towards a fluid complex handling of time, involving much cross-reference backwards and forwards across the chronological span of the action.[2]

The publication of *¡Rebeca!* during the landmark year of 1936 undoubtedly highlights the dangers of narrowly subsuming works of literature under over-rigorous paradigmatic frameworks simply because of their date of publication. Anyone who has read *¡Rebeca!* will have noted that it is radically different to anything published in Spain before. Heavily influenced by French literary surrealism, it is my contention that had *¡Rebeca!* benefited from wider translation and readership, it would have constituted one of the main examples of literary surrealism and been a forerunner to the existential-ist literature of the 1940s.

The 1930s mark a time of upheaval in Gómez de la Serna's personal life. In 1931 he made his first trip to South America, where he gave a series of conferences in Argentina and Chile, including one particular conference on the subject of butterflies. In Chile he partook in a banquet held in a hospital operating theatre, where the wine was served in medical receptacles and the food laid out on an operating table. On a subsequent trip in 1933 he dressed up as a variety of characters including a toreador, Napoleon, Goya, and El Greco to give conferences. He became increasingly isolated from his Spanish peers who were openly supporting the new Republican government. He was becoming evermore detached from the socio-political realities in his home-land, embarking on a literary enterprise which militated against the nor-mative socio-realism re-emerging in the Spain of the 1930s.

¡Rebeca! captures the post-theistic era of modern twentieth-century European society where traditional structures and ways of life were dissolv-ing and changing with the emergence of urban centres and ever-expanding metropolises. In many ways *¡Rebeca!*'s narrative could be considered a-historical in that it makes no direct reference to important political events. Instead, it is heavily psychological and surrealistic, uncovering surface ap-pearances to delve deeper into a disconcerting world dominated by random and inexplicable forces, lonely human forms and a pervasive sense of absurd-ity. The main character Luis is a modern-day anti-hero, emanating from a society not that different from the one decried by Unamuno in *El sentido trágico* (1912), by Ortega y Gasset in *La España invertebrada* (1921), and prophesised by Oswald Spengler in his controversial *The Decline of The West* (1921).

Bearing this in mind, *¡Rebeca!* serves to question the nature of the Span-ish novel within the European context, and invariably prompts the reader to reconsider Spain's contribution to European modernist literature between the two World Wars.

Whilst Spain's contribution to European culture of this period is well known in the field of poetry and the visual arts (Lorca, Cernuda, Alberti, Giménez, Dalí, Picasso, Miró, Gris), its contribution to the genre of the novel has barely been recognised until relatively recently.[3] Contrary to the Euro-pean modernist writers such as Kafka, Proust and Joyce, whose work tran-scended national boundaries, Spanish novelists have languished in the shadows, victims of misrepresentation and ignorance. Gómez de la Serna, who was sensitive to European cultural influences not least because of his two-year sojourn in Paris, needs to be considered within the sphere of Euro-pean literary modernism. Although *¡Rebeca!* was published at a time when literature at large was reverting to a more socially driven narrative style, *¡Rebeca!* has much to tell us about modern western European society and the crisis of consciousness in human understanding.

Despite the profoundly experimental nature of Ramón Gómez de la Serna's 1936 novel *¡Rebeca!*,[4] upon close analysis it becomes clear that many of its themes encapsulate and give voice to central Spanish concerns pertaining not only to the 1930s, but to Spanish history as a whole. At the same time, it clearly follows the broad tenets of European modernism and should not, therefore, be considered in isolation. Although there has always been the temptation to view of Ramón Gómez de la Serna as a kind of literary aberration whose work could not be accommodated within any particular literary paradigm, his narrative fiction should be understood as part of the modernist attempt to break with 19th century realism and naturalism through poetic deconstruction and defamiliarisation. The crisis of consciousness that engulfed Spain between 1898 and 1936, was prompted by very different events to those that influenced the Northern European countries following the First World War. However, this crisis not only brought about radical social change into Spain, but also new ways of perceiving and understanding the surrounding world.

Ramón Gómez de la Serna's experimental novels are a good starting point to understand the tensions and influences at work within the modern Spanish novel, of how the novel draws on both Spanish and European influences, simultaneously breaking with pre-existing literary paradigms whilst asserting and reinforcing the literary tradition. Gómez de la Serna's work captures the fervour of 1920s experimentalism and the new spirit of change that was challenging the artistic world at large. There is no doubt that *¡Rebeca!* constitutes a surrealist novel. If Dadaism had represented the crisis in European consciousness through a destructive annihilation of conventional artistic and literary taste in a deliberate attempt to question and subvert deeply ingrained aesthetic sensibilities, surrealism goes much further by delving into the human subconscious in an attempt to gain a fuller understanding of the human condition. Breton in his first manifesto of surrealism, states that his intention is not only to create a new kind of art, but a new man. This 'new man' was to embody true freedom, which could only be attained once the chains of reason, morals, religion and tradition had been broken.[5]

Although a full account of how surrealism emerged and took shape in Spain is not possible in this context, it may be useful to highlight some of its main tenets.[6] Waldberg defines surrealism as 'a way of knowing, a kind of ethics'. In other words, surrealism is not simply to be understood as a matter of aesthetics, but a particular thought pattern, and new and different way in which to perceive and understand the surrounding world. In what could

equally be a description of some of Gómez de la Serna's *greguerías* Waldberg states: '[...] human figures and objects are divorced from their natural
function and placed opposite to one another in a relationship which is unexpected—perhaps shocking—and which therefore gives each of them a new
presence'.[7] Breton explains that the highest task poetry can set for itself is
the comparison of two distant objects so as to show their concrete unity and
to confer upon each a strength lacking in its former isolated situation: 'the
breaking down of their formal opposition is an essential step toward the realization of their full meaning'.[8] The external world is fused with the interior
world of the author, producing a sense of bewilderment and strangeness, giving expression to a world predicated on chance, serendipity, incongruity,
metamorphosis, mutation and an exploration of the subconscious. Carlos
Marcial de Onis argues that 'El surrealismo representa en la poesía moderna
la culminación del irracionalismo al pretender basarse en lo subconsciente,
en el mundo onírico, desprovisto, por definición, de toda lógica'.[9] Lemaitre
argues that surrealism brings about :

> [...] the desire to rid artistic or literary works of any rigorous connection with the
> external reality that we perceive through reason and senses. At the extreme limit of
> this tendency has appeared the idea of a meaningless, self-contained and justifying
> creation, absolutely unrelated to the normal concepts or shape familiar to our experi-
> ence.[10]

Lemaitre goes on to argue that:

> The revelations of experimental psychology in regard to the working of the subcon-
> scious mind and over the practical applications of the cinema and the phonograph,
> constituted in no small measure to create the impression that every sentiment we en-
> tertain and every solid object we perceive is but a flimsy assemblage ready to
> collapse into fragments at the impact of some new discovery.[11]

Spontaneity, irrationality, flight of thought, incoherence and incursions
into the dream world lie at the heart of *¡Rebeca!*. The quest for love is the
only factor that ultimately gives life any meaning. *¡Rebeca!* is about the ideal
woman who never materialises. The protagonist is consumed with surrealism's notion of *amour fou* which knows no boundaries.

By the time Gómez de la Serna started to write *¡Rebeca!* he was no
longer interested in literary experimentalism simply for its own sake. He was,
instead, arguably more aware of the absurdity of existence as he advanced in
years and was evermore aware of the inevitability of his own death. Similar
to the surrealists, for Ramón the logical and rational world is of less importance than the world of imagination and dreams. Ramón shares the surrealist's interest in the unlimited world of poetic imagination, coincidence

and objective chance, and the non-logical development of plot. Waldberg convincingly argues that one of the main objectives of surrealism is to 'transmute the real' through imagistic ingenuity, a process which lies at the heart of what Ramón sets out to achieve in *¡Rebeca!*. Surrealism frees objects from their natural environment, transforming them into something new. As Baudelaire says: 'The beautiful is what is bizarre'. Gómez de la Serna understood this when he wrote: 'Las cosas quieren decirnos algo, pero no pueden',[12] implying that there is more to the external world than that which meets the eye. It therefore comes as no surprise that in many of his novels more importance is placed on the physical world than on human characters.

In Ramón Gómez de la Serna's essay 'superrealismo', he cites Aragón's well known words used to describe what every surrealist writer should achieve: 'el narcótico de la imagen'. Similar to Aragón, Gómez de la Serna is primarily interested in the way in which imagery can be deployed as a means of questioning and re-evaluating the nature of the universe we live in. Indeed, many of his *greguerías* set out to do just that, juxtaposing random objects, playing with visual associations, creating links and bridges between phenomena, which would not normally be associated in the natural world. For Gómez de la Serna this constitutes one of the ways he breaks away from the traditional confines of narrative convention to create a new and experimental kind of novel through a radically new poetic language.

It is my contention that *¡Rebeca!* (1936) constitutes a crucial novel in the history of twentieth century Spanish literature, not least because Spanish surrealism has been primarily associated with poetry and the visual arts, and to a much lesser extent narrative fiction—the works of Hinojosa and Giménez Caballero are arguably the only other examples of this kind. Camón Aznar argues that 'Rebeca es la novela más superrealista de cuantas ha publicado Ramón y me atrevo a decir que de la literatura europea'.[13] The obsession with the Generation of 27 has led to a distortion of the period as a whole and a bias towards poetry at the expense of narrative. There is no doubt that the poetic tradition in Spain has always been very strong, and that the individual geniuses of Cernuda, Alberti and Lorca created some of the greatest surrealist verse ever written, but this should not be allowed to eclipse what was happening in the field of narrative fiction at the time.

The complexity of *¡Rebeca!* as a novel should not in any way detract from the simplicity of the central themes, which appear in much of Gómez de la Serna's fiction and which are of a universal nature. *¡Rebeca!* is essentially about the quest for love. González Gerth argues that *¡Rebeca!* is '[…] the account of a man's quest for the signs of reality and the personal meaning of life'.[14] In fact, the protagonist Luis is in many ways reminiscent of the quintessentially Spanish character Don Quixote. He lives for an ideal, Rebeca, and is bordering on the insane despite the narrator's claim early on that Luis is not mad 'El no estaba loco, pero quería vivir la locura de la vida con todos sus trastornos y sus esquizofrenias' (p.7). Luis leads a curious and eccentric existence in a world of shifting and uncertain values. He escapes the monotony of everyday life by contemplating objects that at times take on extraordinary characteristics and transport him to various levels of aesthetic fulfilment. Reminiscent of the author himself and indeed of André Bretón, Luis lives surrounded by jumbled memorabilia that is not organised or catalogued in any particular way. The juxtaposition of these objects frequently creates curious associative and double images. The nebula of imagery that pervades the novel is not helped by Luis' self-confessed occupation: that of contemplating daydreams. Thus from the very start of the novel the surrealist obsession with dreams, objects and an unconventional character who leads a marginal existence, form the central crux of the narrative. The prevalence of contemplation and perception over plot, place ¡Rebeca! at the heart of modernist fiction. Gómez de la Serna is not interested in presenting the reader with a carefully calibrated plot; instead he allows it to progress (or perhaps more accurately digress) to show the reader the complexity of the protagonist Luis, and his failed attempt to find a lasting kind of love and friendship with the elusive Rebeca.

It might be argued that Luis is driven by a Platonic and Neo-Kantian obsession with the ideal. He is interested in the ideas behind objects, in the emotions they provoke. His frustrated and ongoing quest to find Rebeca turns him into a solipsist, living in a solitary world made up of his own fantasies and dreams. He smiles at closed doors, picks up old newspapers from the ground, has a curious fascination for erasers and combs and converses with his teapot, which on occasions appears to speak back at him. Luis claims to believe in God, but not in any transcendental or spiritually uplifting way. He sees God as an aloof being who takes little notice of mankind, preferring to remain, at all times, absent.

Luis' existence is enveloped in a sense of absurdity in a world that is not predicated upon rationality and where causality has ceased to exist. The plot is meandering and elusive, the division between what is imaginary and what is real is deliberately obscured. When Luis sits down on one occasion to write Rebeca a letter not knowing her exact whereabouts he writes an arbitrary address on the envelope in the vain hope that it will reach her. At times the phone rings and a mysterious voice claims to be Rebeca, but she never physically appears although materialises in the shape of a teapot or a pipe. His desire to find her will know no limits and lead him into a world of labyrinthine dimensions that should (in the narrator's opinion) be entered without cowardice:

El que tiene miedo de meterse en ese laberinto es un verdadero cobarde. Hay que saber inventar puentes, andar como un sonámbulo sobre tejados de sonambulismo y acertar con pasadizos sobre el abismo. (p.217)

Here the narrator provides the reader with the key to Luis' existence. Like the archetypal surrealist, Luis is the 'sonámbulo', travelling through a world that exists on the frontier between sleep and the waking hour, poetically evoked in this passage by the phrase 'tejados de sonambulismo'. In this semi-conscious somnambulant state, the bizarre is narrated objectively as though it constituted normality, fusing the world of dreams with everyday life in a surrealistic attempt to go beyond surface appearances and uncover a world of imaginary proportions.

To describe this world, Gómez de la Serna does not experiment with language in the same way in which Joyce or Woolfe did. He does not stretch and push language to its limits, nor does he use onomatopoeia as a means of blurring the distinctions between language and music. The Dadaists who used onomatopoeia and sound-words, which when juxtaposed were interesting for the sonorous effect elicited rather than any semantic value, had of course experimented with this. Gómez de la Serna alters normal discourse, not so much through the invention of new words or the amalgamations of sound, but through the juxtaposition and re-combination of words which when brought into friction with each other create images that are difficult to picture. The distortion and defamiliarisation of that which is everyday is a key to understanding what Gómez de la Serna is attempting to achieve in ¡Rebeca!. Consider, for example, the curious double-image that is produced when Luis contemplates some headless mannequins: '[...] alegre de ver las aulas de la pierna exhibidora de medias de pájaro de la luz dentro' (p.83). Logical word associations are done away with; the bizarre imagery, which is elicited in the mind of the reader, is brought about through the combination of disparate words and ideas. The reader is enmeshed in the flux of poetic images brought about by curious word associations. Luis' endless universe of objects serves to reinforce his futile quest to find Rebeca, whom he refers to as 'la que no pude encontrar' (p.121). Boredom, fear, and uncertainty are all expressed through objects, and Luis feels at a loss when things are not interlinked: 'Había perdido la vida al no enlazar cosas que hay que enlazar bien...' (p.135)

At times these visual associations are of a poetic nature and the outside world is recreated imaginatively, without recourse to literary cliché, such as the following description of the sky: 'El cielo depachaba cheques firmados frenéticamente y de prisa como si acordase un presupuesto de destinos' (p.82). On other occasions rational meaning is sacrificed for free association, such as on the occasion when Luis reflects on his failure to find Rebeca: 'Rebeca no aparecía por ningún lado, y eso que encontró seres extra-ordinarios como la mujer metida en la jaula del canario mientras el canario como un chulo picoteaba las flores del tapete de la mesa de las tertulias' (p.209). As Caws has noted:

> Surrealism insults reason for the benefit of spontaneity, logic for the benefit of the lyric sense of the marvellous, and everyday reality for the glorification of the *insolite*, in which elements of the real are transfused with the light of the 'super-real' by the inexplicable and unexpected workings of objective chance![15]

The importance of poetic discourse that disrupts normal word associations does away with well-worn clichés and transforms mundane reality into a vibrant succession of unconventional images, as exemplified in a letter that Luis enigmatically addresses to 'Tú de mi vida'. It is worth considering this passage in some detail as it is highly revealing of Gómez de la Serna's aesthetics:

> Te escribo esta noche porque no quiero tener más tiempo oculto mi secreto.
> Te escribo al amor de la lumbre del amor porque los radiadores son órganos muertos ya a esta hora. El organista de la calefacción central economiza nuestras veladas y en los tubos platinados solo hay agua fría.
> Quisiera definir el amor esta noche en esta carta frenética que te escribo.
> Reduces el mundo a tu figura. Parece que se empequeñece hasta desaparecer en el fondo de un automóvil que ha mandado parar tu mano enguantada, pero después se va agrandando como si fuese foco de telescopio, lente insuperable.
> Veo tu luz, no de estrella, que las estrellas están muy lejos; veo tu luz, que es una luz lustral, intransfundible, por lo que quiero tenerte cerca y que no nos separemos más.
> Tengo que adivinar algo de tu corazón que no sepa tu corazón. Anunciarte a ti tus propios proyectos.
> Quizá duermes ya... En tu sueño hay jardines dormidos y se escapan de él olores ahogados de flores en reposo. Me aprovecharé para convencerte, de la condescendencia que tienen las sonámbulas a las que se puede retener por las manos blancas como por el borde de una túnica.
> Sonámbula, me comprenderás mejor si no callo por respeto a tu fantasma ideal.
> Sabemos que nos engaña la vida y nos consolamos los dos de ese engaño. El amor está lleno de tristeza de perderse, pero no hay otro camino para recobrarse. Con que sepamos solo un minuto la evidencia de que vivimos, nos seremos deudores eternos.
> Monja de tu claustro tienes miedo de asomarte a la celosía, pero mis palabras encontrarán el revés de la rejilla entrecruzada que te oculta.
> El amor hace vivir el presente como si fuese un tiempo inmortal.
> El amor es estar muerto de amor, no saber lo que sucederá, no contar con nada. Cargarse de un desinterés que supere las mayores riquezas, estar en una actitud suspirante en que esté la suspiración plena del alma.

Ir andando en sueños para encontrar alguna vez el despertar o nunca. ¡Qué más
da empalmar un sueño breve con un sueño largo! Morir de amor es después de todo
emprender el estado que a de ser más duradero en nosotros [...]. (p.218–219)

The surrealist notion of *l'un dans l'autre*, of one thing within another is
deployed in this passage. Love, radiators, and organ pipes are elicited in a
single sentence. Luis admits to writing 'esta carta frenética', reminiscent of
automatic writing whereby meaning is freed from the restrictions of rational
thought. Although it would be wrong to assume that this letter constitutes a
stream of consciousness (a phenomenon which is very rare in Spanish literature) it resonates with free association and a reversal of normal hierarchies
and established codes of normal word association. For Luis, the world is seen
only through his idea of Rebeca: 'reduzco el mundo a tu figura', but then the
figure of Rebeca is associated with a car, a gloved hand and a telescope to
create an ever-shifting and complicated semantic structure. Not all the imagery makes such demands on the reader. Further on in the letter, the light
Rebeca represents is logically compared to that of a star. But this image is
not long lasting. In almost immediate succession the reader is transported
back to the realm of dreams with the clause 'Quizá duermes ya...' and a
world of dormant gardens, the entangled scent of flowers and figures who
walk in their sleep are poetically brought together. Despite the flux of disparate poetic imagery, the centrality of love is clearly conveyed. It is love that
transforms the present into eternity ('El amor hace vivir el presente como si
fuese un tiempo inmortal') and is something that should be felt and lived
without hindrance or boundaries: 'El amor es estar muerto de amor, no saber
lo que sucederá, no contra con nada'. In a sense, this is no different to the
surrealist concept of *amour fou*, which knows no boundaries and accepts no
limitations placed on it by convention, religion or society, and lies at the
heart of what Caws understands as 'the surrealist aim':

> The surrealist aim could be loosely defined as the intention of transforming (with all
> the deliberately alchemical force which attaches to the latter verb) sets of static polar
> contraries into powerful juxtapositions, intellectually uncomfortable to contemplate,
> shocking to the normal perception in their intense irrationality (it is to this sort of ir-
> rationality that the adjective *l'amour fou* refers).[16]

Luis' irrational and uncontrollable love for Rebeca prompts a friend of
his to warn him of the potentially dangerous effect she is having on him.
However, Luis pays no attention to his warning:

> El necesitaba a Rebeca para compartir con ella el sacrificio de no comer, la
> afrontada amenaza del destino, el quedarse en casa el día de lluvia torrencial, la

preocupación de las historiadas puertas del portal, el sentimiento del cancer sonrosado, la pena de no tener maleta de cuero. (p.144)

The poetic nature of this passage lies in its ability to alternate between transcendental notions such as 'destiny', and the in-transcendental objects of everyday life such as the 'maleta de cuero'. All hierarchies are broken down as these elements are recombined together. Luis' outlook on life, in the final analysis, is one of diminished expectations. He sees the answer to life's questions in exploring the here and now. He finds some degree of solace in the material world of objects. The image of the bell jar evoked at the end of this particular episode to some extent symbolises Luis' condition:

> —¿Vienes triste?
>   —He estado viendo fanales.
>   —¿Fanales de qué?
>   —Fanales de crystal...Parecen tener almas sin destino. (p.81)

Luis' lack of belief in his fellow human beings to some extent explains his interest in the material world. However, this material world is ultimately meaningless and devoid of any purpose, save the aesthetic value it may seem to possess. Rebeca becomes Luis' only hope and dream, and in his mind she is the only one who can help him cope with life's uncertainties.

His attempt to find her frequently leads him into a borderline world of shadows. On one occasion he challenges Rebeca to sit in the shadow of the chair projected on the wall, but she is unable to as the shadow falls on various objects. His obsession with Rebeca causes him to end up in the courtroom where he has to defend himself after a bizarre sequence of events. Whilst sitting in a tavern, an *agent provocateur* runs in with a gun and the words 'maldito sea Rebeca' are heard, which cause Luis to hurl his glass at the intruder. When the police arrive on the scene and question Luis about his reaction at hearing the words uttered by the man with the pistol, Luis answers: '—Para mí, Rebeca es el más alto ideal'. (p.125). When the police then ask Luis to explain who Rebeca is, Luis replies saying that it is impossible to know. He is subsequently ordered to appear before a judge. In his defence Luis says:

> Señor juez, hay una clave de nuestra vida que lleva un nombre...Para mí es Rebeca...Está entre las páginas de un libro, es la imagen que triunfa de una revista que hemos tirado, está en el vaso de agua que bebimos con más sed... (p.128)

Rebeca is everywhere, and can, at any time, turn into anything, but at the same time she is nowhere to be found: 'Rebeca no está en ninguna parte' (p.141).

It would be difficult for any critic to deny that ¡Rebeca! is an experiment
in literary surrealism written at a time when experimental fiction was becoming increasingly unfashionable. The paradox is that ¡Rebeca! encapsulates
and evokes a very Spanish quest: how to reconcile everyday reality with the
ideal. Cervantes' genius lay in his ability to grasp this inherent human preoccupation, which the Spanish adopted as their own. The brilliant characterisation of Don Quixote and Sancho, representing the ideal versus the
pragmatic has resonated in the Spanish consciousness through the centuries.
In this sense Ramón Gómez de la Serna's ¡Rebeca! could be understood as a
continuation of the same tradition and quest, as represented by Luis' obsession with finding ideal love in the inscrutable, and ultimately unattainable
ideal represented by Rebeca. Similar to Cervantes' character, the protagonist
of ¡Rebeca! is both profoundly Spanish and yet universal at the same time in
terms of the ontological questions his existence poses. Gerald Brenan may
have been right when he stated that the main theme of Spanish literature is
disillusion. Despite Gómez de la Serna's immersion in the European avant-
garde vortex, Gómez de la Serna's literary works not only capture the spirit
of the times under the guise of avant-garde humour, but in the process uncover the futility of the human condition.

Whilst the authors of the so-called 'avanzada' believed that the best way
to criticise a divided and rapidly disintegrating society was through the
means of social realism, Gómez de la Serna was unable to break free from
his avant-garde prism. And in a sense nothing gives voice more eloquently to
the fragmentary world of 1930s Spain and Europe, of the modern man seeking for some kind of meaning in a world which was heading once again
towards war, than the futile quest of Luis in *¡Rebeca!*. Luis represents the
post-theistic individual who cannot rely on history or religion as a means of
giving meaning to his world. His universe is one that is not predicated on
rationality. Underneath the incongruous humour and wordplays lies a world
that is ultimately inexplicable and impossible to reconcile. It is not surprising, therefore, that surrealism is the means through which Gómez de la Serna
comes to this state of existential disillusion, or 'desengaño' (to use the vo-
cabulary of the Spanish literary tradition), as his attempt to reconcile two
distant incompatible realities is ultimately futile.

In Gómez de la Serna's narrative fiction reconciliation is seldom found.
The surreal fantasies and chimerical dreams of Luis are ultimately unfulfilled. The 'desengaño' which underpins *¡Rebeca!* is taken to its extremes
several years later, when Gómez writes his most existential and prophetic
novel ever, with a title which could serve as a description of the quintessen-
tial Ramonian fictional character: *El hombre perdido* (1947).

¡Rebeca! marks the first phase in this experimental apotheosis, and what better way to represent the profound contradictions embedded in Spanish society during the cataclysmic year of 1936, and the ultimate impossibility to resolve them?

Notes

1   See José Díaz Fernández, *El Nuevo romanticismo* (Madrid: Velasco, 1930).
2   David Lodge, *The Modes of Modern Writing*, (London: Edward Arnold, 1977) p.45.
3   See Francis Lough (Ed), *Hacia la nueva novela: essays of the Spanish Avant-Garde*, (Oxford: Peter Lang, 2000).
4   Ramón Gómez de la Serna, Rebeca [1936] (Madrid: Espasa Calpe. 1974).
5   Andre Breton, *Manifestos of Surrealism*, translated by Richard Seaver and Helen R. Lane (Michigan: The University Press, 1969).
6   For a comprehensive study of how surrealism took shape in Spain see C.B. Morris, *Surrealism and Spain (1920–1936)* , (Cambridge: University Press, 1972) and Robert Harvard, *A Companion to Spanish Surrealism* (London: Tamesis, 2005).
7   Patrick Waldberg, *Surrealism* (London: Thames and Hudson, 1997) p.8.
8   André Breton, cited in Mary Anne Caws, *The Poetry of Dada and Surrealism: Aragon, Breton, Tzara, Eluard, Desmos* (Princeton: University Press, 1970) p.18.
9   Carlos Marcial de Onis, *El surrealismo y cuatro poetas de la Generación del 27*, (Madrid: Ediciones José Porrúa Turanzas, 1974) p.17.
10 Lemaitre, cited in Onis, ibid, p.18.
11 ibid, p.19
12 Ramón Gómez de la Serna, 'Las cosas y 'El Ello' (1934) in Ana Martínez Collado Una teoría personal del arte: antología de textos de estética y teoría del arte de Ramón Gómez de la Serna (Madrid: Tecnos, 1988).
13 Camón Aznar, op cit, p.368.
14 Miguel González Gerth, A Labyrinth of Imagery: Ramón Gómez de la Serna's 'Novelas de la nebulosa' (London: Tamesis, 1986) p.65.
15 Op Cit Caws, p.18.
16 ibid, p.14, 15.

Chapter 6. The 1940s and Beyond

Man is nothing else but what he makes of himself.
Jean-Paul Sartre (1905–1980)

What will attract me to a new book, is not so much new characters as a new way of presenting them. This novel must end sharply, not through exhaustion of the subject, but on the contrary through its expansion and by a sort of blurring of its outline. The blurring occurs precisely along the margins between art and life.
Andre Gide (1869–1951)

It is always consoling to think of suicide: in that way one gets through many a bad night.
(Friedrich Nietzsche)

For we are old and the earth's passion dieth;
we have watched him a thousand times,
when he wanes an old wind crieth,
for we are old, and passion hath died for
us a thousand times, but we never grow weary.
Ezra Pound (1885–1972)

El hombre perdido (1947) is arguably one of Gómez de la Serna's best novels.1 It draws on the modernist obsession with abstraction, disintegration and the depiction of a universe which is not predicated on rationality. Nietzsche had argued half a century earlier that man's instinct must not be curtailed or restricted by rationality, which in his opinion only produces a mediocre and homogonous society characterised by uniformity. The individual was to rise above this state of 'anomie' (to borrow Emile Durkeim's terminology) through the will to power. Gómez de la Serna's individualistic characters do not form part of the fabric of society, nor do they believe in society. The nameless main character of *El hombre perdido* is no exception. Similar to Dostoevsky's characters, the protagonist of *El hombre perdido* is driven at times by an irrational impulse, is highly individualistic and drifts in isolation through a world where rationality is on the demise. The 'lost man' of *El hombre perdido* is alone, his interaction and communication with others is quirky but seldom meaningful, his world is devoid of ultimate purpose or meaning, but one where the bizarre is recurrently fore-grounded. The society presented is post-theistic, where all over-arching narratives have been dissolved, replaced by a fragmented and listless society through which the individual wanders alone with no direction or sense of purpose. Although Ramón Gómez de la Serna was open about his disdain for Sartrean Existentialism, with its bleak vision of the human condition and pervasive despair, *El hombre perdido* (1947) is very much a novel in tune with its time, and is arguably the most 'existential' of all Gómez de la Serna's novels. 2 *El hombre perdido* marks a new level of maturity in Gómez de la Serna's writing. Experimentation for its own sake is no longer the order of the day, instead, a heightened awareness and growing questioning about the human condition is voiced—albeit indirectly—through an experimental prose style very different to the kind of fiction that was emerging in 1940s Spain. The stark realism of the fiction produced by Spanish authors in the 1940s was understandably bleak in its outlook, in the wake of the Spanish Civil War and the enforced establishment of the Francoist dictatorship. The *tremendismo* of the nineteen forties depicted a grey monochromatic world where freedom and the creative voice had been silenced. The evolution towards the behaviourist novel of the 1950s, stemmed from an 'objective' documentation of every day life as seen for example in García Hortelano's lack-luster novel *Nuevas amistades* (1959) attests the bareness of the Spanish novel of that time. *El hombre perdido* does not fit into this category. His major work of this decade—and arguably his most important work of all time—does not sit comfortably within the paradigmatic framework of 1940s social realism and *tremendismo*. *El hombre perdido* is experimental in the extreme, yet at the same time poses serious questions about the human condition, portraying a world of shifting certainties, within a disjointed narrative which breaks with all linearity and causality. If there was ever a stronger argument to counter the over-simplistic assumption prevalent in Spain at the end of the 1920s and throughout the 1930s that the socially responsible author is obliged to denounce society through a realistic prose-style, it is to be found in this remarkable and challenging novel.

It must of course be remembered that Gómez de la Serna was not living in Spain at the time, as he had left in 1936 for Buenos Aires, where he was to remain until his death in 1963. In 1936 Gómez de la Serna had barricaded himself into his Madrid apartment, placing his bookshelves against the door and mattresses against the windows, alarmed and afraid by the social unrest and impending doom which was to spread throughout Spain. One of the last visits Gómez de la Serna made before his departure from Madrid was to see his old friend Ortega y Gasset, who was extremely ill. This was shortly after the brutal murder of Calvo Sotelo, which was to leave a lasting impression on him. In his autobiography, Gómez de la Serna expresses his despair with the cycle of violence repeated in Spain, which he sees as a recurrent malaise:

> Los españoles, deduje entonces, cada cien años quieren matarse unos a otros. Lo intuí viendo que lo único que podíamos leer en esos días era 'La Biblia en España'

de Jorge Borrow, con sucesos parecidos en 1836 a los que sucedían en 1936, o sea
que hasta el año 2036 no se volverá a dar el mismo peligro. (*AM*, p.610)

He thus decides to leave Spain, opting to board the 'Bell Isle' ship at
Bordeaux, which was heading to South America. He sent thirty parcels of
books to Buenos Aires, and handed over the keys of his apartment to his
'portera' giving her permission to keep all his belongings once seventeen
days had elapsed. He managed to obtain a passport on the eve of his departure with the excuse that he was due to attend the International PEN conference in Buenos Aires. On the train down to Alicante (August 1936) the
militia men allowed him through, stating 'Este es el que habla por la radio los
Domingos, que pase' (*AM*, p.612). Once in Alicante he boarded a Ship to
southern France, and after crossing France he finally boarded the 'Bell Isle'
in Bordeaux, docking briefly in Lisbon before finally arriving in Buenos Aires.

In his autobiography he reflects on being an immigrant and frequently
thinks about all that he had left behind. It is understandable that he experienced loneliness and an acute sense of separation, forever removed from
his family and close friends: 'Ver en perspectiva todo lo que se tuvo
abrumadoramente encima, despedirse de la familia para siempre; verse ya a
una media separación absoluta de lo que se tuvo' (*AM*, 615). This is important to bear in mind when considering *El hombre perdido*. Whilst it will
become evident that as a novel it echoes a sense of absurdity not altogether
far removed from existentialist writing of the times, it must be remembered
that its creation coincided with a time in Gómez de la Serna's life when he
was alone and far removed from his family and natural surroundings, which
have always been such an important influence in his work. It is interesting to
note that Gómez de la Serna's final novel *Piso bajo* (1961) is set in Madrid,
despite the fact that Gómez de la Serna was living in Buenos Aires. It is almost as if the author has come in a full circle, ending back where he began,
chronicling the life in Madrid, its streets, its people, its peculiarities and
traits, through a creative and imaginative prose style.

Nietzsche, Existentialism and El hombre perdido *(1947)*

On a formal level, *El hombre perdido* is a novel out of kilter with its time,
although thematically it shares common ground with the European novel of
the 1940s and to some extent foreshadows and pre-dates the *Nouveau Roman*. That *El hombre perdido* differs considerably from the *tremendista*
novels of 1940s Spain is hardly surprising given that Gómez de la Serna had
been fortunate enough to have escaped the terrors of the Spanish Civil War

and was therefore not subjected to living in Spain during the sombre hunger-years of the 1940s when the Francoist regime was at its most repressive. With personal friends on both sides of the political spectrum he was to re-affirm his long-standing aloofness from the political debate. This stance did not ingratiate him with much of the community of Spanish exiled authors who understandably saw his position as comfortable and convenient. There is no point in attempting to argue differently. Despite Gómez de la Serna's early flirtation with anarchism in his youth—in my view more aesthetic than ideological—Gómez de la Serna was a deeply entrenched middle class cons-ervative who would never be comfortable with the revolutionary rhetoric of the left. It is one thing to espouse anarchist ideals from a position of social comfort and well-being, and quite another to pursue the full implications of its doctrine and ideology. There can be no doubt that Gómez de la Serna was politically conservative. His trip to Spain in 1949 is confirmation of this. The fact that Rafael Alberti ignored him when he saw him wandering the streets of Buenos Aires attests to the political differences which were dividing the Spanish writing community both at home and abroad. Moreover, it is impor-tant to remember that that during his trip to Spain in 1949 Gómez de la Serna visited his old friend and founder of *La gaceta literaria,* Ernesto Giménez Caballero, who invited him to his literary *tertulia* held in the Café de Oriente. By this stage it was public knowledge that Giménez Caballero was a fully fledged apologist for the Spanish Right. Whilst in the 1920s during the hey-day of literary experimentalism and the reception of avant-garde ideas and manifestos into Spain numerous authors who were associated with the Gen-eration of 1927 contributed to Giménez Caballero's avant-garde literary jour-nal, it was deemed by many another thing altogether to continue to be associated with a figure who had become hardened into an unacceptably ex-tremist ideological position. To his critics, this confirmed their suspicions about Gómez de la Serna, although in my view simply confirms his aloofness to the political debate and his attempt to maintain personal friendships from across the political divide. Accepting an invitation from a regime that had been responsible for the death of his friend and compatriot Federico García Lorca, had imprisoned his avant-garde companion Antonio Espina, and had forced into exile most of the liberal writers who were acquaintances of his during the literary *soirées* of the 1920s, was bound to anger many on the cen-tre-left. Despite this, it must also be remembered that Ramón Gómez de la Serna entertained communist writer Pablo Neruda at his residence in Buenos Aires during the 1940s, and was still highly revered by his republican friend and writer José Bergamín, in exile in Mexico. Nevertheless, despite Gómez de la Serna's political ambiguity and possible misjudgement, his work in the 1940s is a-political, and focuses on existential and ontological questions concerning the human condition. He captures the mood of pervasive emptiness and sense of absurdity of a world that was perilously bent on self destruction.

In the prologue to *El hombre perdido*, Gómez de la Serna claims that there is a fifth dimension to life which needs to be experienced if we are to grapple with life in its fullness. He argues that this further dimension to the real world is not necessarily surreal, or 'sub-real' (as he writes) but 'lateral'. Behind the everyday world of objects lies another world to be discovered: 'La realidad tal cual es, cada vez me estomaga más y cada día que pasa me parece más una máscara falsa de otra realidad ni tocada por la confidencia de la pluma' (p.8). This arguably derives from a modernist impulse to depart from the need for fictional verisimilitude as a means of liberating the novel from its nineteenth-century conventions—a stance which Gómez de la Serna adhered to throughout his life, never espousing socio-realism as a possible literary approach. It therefore comes as no surprise when reading the prologue to *El hombre perdido* that Gómez de la Serna states: 'Cada vez me indigna más la glosa naturalista y monótona de la vida, sin lo inesperado, sin lo escardado, sin eso que no es desesperado chiste sino incongruencia fatal, verdadero trastrueque sin cinismo y solo por azar' and goes on to argue: 'Lo que menos merece la vida es la reproducción fiel de lo que aparenta suceder en ella. En salvarse a la lógica sin perderse por eso en lo ilegible está las escapada a la dura y mezquina realidad' (p.8). This concerted decision to go beyond the immediate confines of everyday existence, to uncover a deeper reality below the surface of things is deliberate, borne from the belief that mundane everyday reality and what appears to make sense is what actually leads to madness, not the other way round: 'Sólo en la reconstrucción en el más allá cerebelosos se podrá encontrar el sentido de lo sin sentido. El fracaso de lo que aparenta tener sentido es que cada vez se desorganiza más y lleva más a la disoluta locura' (p.8). His philosophy derives from a deep-seated awareness of his inability to understand life:

> ¿Quién sabe cómo es la vida? Nos sorprenderá siempre como lo más inesperado viendo que lo que parece no es lo que parece, sino otra cosa, ni más buena ni más mala, sino simplemente *otra cosa*, siendo por eso lo que hay que estar preparando a saber que nada es lo que es y así nos salvaremos a la traición última. (p.9)

He sees the artist as someone who has the duty to give voice and shape to the oneiric dimension of reality: 'Nuestra misión es de escultores que plastifican lo que de sueño de la realidad hay en la realidad', a quest which he does not claim to be exclusive to modernist writers, but also to Shakespeare, and indeed Cervantes.

Gómez de la Serna argues that he has modified the narrative conventions of the novel to better convey his literary objectives. He informs the reader

that altering the chapters of his so-called 'novelas de la nebulosa' (reminiscent of Unamuno's 'nivolas') does not alter in any way the overall meaning
of the novel. His objective as an author is to 'buscar cosas menos conven-
cionales' (p.10) asserting that 'Yo recojo algo del caos de nuestra época [...]'
(p.11). He sees *El hombre perdido* as part of a narrative trajectory which
started with *El incongruente* written in 1922, *El novelista* in 1923 and continued in 1936 with his surrealistic novel *¡Rebecca!*. He defines these novels
as novels of the 'nebulosa' which in his own words share the following characteristics:

> Las novelas de la nebulosa han de ser escritas en estado nebulítico—más allá del
> estado sonambúlico—y con fervor de arte, pues no se trata de una obra de fenome-
> nología disparatada, sino de una obra literaria que sirva para detener y calmar la
> muerte, mimando sin tesis alguna la evidencia de que el hombre, en definitiva, vive
> perdidamente perdido. (p.12)

He goes on to define his 'hombre perdido' in a little more detail:

> Mi *Hombre perdido* es el hombre perdido por bueno, el que no quiso creer en lo
> convencional, el que no cejó en su nausea por la lucha por la vida sórdida y
> agremiada, el que en vez de lo regular y lo escalonado prefiere lo informe, la pura
> ráfaga de observaciones, alucinaciones y hojas secas que pasan por las páginas del
> libro, confesionario atrevido y displicente de la vida.
>   Mi hombre perdido es una multitud innumerable de hombres perdidos que
> necesitaban este libro que no es una burla sino que es la lectura que urgían los que
> no pueden leer otros libros y exigían éste para compensar la acidez y la desgana del
> estado apático en que les ha sumido el mundo idiota y falaz. (p.14)

Central to Gómez de la Serna vision of life is the notion that the universe
is not predicated on rationality, but irrationality. The instincts and whims of
individual characters are what drive them forward. This is clearly reminiscent
of Nietzschean thought, whereby rationality is seen as a negative force which
curtails the true essence of being, the freedom and individuality of man. Only
by following the driving force of instinct can man be set free from the medi-
ocrity, uniformity and sameness of his world. Nietzsche does not believe in
absolute truth, rather that our experience is moulded through our 'will to
power', that is our desire to triumph, to be strong and to rise above the en-
slaving instincts of guilt. Although Gómez de la Serna's lost man of *El
hombre perdido* is not driven by a Nietzschean 'will to power', his individuality does enable him to rise above the predictable and mediocre existence of
the average modern-day man. Gómez de la Serna was himself middle class
with a strong sense of individualism and did not believe in the fabric of society. His characters confirm this in every novel. Of course, this is not simply a

modernist nor indeed solely a Ramonian trait: Fyodor Dostoevsky's characters are often driven by a seemingly irrational impulse, based on whims and
individualism which not only sets them apart from their fellow man but becomes a hallmark of their freedom. The reaction against Positivism during
the last quarter of the nineteenth century serves as a precursor to modernism's eschewal of scientific reason as a solid foundation upon which to
predicate and understand existence. Disintegration and abstraction become
the central features of the modernist work, depicting a world of drift and isolation. In this sense *El hombre perdido* is a novel which characterises this
epoch.

As will become clear over the next few pages, the protagonist of *El hombre perdido* (whose name is never revealed throughout the novel and who I
will from now on refer to as 'the lost man') is portrayed as being alone in the
universe. His interaction with the bizarre society that surrounds him is, for
the most part, meaningless and quirky. The lost man inhabits an alien and
unfamiliar world, devoid of ultimate meaning, and his existence lacks purpose. In this sense he could be seen as a quintessentially modern character,
post-theistic and rudderless.

Although I do not claim that *El hombre perdido* is an existentialist work
per se, even a superficial reading of the novel would suggest an affinity
which needs to be explored. Taking Jones' definition of Existentialism as a
starting point, I will then go on to argue that Gómez de la Serna's *El hombre
perdido* adopts some of Existentialism's main tenets, whilst rejecting others.
Jones argues that Existentialism:

> [...] rejects philosophical abstractions, preferring instead to consider man within a
> concrete situation. The existential hero (or anti-hero) feels out of step with contem-
> porary reality, where both objects and people confirm his idea of the absurdity of
> existence. His lack of communication particularly and the threat of the 'other' cause
> loneliness, deception, anguish, and finally alienation, with the ultimate realization
> that he alone is responsible for the answers to his problems. Certain events (e.g.
> death, suffering, guilt) provide an opportunity for a more transcendental decision;
> these are called 'limit-situations'. Such decisions mark the difference between exis-
> tence and essence, or the desire for authenticity and self-definition. One defines
> one's essence through the act of conscious choice and the assumption of responsibil-
> ity for one's actions.[3]

El hombre perdido depicts an irrational world, within which the characters move freely but are not accountable to anyone. Differing from the
Existentialist philosophy, the characters in *El hombre perdido* feel no moral
compunction to follow a particular decision through and seldom make
choices which bring about negative consequences.

Throughout *El hombre perdido*, responsibility is not necessarily the corollary of choice and the idea that the individual must accept responsibility for their actions is alien to Gómez de la Serna. And rather than denying the existence of God, the protagonist of *El hombre perdido* (who remains nameless throughout) sees him as a being who has distanced himself from his creation: 'Yo creía en el Dios que no quiere saber nada de la tierra y el que no le importan ni oraciones ni blasfemias'. (p.144) Sherman H. Eoff defines Existentialism as '[...] a refusal to seek an explanation of human existence in a causal chain of becoming...Human existence is visualised not as a process but as a situation, in which relationships are horizontal rather than vertical'.[4]

For the protagonist of *El hombre perdido* there are no over-arching narratives, not one single formula to understand existence, living in a post-theistic era he sees his life as multidimensional, characterised by uncertainty and drift, where chance plays a central role: 'Este es el misterio de la vida, el de la incierta ubicuidad que nos tocó en suerte porque nuestro destino no ha estado solo en un sitio, sino en varios' (p.121) This is why when he meets the vagabond Herreros on several occasions throughout the novel, he claims to not know where he is going: 'Como siempre, no sé a donde'. (p.144)

The lost man is a drifting, aloof, modern-day character inhabiting a world which is beset by the bizarre and which departs from the customary. Like the author himself, he also claims to be apolitical:

> Yo tenía descontado que no había nacido para la Guerra ni para entrar en un partido político, pero los dos azares me amenazaban y era gracioso como pasaban por encima de mí sin tocarme.
>
> Mi destino seguía siendo independiente y libre, pero por eso yo me volvía más irreal y buscaba combinaciones que me demostrasen viviente y capaz de entrar en todas las combinaciones de la vida, las más imprevisibles, las más fantásticas.
>
> Gracias a reunir todo lo imaginable podré vivir un minuto de superrealidad y tocar las orillas del sobrevivir.
>
> Me prestaba a todo, bajaba a los subterráneos del subconsciente sin miedo, reunía la realidad del vendedor de muebles, con la realidad de la plancha eléctrica. (p.162)

His existence delves into the surreal, openly accepting that he lives in a world where 'todas las combinaciones de la vida, las más imprevisibles [...]' are at play, which is no different to the surrealist's fascination with juxtaposition, whimsical associations re-combining the elements of the surrounding world and re-constituting them into new poetic forms which stand out for their strangeness. The open admission on the part of the protagonist that he frequents the subconscious depths, represented by going underground should dispel all doubts that *El hombre perdido* is a surrealist novel. The lost man is fascinated with what lies beneath the surface of things, a fascination that is emblematically evoked when he travels with Herreros on the underground. In his world, the bizarre and the improbable are fore-grounded: at one particular juncture in the novel he travels to an unknown house where a party is taking place. When he arrives he asks the owner of the house:

> —Antes de beber este whisky hecho con papel de periódico le pediría permiso para marcharme volando por el balcón.
> —Concedido—dijo el señor y el joven abrió el balcón y salió volando. (p.16)

On another occasion he holds a conversation with an aubergine, and feels that he is being pursued by a fountain. Further on in the novel he opens a piano and finds it full of gloves. Life is reduced to the here and now, to the objects that surround him: 'Me prestaba a toda investigación para ver si conseguía saber si la vida es trapo o zapato, caja de píldoras o botella de vino' (p.57). In his solitude he speaks to himself, although he does claim to believe in some sort of a God. At times the melancholy of his solitary world is expressed poetically: 'Aquella tarde en que el cielo se cubrió de rosas secas y engurruñadas yo sabía que me iba a suceder algo en mi copiosa soledad' (p.54). He feels engulfed in a sense of mystery, as a storm approaches. He believes he can see the figure of a woman in the curtains, and then he sees her outside his window with her finger over her lips as if asking him to remain quiet. He believes that she is there because of the storm: 'Si la humanidad no fuese tan aturdida comprendería que en la excitación de la tormenta hay enlaces verdaderos con buenas mozas que vienen empujadas por el nublado como truchas dobladas'. (p.56)

In the opening chapter of *El hombre perdido* the protagonist encounters a man walking down the street wearing a wig. After engaging in conversation it emerges that the character wears a wig in an attempt to disguise himself from the police, as he physically resembles a criminal they are attempting to arrest. His days are spent wandering the streets and hiding in his dilapidated house on the banks of the river, where he claims that Goya used to sometimes hide. He keeps the key hidden under his wig, and allows the protagonist to accompany him home providing he departs by two o'clock. In his house he has Goya originals which he never will sell because he is unsure as to how they came into his possession and he is fearful of being arrested. This mention of criminality causes the protagonist to reflect on his own guilt. He believes himself to have committed a crime, maybe in his youth, and feels that the only way he will be able to find himself is by discovering the crime he had committed: 'Solo sabiendo el crimen que cometí me encontraría a mi mismo' (p.28). The protagonist's self-questioning leads him into philosophical questioning: he asks himself if his recollections from the past are actually real, or whether they pertain to the world of dreams, which leads him to ask; '¿Se vive la vida que estamos viviendo?' (p.29) He seeks for answers to his questions in inanimate objects which reassure him that he is awake. He is driven by curious whims and ideas, such as that of finding a ship in the middle of the city. After finding the ship he speaks with its crew and it transpires that it had been deliberately steered into the city to get away from the monotony and predictability of simply sailing on the sea. Those with a preponderance to suffering from being sea sick are its regular customers, enjoying the pretence of being at sea without the physiological effects. His daily encounters cause him to ponder on existential questions about the nature of human existence: 'Con lo que hay, tenemos necesidad de fomentar lo que no hay. La vida no es cierta en ningún momento y lo 'único cierto es que hay algo que nos empuja como torrente a una velocidad inconcebible' (p.32). But this concept of speed is not portrayed as something altogether negative, instead it is to some extent glorified futuristically and is emblematic of life which must move forward: 'Sólo vivo estos últimos tiempos el drama de los ferrocariles...Me he dedicado a vivir en los tres kilómetros que ocupa el arsenal de coches viejos y los talleres ferrocarrilleros...Nada más interesante ni más circulatorio... A mí que me picaban las piernas por falta de circulación, ahora circulo lo que es una gloria...' (p.33). For the protagonist trains represent life itself: '[...] Un ochenta porciento de los trenes no saben a dónde van y solo representan con su marcha veloz la inquietud de la vida [...]' (p.34).

In customary Ramonian fashion, *El hombre perdido* bears recognisable traits with his previous novels in terms of characterisation and the way in which the various characters interact. When the protagonist meets the elusive Adoración in chapter five, their love is reminiscent of the surrealist notion of 'amour fou', which knows no boundaries and needs to be pursued at any cost, with delirious intensity if necessary:

> —¿Me quieres hasta la locura?
> —¿Por qué hasta la locura?
> —Por que hasta la sensatez es poco...No es apenas nada...Si no me quieres déjame morir. (p.36)

The lost man is not curtailed by living life under the guidance of reason, but is propelled instead by what modernist theorizer Amédée Ozenfant (1886–1966) saw as the central tenets of modern art:

> Being no longer controlled by the powerful impulses of 'common sense', and the 'normal', the valves of our unconscious open, and permit the fusion of our slumber-

ing, suppressed, or un-witted potentialities. Thus a world of new sensations and awareness comes into being.[5]

The lost man experiences sentiments not too dissimilar to those mentioned by Ozenfant: 'Me sentí frenético de ausencia y commencé a vivir sueños de delirio y vigilias de delirio' (p.42) His deranged and confused mind cause him to see things which are not there, and as he wanders aimlessly along the streets of his city he shouts out incongruities, saying that he can see crocodiles, and human figures who metamorphose into ducks, reminding the reader that he lives in a surrealist world where things can change and transform into other things. He repeatedly ponders about death, although asserts that he will welcome it as it is a state where one can obtain freedom from pain. The protagonist is a more philosophical and existential character than Gustavo in *El incongruente* (1922), whose incongruous lifestyle seldom leads to any questioning. In *El hombre perdido* there are recurrent references to death and the brevity of life, and the pervasive sense that man is a small being in a universe which is largely founded on irrationality: '¡Cómo se es de pequeño en la vida! Tan pequeño como lo que desapareció' (p.41). Furthermore, he does not simply believe that he will one day disappear, but that he has already disappeared: '—No es que vaya a ser un desaparecido— no es que vayamos a ser unos desaparecidos—es que lo soy ya—es que los somos ya.' (p.44) and ultimately, his only refuge is to be found in the world of matter, the objects that surround him and the 'here and now'. Unrequited love and his failure to engage in meaningful human relationships cause him to become increasingly withdrawn and inward looking, eventually leading him to fall in love with the wash-basin in his bathroom:

Sentía encerrada mi vida en una lata de conservas estañada. Tenía jugo para vivir toda la vida jugosa, pero me sentía más perdido que nunca.
    Como una aberración de aquel encierro comencé a amar el lavabo del cuarto de baño, su porcelana aséptica, sus grifos relucientes, su conjunto de pila limpia, con el brillo lunar de la porcelana, con la fidelidad inoxidable de las canillas.
    Si yo pudiese decirlo lo diría:
    —¡Me he enamorado de los muslos de porcelana de mi lavabo, del grifo que responde a la mano que le hace echar agua o lo detiene a la voluntad!
    Es todo el conjunto del objeto metálico, unido al fondo acuoso de la tierra, comunicante teléfono con ríos y manantiales.
    Interiormente me daba ánimo recurriendo al lavabo perfecto y puro, con sus delicadas y suaves curvas, de hombros de jabón.
    Fue mi último recurso y salvación: la respuesta del lavabo incontaminado, gracioso por su cuenta, sin reservas en su material macizo, compacto y refulgente.
    Muchas veces me encerraba en el cuarto de baño sólo para contemplar las reberondas y gimnásticas plasticidades y los robinetes niquelados. (p.215)

In this passage Ramón Gómez de la Serna takes poetic defamiliarisation to new heights. By describing the life of the 'lost man' as being enclosed like fruit in a tin, he brilliantly evokes the sense of his world closing in on him, and his pervasive feeling of loneliness and the awareness that he is ultimately lost. Having lost all faith in human relationships, and although he never denies the existence of God, he does not relate to him in any meaningful or spiritually uplifting way; his only recourse is to the material world, in particular, to the wash-basin in his bathroom. In an ironic and avant-gardist play of images: the wash-basin, which supplies water replaces the Biblical notion of salvation through partaking of 'the water of life', equated in scriptures with Christ himself. 'The lost man's' progressive fixation with the wash-basin confirms his modern-day characteristics: an individual who no longer relies on the comfort of a transcendent God, but on the material world of the 'here and now', even though the material world takes on a certain poetic meaning and significance. In this sense, 'the lost man' is no different to don Pablo in *El secreto del acueducto* who is fixated by the Segovian aqueduct (interestingly, like the wash-basin, another means for channelling water). With brilliant, ironic avant-garde humour, the wash-basin takes on human characteristics: 'delicadas y suaves curves, de hombros de jabón', and he confesses to it becoming his last hope and only possible salvation: 'Fue mi ultimo recurso y salvación: la respuesta del lavabo incontamindo [...]'. The wash-basin becomes associated with salvation in a parodic and ironic avant-garde twist, replacing Christ the giver of the water of life, by the physical non-transcendental wash-basin in 'the lost man's' bathroom. Reminiscent of the restaurant scene in *La mujer de ámbar* when the sacrosanct act of marriage is ironically and imaginatively reduced to a tacky restaurant setting, in *El hombre perdido* the quest for salvation and hope is reduced to a progressive fascination and existential dependence on his wash-basin.

In the final chapter of *El hombre perdido* there is a growing realization on the part of the protagonist that he is ultimately unable to escape his world: 'Mi insistente deseo de evasión no había encontrado oportunidad ni recodo pero ya estaba cansado de esa vida de creer ir a lograr lo que nunca se hacía efectivo' (p.216). He feels drawn to the railway tracks adjacent to a train station where vagabonds live in the carriages, surrounded by abandoned merchandise: 'No tenía que tener más que el valor de quedarme, de tirarme en la camada de los vagabundos que no se ven unos a otros—tan extensa es su cama—y esperar al día siguiente sin pensar en nada'. (p.218)

The novel ends with the protagonist lying down between the rail tracks. The next day there is a newspaper article which reports his death:

En los terrenos baldíos que marginan la red ferroviaria del sur ha aparecido el
cadáver de un hombre tan destrozado que no ha podido ser identificado.
   Parece ser que debió ser atropellado, mientras dormía, por uno de los trenes de
carga compuestos de innumerables vagones que llevan las mercancías al Kilómetro
no. 5 donde se forman las expediciones definitivas. (p.221)

The factual medium of the newspaper, coldly reporting the last movements of the lost man contrasts with the style adopted in the rest of the novel,
deliberately demarcating the limit between the bizarre and the dream-world,
and the actual realities of the world in which he was living. At the same time,
it is possibly the only way to end the novel, which is written in the first person, a curious departure for Gómez de la Serna as most of his novels are in
the third person. As the reader is informed, a body is found, although it is not
possible to identify it because it has been mangled beyond recognition, but is
presumably the body of the lost man. His death brings about the end of the
narrative, so it is fitting that the dream-infused prose typical of much of the
novel gives way to the rational documentation of the newspaper article. For
the first time in the novel, time and place are not distorted but real. The death
of the lost man brings about the death of the ideal, but the outside world built
on rationality and logic prevails. This is of course analogous with the end of
Don Quixote: Don Quixote dies, leaving the practically minded Sancho.
Similar to other of Ramón's works, despite its experimental prose and modernist devices, *El hombre perdido* simultaneously draws on the Spanish
literary tradition, eliciting, in the final analysis the themes that have accompanied Spanish literature since its beginnings: dream versus reality, 'engaño'
versus 'desengaño', life versus death. *El hombre perdido* represents a crucial
work of its time as it re-engages with the big themes of old, but through a
modernist medium, questioning man's position in a universe which is ultimately presented as meaningless and absurd. It therefore deserves to be
considered with the great Existentialist novels of the twentieth century, and
should cause us to re-examine our claims about the Spanish literature of the
1940s.

A brief consideration of Piso bajo *(1961)*

The widespread assumption that Spain produced very little of any real literary worth during the sterile and uninspiring years of the 1950s is by no
means challenged by Ramón Gómez de la Serna's last, and highly disap-
pointing novel, *Piso bajo* (1961). It has been noted that the novel of 1950s
Spain is largely barren and of limited horizons. Living in self-imposed exile
since the outbreak of the Spanish Civil War in July of 1936, it comes as no
surprise that Ramón Gómez de la Serna's *Piso bajo* (1961) is imbued with

deep-seated nostalgia for his beloved Madrid and steeped in over-romanticised memories. The prose-style is drab, made up largely of clichéd *greguerías*. Gómez de la Serna is clearly writing from memory, a few years before his death having visited Spain only once since 1936. This undoubtedly accounts for the melancholy and sombre tone of the novel, written by Ramón as he approached the age of seventy. The main characters of the novel are the philosopher-scientist Don Pedro Savedra, his wife Conchita and his profligate daughter Olvido. They live together on the ground floor of an apartment and much of the novel consists of descriptions of the surrounding streets and neighbourhoods. It is a novel of nostalgia, which looks to the past in search of some form of comfort. Don Pedro Savedra—another prototypical Ramonian character—is obsessed with his physical surroundings rather than human relationships. He thus describes his life through inanimate objects and architecture [remisniscent of Don Pablo in *El secreto del acueducto* (1922)]: 'Don Pedro recordaba todos los portales en que se definió su vida'; 'Siete portales componían el calvario de su vida [...]' (p.31) and 'De su vida pasada sólo le quedaban los portales' (p.33). His sense of worth derives from his surroundings and the comfort of the familiar Madrid streets, cafes and buildings. At no juncture is there any mention of the socio-political situation. Don Pedro is self-obsessed, highly individualistic in his outlook, and claims that he cares little for others around him: 'No le importaba nada de lo que sucedía en el mundo ni a su alrededor [...]' (p.22). The philosophy which underpins his understanding of life features in his book *Alam en el espacio* which deals with the world of atoms and protons. This was a fascination of Gómez de la Serna's since his early years as a writer and a theme which inspired the short story written in 1927 about a scientist who splits the atom with devastating effects, *El dueño del átomo*. This fascination with the world of atoms and molecules is logical given the prominence of the material world not just in *Piso bajo* but in all of the author's novels. Objects are not just as they are perceived with the naked eye, but within them contain a world of energy which although is not apparent, constitutes their very nature. Don Pedro affirms this in his own words in chapter five—which could be understood as central to his obsession with the physical world of matter not only in *Piso bajo*—but in his fiction as a whole:

—Todo tiene su ritmo secreto, su girar íntimo, sus cargas memorables de electricidad positiva y de electricidad negativa. Todo necesita eso para sentirse materia. ¿Cuánto más no habrá que suponer necesario para sentirse espíritu? Las cosas no están paradas, las cosas viven, están en movimiento perpetuo, las hemos dado una forma engañosa, que nos ha distraído durante siglos, pero ellas tienen sus formas invisibles y no son compactas más que provisionalmente, sólo para contentar nuestro deseo decorativo o práctico. Las materias esenciales no tienen nada que ver con esas formas artificiales que las damos. (p.44)

The world depicted in *Piso bajo* is a monotonous world of non-events which are brought into the foreground of the novel. In such a world it is understandable that the object world takes on a special fascination. The attempt to go beyond the mere 'here and now' is what propels Don Pedro to search for the hidden properties within things. But it is not only objects that stimulate his interest. The narrator informs the reader that Don Pedro is consoled by space: 'Le consolaba el espacio.—Mientras haya espacio me salvaré de toda angustia [...] Ustedes saben que yo me adelanté a todos los filósofos alemanes en la idea de la consolación compensativa del espacio'. (p.45)

Piso bajo differs greatly from the complexity and depth of *El hombre perdido*. Despite shared characteristics in terms of themes and character prototypes which Gómez de la Serna cannot avoid in any of his fiction when reduced to the lowest common denominator, *Piso bajo* lacks experimentation and reads as a drab and uninspiring novel. As its very title suggests, it is a novel of limited horizons and low expectations, confirmed in the words of one of the characters: '—Somos pobres, tenemos sueños modestos [...]' (p.92), which compels Olvido to sleep face down on days when she feels melancholy: 'Olvido, en los días muy malos—en algún lado había eclipse de luna— se acostaba en la cama, hacia abajo, como si mirase a los horizontes del futuro [...]' (p.95). *Piso bajo* lacks a convincing narrative—which comes as no surprise for those acquainted with Gómez de la Serna's fiction—but in addition elicits very little linguistic interest. Towards the end of the novel Don Pedro is lying in bed feeling and overwhelming sense of 'desengaño' (p.145) when he thinks about life. In his own words he conveys his sense of dissilusion as he ponders on the nature of human existence: 'Todos creen que la vida es una apariencia y la vida es la más profunda desapariencia, todo en ella es verdad, demasiado verdad'. (p.145). He comes to the realization that everything is fleeting and ephemeral and that there is no ultimate hope for the future. He inhabits a world of dissipating atoms and empty spaces: 'Su vida había sido atrevida, pero siempre entre Dios y la muerte, dándose cuenta de que el hombre está entre paréntesis de muertos'. (p.147) In the final pages of *Piso bajo,* Don Pedro is dying, his daughter Olvido is living in a convent, and ultimately the surrounding world of dissipating atoms and empty spaces offers no solace or consolation. It reads very much as a novel written by an author who has realised that he is close to death, imbued with a deep-seated 'desengaño'.

It was only a few years later that Gómez de la Serna was to die in Buenos Aires, estranged from his country, a kind of 'hombre perdido' in a distant and fading world.

Notes

1   Camón Aznar states that: 'Es ésta la novela central en la producción de Ramón. La que nos aclara su estética, su pensamiento y hasta su técnica de escritor. Es la obra que todo creador produce en la segunda mitad de su vida'. *Ramón Gómez de la Serna en sus obras* (Madrid: Espasa Calpe, 1972). Miguel González Gerth argues that *El hombre perdido* 'represents the culmination of Ramón's bold literary vision and inventiveness'. *A Labyrinth of Imagery: Ramón Gómez de la Serna's 'Novelas de la nebulosa'* (London: Tamesis, 1986) p.93.

2   Many years later Ramón, writing on Dalí, shows his continuing contempt for Sartrean Existentialism: 'El destino del surrealismo era el de empalmarse con otra doctrina más alta y más nueva que no fuese de ningún modo el chabacano y monstruoso existencialismo sartriense'. In *Dalí* (Madrid:Espasa Calpe,1985) p.95.

3   Margaret F.W. Jones, *The Contemporary Spanish Novel 1939–1975*, (Boston: Twayne, 1985) p.17.

4   Sherman E. Eoff, *The Modern Spanish Novel*, (London: Peter Owen, 1961) p.213.

5   Harrison and Wood Op Cit, p.369.

Chapter 7. The Poetics of Abstraction

Existence and the world are eternally
justified solely as an aesthetic phenomenon
(Friedrich Nietzsche)

It's a seat…But the word stays on my lips: it
refuses to go out and put itself on the thing.
Things are divorced from their names…
I am in the midst of things, nameless things.
Alone, without words, defenceless, they surround me, are beneath me, behind me,
above me […]
And then, all of a sudden, there it was, clear as day: existence had suddenly unveiled
itself. It had lost the harmless look of abstract category: it was the very paste of
things…the diversity of things, their individuality, was only an appearance, a veneer.
This veneer had melted, leaving soft, monstrous masses all in disorder—naked, in a
frightful, obscene nakedness.
[‘Roquentin’, in La Nausea (1938) Jean-Paul Sartre]

It is possible to read western history
as a record of the breakdown of
order leading towards disintegration.
Roland Stromberg

The individual has become a mere cog in an enormous organization of things and
power which tear from his hands all progress, spirituality, and value in order to
transform them from their subjective form into the form of a purely objective life.
George Simmel (1858–1918)

In *The Birth of Tragedy* Nietzsche famously stated that 'Existence and the
world are eternally justified solely as an aesthetic phenomenon',[1] re-asserting
the importance of the aesthetic ideal over moral, ideological, religious and
social considerations. With these words Nietzsche gives voice to the pervasive mood emerging at the turn of the century and which would come to
dominate the first third of the 20th century. Ramón Gómez de la Serna's narrative fiction is not an isolated literary phenomenon, divorced and detached
from the world in which he was living, but a product of the ideas and influences that fuelled the modernist enterprise. These words by Nietzsche to
some extent sum up the main thrust of Gómez de la Serna's narrative fiction
from his early beginnings in 1909 to his last novel in 1961. His trajectory as
a writer and the evolution of his narrative style never departed from the absolute certainty that art was to occupy a place of central importance. Similar to
Oscar Wilde, Gómez de la Serna re-asserts the importance of art over life

itself, abstracting the real through a poetic re-interpretation of the surrounding world, whereby the poetic construct not only competes with Nature but overshadows it.

Ramón Gómez de la Serna's works need to be understood as part of the modernist enterprise. The fragmentary nature of their narrative, the estrangement from normality of many of his main fictional characters coupled with their sense of rootlessness and detachment from society at large place them at the heart of modernism. Throughout his narrative fiction there is an attenuation of the rational world replaced instead by a sense of progressive irrationality, clearly in keeping with the prevailing mood throughout Europe at the turn of the century and beyond, a mood captured by Richard Weston in his study on modernism:

> The Age of reason seemed to be giving way to a new Age of Unreason and, doubting that there could be rational answers to the big questions about life and disenchanted by traditional religion, people turned in surprising numbers to new systems of belief [...].[2]

Ramón Gómez de la Serna's narrative fiction captures modern day life, feeding on the progressive sense of irrationality and unreason which arose as a reaction to 19th century positivism and literary naturalism. Bearing in mind ¡Rebeca! (1936) and El hombre perdido (1947) Gómez de la Serna should be considered one of the greatest surrealist writers of all times. His worth as a writer lies in his unparalleled ability to champion subjective perception and the poetic defamiliarisation of reality. Intoxicated by the changing ideas in art at the turn of the century; from Impressionism to the formal innovations afforded by cubism; coupled with the promotion of absurdity and incongruity associated with Dadaism, to the mental and verbal liberty brought about by surrealism; Gómez de la Serna's narrative fiction is a fascinating record of experimental writing very much a product of his time, undoubtedly influenced by the emerging ideas during one of the most interesting periods of European literature. And yet, paradoxically, he remains very Spanish, deeply entrenched in tradition, in the same way that Picasso and Dalí did. It is the conflux of such diverse influences which make his work so interesting, and so crucial for understanding the evolution of the Spanish novel.

As Gómez de la Serna matured as a writer his work took on a more profoundly philosophical message, as we have seen in his most accomplished novels ¡Rebeca! (1936) and El hombre perdido (1947). These are, in my view, undoubtedly Gómez de la Serna's best novels, different in terms of style and substance to many of his 1920s works. The use of surrealism to evoke the main theme in all of his work: the failure of the erotic dream, imbues these works with a metaphorical brilliance and linguistic ingenuity;

whilst simultaneously suggesting ontological and existential issues in a manner rarely seen in his earlier fiction. Although he was not an atheist and did purport to have some kind of faith, there is no doubt that his fiction describes a post-theistic society, where the individual is central, having lost all traditional bearings. If they do believe in a God, it is a God who has absented himself from human experience. He champions the avant-garde as a new and innovative way of understanding man's position in the universe, showing how man can rise above a normalised existence through his creative imagination, poetic wit and humour. The incongruity of Gómez de la Serna's fictional characters is Chaplinesque in the exaltation of quirky behaviour, driven by absurd whims which set them apart from the crowd enabling them to retain their individuality. However, in his later novels this humorous treatment does not mask an underlying feeling that life is ultimately absurd and meaningless. The individual may be presented as autonomous and at the centre of the universe, but is ultimately trapped in a world which offers no more than the ephemeral allure of the object world. Gómez de la Serna, like no other author, glorifies the material world and is gripped by the poetic possibility afforded by its literary manipulation. Whether we consider Pablo in *El secreto del Acueducto* (1922) who is fascinated and transfixed by his surroundings which are poetically and subjectively recreated in his mind, to Palmyra in *La quinta de Palmyra* (1923) who inhabits a decadent and aestheticised world of gardens and lush surroundings, to Luis in *¡Rebeca!* (1936) who has a conversation with a teapot, and the nameless protagonist in *El hombre perdido* (1947) who falls in love with the washbasin in his bathroom; Gómez de la Serna is transfixed by the material world. This world is brought to life through poetic re-creation and metaphorical association in the form of the *greguería*, but is, in the final analysis, non-transcendental. His characters are therefore lopsided, uni-dimensional lacking any human or spiritual depth. They are largely aesthetic creations in a human form. This does not mean that they are completely divested of all human traits: they feel the need for love, they experience loneliness, unease and even exhibit some kind of existential questioning in his later fiction; but they are overwhelmingly driven by an aesthetic impulse, in an increasingly meaningless world. They drift in isolation, in state similar to that which Emile Durkeim described as 'anomie'. It therefore comes as no surprise that most of Gómez de la Serna's novels end pessimistically, despite the use of humour which is deployed by Gómez de la Serna as a way of coping with life's absurdities, a means of shunning and avoiding ontological and metaphysical issues. But in so doing he creates aesthetic creations which appeal to us on the basis of their unconventional behaviour and who are interesting for their approach to life, but not one with which the reader can easily identify. They are interest-

ing as avant-garde creations. Gómez de la Serna does not create literary he-
roes with human traits, but modern-day individuals who are out of kilter with
their world. They defy the established norms and strict moral codes and share
traits with Roland Stromberg's definition of modern man:

> The individual who feels bewildered and alone in a huge, impersonal world, who has
> lost the guidance of tradition and religion, and can find no source of values outside
> of self, who has lost contact with the community—such a person is surely all too
> typical of modern urbanised and industrialised society [...].[3]

In this kind of society the pursuit of hedonistic and aesthetic pleasure becomes one of the main reasons for existing. The world is refracted through an
aesthetic prism, through which it is poetically distorted.

It is no wonder that the writer George Orwell years later looked back on
the modernist enterprise and remembered it for its exaltation of linguistic
ingenuity, but at the expense of disengaging with political issues:

> What is noticeable about all these writers is that what 'purpose' they have is very
> much up in the air. There is no attention to the urgent problems of the moment,
> above all no politics in the narrower sense...when one looks back at the twenties...
> in 'cultured' circles art for art's sake extended practically to a worship of the mean-
> ingless. Literature was supposed to consist solely in the manipulation of words.[4]

Obviously Lukács and Orwell were staunch critics of modernism, and
their extreme political views are well known. It is true that they failed to see
the positive side of modernism, such as the liberation of the human imagination through startling poetic imagery and flight of imagination. To restore
some balance it may be useful to cite Jameson's view of modernism, which
takes issue with Lukács' (and for that matter Orwell's) politically driven disdain of modernism:

> Lukács is not wrong to associate the emergence of modernism with the reification
> which is its precondition; but he oversimplifies and deproblematizes a complicated
> and interesting situation by ignoring the Utopian vocation... the mission to return at
> least a symbolic experience of libidinal gratification to a world drained of it, a world
> of extension, grey and merely quantifiable.[5]

But it is also true that the unremitting stride towards the poetic and subjective world of the senses ultimately fails to address man's spiritual need,
and does not answer the ontological questioning and *raison-d'être*. Herein
lies the dilemma. It is therefore hardly surprising that most of Gómez de la
Serna's characters end up living estranged lives on the margins of society,
very often alone.

Writing between two World Wars, The Spanish Civil War and the ensuing Francoist dictatorship, Gómez de la Serna's fiction shuns socio-realism,
adopting instead a modernist approach to writing; Schopenhauerian in the
importance accorded to aesthetic contemplation (although without the persistent mood of despair). As Roger Shattuck argues, modernism presents '[...]
man's need for divinity and spiritual values within the material world, above
all within himself [...] the work itself becomes the means, the locus of the
search.'[6]

Ramón's deconstruction of the material world, and his quest to transform
objects through the *greguería* is carried out with a near religious fervour. The
attempt to satisfy a spiritual quest with a material answer is what causes the
characters' neurosis and insanity. It is no coincidence that most of Gómez de
la Serna's characters become steadily insane. The momentary transcendence
afforded by the object world is never enough to quench the existential search.
As Leopoldo Alas Clarín stated: 'We are worms, we are told, of this planet,
and our ephemeral lot is joined with the soil as though we were slaves to
lumps of dirt'.[7] T.S Eliot saw the human condition as 'Shape without form,
shade without colour, paralysed force, gesture without motion'. Georg
Lukács argued: 'Man is reduced to a sequence of unrelated experiential
fragments; he is inexplicable to others and himself.' All of these authors express the ultimate absurdity and futility of the human condition. As the 19th
century view of the world gave way to a modernist world where the individual is out of kilter with society and his environment, in Lukác's words
'the ontological view governing the image of man in the work of leading
modernist writers [...] is by nature solitary, asocial, unable to enter into relationships with other human beings'.[8] Gómez de la Serna's characters share in
this malaise: Don Pablo in *El secreto del Acueducto* replaces human relationships with his fixation with the aqueduct. The characters of *Cinelandia* are
transient and superficial living in a modern world where human relationships
are shallow. Palmyra in *La Quinta de Palmyra* lives for an aesthetic ideal,
similar to Lorenzo in *La mujer de ámbar*. The protagonist of *¡Rebeca!* pur-
sues an ideal which ultimately never materialises. The main character of *El
hombre perdido* dies alone, stretched out on a railway track. In true modernist fashion, there is an underlying hollowness to modern man in all of Gómez
de la Serna's characters. As Lukacs suggests regarding the nature of modern
man: 'The disintegration of personality is matched by a disintegration of the
outer world'.[9] Gómez de la Serna's modernist fiction shows us man's position in a world where religion is progressively called into question, and
where there is a disintegration of old orders, and a renewed interest in the
fragment, the part, detached from the organic whole. And whilst this experimental kind of literature is difficult, and constantly questions traditional

notions of what constitutes a novel, it is essential, to anyone in understanding the evolution of the genre. Regarding the European experimental novels of the 1920s and 30s Jeanette Winterson stated that:

> To assume that modernism has no real relevance to the way that we need to be developing fiction now, is to condemn readers and writers to a dying Victorian twilight. To say that the experimental novel is dead is to say that literature is dead. Literature is experimental. Once the novel was novel; if we cannot continue to alter it, to expand its boundaries without dropping it into even greater formlessness than the shape tempts, then we can only museum it. Literature is not a museum, it is a living thing.[10]

Gómez de la Serna needs to be understood as a champion of experimental literature, as his works give voice to the complexities of modernity and its effects on the individual. His work captures the exuberance and humour of the roaring twenties, and at the same time evokes the absurdity of human life. In a letter to himself he captures this, and it is worthwhile including this quotation in full:

> Querido Ramón:
>   Somos una humanidad catastrófica. Estamos en las vísperas de la Guerra más descerrajada de la historia y no sabemos más que vamos a ser arruinados y correremos de un lado a otro intentando seguir viviendo hasta el final.
>   Es la tercera vez que sucede una cosa así en nuestra vida y siempre sospechamos que no nos volveremos a ver. ¡Ojalá encontremos un puente o una islita en que mantenernos en pie mientras que se inunda todo!
>   Todos están como inconscientes sin querer borrar de su cabeza la idea de lo que comprarán el mes que viene.
>   Los días son aparentemente iguales, todas las minucias de la vida dan su noticia, lo maquinal trabaja como si no le fuese a faltar esencia para sus motores.
>   El bárbaro no piensa en lo que pueda pasar, en lo que se derrumba, en que se apague la luz en el hogar, en que todo se tumbe y se desparrame. Como siempre, van asaltar la vida tranquila, a intentar apoderarse de sus frutos, de sus honestidades, de sus rotas armonías.
>   Todo se atrabucará y probablemente ya no podré resistir el embate, defendiendo la dignidad que ha procurado que quede en pie a través de dos guerras. Esta vez va a ser la pavorosa, la asoladora, la que ni siquiera tendrá ese rabo de bayoneta que fue su última piedad.
>   Todo va a estar tirado por el suelo, revuelto, ayeante, y, sin embargo, en vísperas nada menos que de eso, nunca ha estado menos alarmada la humanidad, como si en su inconsciente supiese que este es el último respiro que va a tener, no presagiando la noticia, no dándole vueltas […] Este escepticismo es el repeluzno profundo de la hora visperal.
>   Abrazos resignados de Ramón.[11]

In his fiction Gómez de la Serna captures the essence of the modern world and man's position in it. But the early enthusiasm with modernity and all it had to offer does not, in the final analysis, satisfy the existential and ontological questions of life. Therein lies his dilemma; a sentiment which pervades his every novel.

Notes

1   Rüdiger Safranski, *Nietzsche: A Philosophical Biography*, trans. by Shelley Frisch (London: Granta Books, 2002) p.73.
2   Richard Weston, *Modernism* (London: Phaidon, 1996) p.60.
3   Roland N. Stromberg *An Intellectual History of Modern Europe* (New York: Appleton-Century-Crufts, 1966) p.226
4   George Orwell, 'Inside the Whale' (1940), rpt. in Sonia Orwell and Ian Angus (eds.), *The Collected Essays, Journalism and Letters of George Orwell* (Harmondworth: Penguin, 1970) Vol I, p.557.
5   Frederic Jameson, *The Political Unconscious; Narrative as a Socially Symbolic Act* (London: Methuen, 1981) p.63.
6   Roger Shattuck, *The Banquet Years: The Origins of The Avant-garde in France 1885-1918* (London: Jonathan Cape, 1969) p.326
7   Sherman H. Eoff, *The Modern Spanish Novel*, (London: Peter Owen, 1961) p.71
8   Cited in Harrison and Wood, op cit, p.684.
9   Ibid, p.684
10 Jeanette Winterson, *Art Objects: Essays on Ecstasy and Effrontery* (New York: Alfred A. Knopf, 1996) p.188.
11 Ramón Gómez de la Serna, *Nuevas páginas de mi vida* (Madrid: Alianza Editorial, 1970) pp.177–119.

Bibliography

Primary Sources

Gómez de la Serna, Ramón, *El ruso* [1913], in *El dueño del átomo* (Madrid: Historia Nueva, 1928).
——— *Greguerías selectas* (Madrid: Calleja, 1919).
——— *El doctor inverosímil* (Madrid : Alrededor del Mundo, 1921).
——— *El doctor inverosímil* [1914] (Barcelona: Destinolibro, 1981).
——— *El Rastro* [1915] (Madrid: Espasa Calpe, 1998).
——— *La viuda blanca y negra* [1917?] (Madrid: Biblioteca Nueva,1921).
——— *La viuda blanca y negra* (Madrid: Cátedra, 1988).
——— *Senos* [1917] (Barcelona: Círculo de Lectores, 1968).
——— *Senos* (Madrid: Prodhufi, 1992).
——— *Pombo* [1918–1924] (Barcelona: Editorial Juventud, 1960).
——— *La Sagrada cripta de Pombo* [1918–1924] (Barcelona: Editorial Juventud, 1960).
——— *El alba y otras cosas* (Madrid: Calleja,1923).
——— *El miedo al mar* [1921], in *La malicia de las acacias*. (Valencia: Ediciones Sempere, 1924).
——— *El secreto del Acueducto* (Madrid: Biblioteca Nueva, 1922/3).
——— *El secreto del Acueducto* (Madrid: Cátedra, 1986).
——— *El incongruente* (Madrid: Espasa Calpe, 1922).
——— *El incongruente* [1922] (Barcelona: Ediciones Orbis, 1982).
——— *La hija del verano* [1922], in *El dueño del átamo* (Madrid: Historia Nueva, 1928).
——— *El Gran Hotel* [1922] (Barcelona: Al Monigote de papel, 1942).
——— *La gangosa* [1922], in *La malicia de las acacias*. (Valencia: Ediciones Sempere, 1924).
——— *El olor a las mimosas* [1922], in *El dueño del átamo* (Madrid: Historia Nueva, 1928).
——— *La hija del verano* [1922], in *El dueño del átamo* (Madrid: Historia Nueva, 1928).
——— *El hombre de los pies grandes* [1922], in *El dueño del átamo* (Madrid: Historia Nueva, 1928).
——— *El Chalet de las Rosas, La quinta de Palmyra* [1923], ed. by María Martínez del Postal (Barcelona: Bruguera, 1968).
——— *La Quinta de Palmyra* [1923] (Madrid:Espasa Calpe,1982).
——— *María Yarsilovna (falsa novela rusa)* (1923), in *Revista de Occidente*, no. 1 (September, 1923), 183–201.
——— *Los dos marineros (falsa novela china)* (1923), in *Obras selectas* (Madrid: Editorial Plenitud, 1947), pp.319–365.
——— *Cinelandia* (Valencia: Sempere,1923).
——— *Cinelandia* (Madrid:Valdemar,1995).
——— *El novelista* [1923] (Madrid: Espasa Calpe, 1973).
——— *La malicia de las acacias* (Valencia: Ediciones Sempere, 1924).
——— *El joven de las sobremesas* [1923], in *La malicia de las acacias* (Valencia: Ediciones Sempere, 1924).

────── *Los gemelos y el guante* [1923], in *La malicia de las acacias* (Valencia: Ediciones Sempere, 1924).

────── *La saturada* [1923], in *El dueño del átomo* (Madrid: Historia Nueva, 1928).

────── Ramón Gómez de la Serna, 'Realidades', *España* no.24 (Agosto 1923), pp.69–75.

────── *De otra raza* [1924], in *La malicia de las acacias* (Valencia: Ediciones Sempere, 1924).

────── *Aquella novela* [1924], in *La malicia de las acacias* (Valencia: Ediciones Sempere, 1924).

────── *La capa de don Dámaso* [1924], in *El dueño del átamo* (Madrid: Historia Nueva, 1928).

────── *La fúnebre (falsa novela tártara)* (1925), in *Seis falsas novelas*, ed. Iona Zlotescu (Madrid: Mondadori, 1989), pp.73–88.

────── *La virgen pintada de rojo (falsa novela negra)* (1925), in *Seis falsas novelas*, ed. Iona Zlotescu (Madrid: Mondadori, 1989), pp.89–114.

────── *La mujer vestida de hombre (falsa novela alemana)* (1925), in *Seis falsas novelas*, ed. Iona Zlotescu (Madrid: Mondadori, 1989), pp.115–139.

────── *Caprichos* [1925] (Madrid: Espasa Calpe, 1962).

────── *Gollerías* [1926] (Barcelona: Bruguera, 1968).

────── *El torero Caracho* [1926] (Madrid: Espasa Calpe, 1969).

────── *La casa triangular* [1925], in *El dueño del átamo* (Madrid: Historia Nueva, 1928).

────── *El dueño del átomo*, in *Revista de Occidente*, no. 12 (April, 1926), 59–84.

────── *El hombre de la galería*, in *Revista de Occidente*, no. 13 (August, 1926), 299–316.

────── *El hombre de la galería* [1926], in *El dueño del átamo* (Madrid: Historia Nueva, 1928).

────── *El gran griposo*, in *Revista de Occidente*, no.16 (September, 1927), 57–78.

────── *El gran griposo* [1927], in *El dueño del átamo* (Madrid: Historia Nueva, 1928).

────── *El defensor del cementerio*, in *Revista de Occidente*, no.17 (August, 1927), 34–51.

────── *El hijo del millonario (falsa novela norteamericana)* (1927) in *Seis falsas novelas*, ed. Iona Zlotescu (Madrid: Mondadori, 1989), pp.143–162.

────── *La mujer de ámbar* [1927] (Madrid:Espasa Calpe,1981).

────── *Goya*, [1928] (Madrid: Espasa Calpe, 1972).

────── *El caballero del hongo gris* [1928] (Madrid: Alianza Editorial, 1970).

────── *La nardo* [1930] (Barcelona: Bruguera, 1980).

────── *El hijo surrealista*, in *Revista de Occidente*, no.30 (October,1930), 27–52.

────── *Ismos* [1931] (Madrid: Ediciones Guadarrama, 1975).

────── *Policéfalo y señora* [1932] (Madrid: Espasa Calpe, 1932).

────── 'Ensayo sobre lo cursi' [1934], in *Una teoría personal del arte: antología de textos de estética y teoría del arte de Ramón*, Ana Martínez Collado (Madrid: Tecnos, 1988), pp.25–34.

────── 'Las cosas y el ello' [1936], in *Una teoría personal del arte: antología de textos de estética y teoría del arte de Ramón*, Ana Martínez Collado (Madrid: Tecnos, 1988), pp.35–43.

────── *El Greco: el visionario y la pintura* [1935] (Buenos Aires: Losada, 1960).

────── 'Las palabras y lo indecible', *Revista de Occidente*, no.51 (April, 1936), 63–64.

────── *Dalí* [1941] (Madrid: Espasa y Calpe, 1985).

────── *Nuevos retratos contemporáneos y otros retratos* [1945] (Madrid:Aguilar,1990).

────── *Quevedo* (Madrid: Biblioteca Nueva, 1950).

────── *Quevedo* [1950] (Madrid: Espasa Calpe, 1962).

———— *Lope viviente* [1954] (Buenos Aires, Espasa Calpe,1954).

———— *El hombre perdido* [1947] (Madrid: Espasa Calpe, 1962).

———— *Obras selectas* (Madrid: Editorial Plenitud, 1947).

———— *Automoribundia* (Buenos Aires: Editorial Sudamericana, 1948).

———— *Nuevas páginas de mi vida: lo que no dije en Automoribundia* [1957] (Madrid: Alianza Editorial, 1970).

———— *Piso bajo* (Madrid:Espasa Calpe,1961).

Secondary Sources

Alberti, Rafael, 'Ramón orquesta sólo de trombón', Suplemento CULTURAS, *Diario 16*, 2 July 1988, p.1.

Alfaro, José María, 'Algunos recuerdos melancólicos', *ABC literario*, 2 July 1988, p.6.

Alfaro, José María, 'El tiempo de vanguardia', Suplemento EXTRA, *El País*, 30 June 1988, p.2.

Alfaro, José María, 'El rastro de Ramón', *Insula*, 196 (1963), 12.

Angel García Pintado, 'Aritmética del humor', Suplemento EXTRA, *El País*, 30 June 1988, p.3.

Ayala, Francisco, 'Como Lope, otro escritor torrencial y fluente', *Lateral*, 24 (1996), 3.

Ayala, Francisco, 'Un mundo ficticio', Suplemento CULTURAS, *Diario 16*, 2 July 1988, p.3.

Bacarisse, Mauricio, 'Kinescopio:el elogio a lo pasajero', *España* 296 (1921), 12–13.

Baroja, Pío. *La caverna del humorismo* (Madrid: Colección Selecta, 1919).

Barrera López, José María, 'Afinidades y diferencias: Ramón y el Ultra', *Cuadernos Hispanoamericanos*, 450 (1988), 29–37.

Benito Fernández, José, 'Ramón periodista', *Quimera*, 27 (1983), 37–40.

Bloom, Harold. *The Anxiety of Influence: A Theory of Poetry* (New York: Oxford University Press,1973).

Bonet, Juan Manuel, 'Ramón y los cubistas', Suplemento CULTURAS, *Diario 16*, 2 July 1988, p.5.

Bóveda, Xavier, 'Un automóvil pasa', *Grecia*, 15 (1919), 31.

Breton, André, *Manifestos of Surrealism*, trans. Richard Seaver and Helen R. Lane (The University of Michigan Press, 1972).

Bryfonski, Dedria; (ed.) *Contemporary Literary Criticism: Excepts from Criticism of Works of Today's Novelists, Poets, Playwrights, and other Creative Writers*, Vol IX (Michigan: Sale Research Company, 1978).

Buckley, Ramón, and Crispin, John, *Los vanguardistas españoles: 1925–1935* (Madrid: Alianza Editorial, 1973).

Buñuel, Luis, *My Last Breath*, trans. Abigail Israel (London: Johnathan Cape, 1982).

Bürger, Peter, *Theory of The Avant-garde*, trans. Michael Shaw (MUP: 1984).

Calderón, E.Correa, 'Ramón en el recuerdo', *Insula*, 196 (1963), 3.

Calvo, Luis, 'Como un niño genial', *ABC* literario, 2 July 1988, p.8.

Camón Aznar, José, *Ramón Gómez de la Serna en sus obras* (Madrid: Espasa Calpe, 1972).

———— *Los libros de arte en la obra de Ramón Gómez de la Serna* (Madrid: Editorial Maestre, 1968).

Cano Ballesta, Juan, *Literatura y tecnología: las letras españolas ante la revolución industrial: 1900–1933* (Madrid: Orígenes, 1981).

Cansinos Assens, Rafael, 'Huidobro y el Creacionismo', *Cosmópolis*, 1 (1919), 68–73.

Cansinos Assens, *La novísima literatura*, 2nd ed (Madrid: Editorial Paez, 1925).

188 THE DILEMMA OF MODERNITY

Cardona, Rodolfo, *Ramón: A study of Gómez de la Serna and his works* (New York: Eliseo Torres and Sons, 1957).

Caws, Mary-Anne, *The Poetry of Dada and Surrealism: Aragón, Breton, Tzara, Eluard, Desnos* (Princeton: University Press, 1970).

Cernuda, Luis, *Estudios sobre poesía española contemporánea*, (Madrid: Ediciones Gudarrama, 1957).

Chacel, Rosa, 'Evasión', Suplemento CULTURAS, *Diario 16*, 2 July 1988, p.5.

Charpentier Saitz, Herlinda, Las 'Novelle' de Gómez de la Serna (London: Tamesis, 1990).

Conte, Rafael, 'Talentos desconocidos', Suplemento EXTRA, *El País*, 30 June 1988, p.7.

Cortázar, Julio, 'Los pescadores de esponjas', *Lateral*, 24 (1996), 1–2.

Crespo, Angel, 'Invitación a la movida', Suplemento CULTURAS, *Diario 16*, 2 July 1988, p.4.

Darío, Rubén, *Prosas profanas* (Caracas: Biblioteca Ayacucho, 1977).

Dennis, Nigel, *Studies on Ramón Gómez de la Serna* (Ottawa: Dovehouse Editions, 1988).

——— 'En torno al martirologio', Suplemento CULTURAS, *Diario 16*, 2 July 1988, p.5.

Díaz Fernández, José, *El nuevo romanticismo* (Madrid: Velasco, 1930).

Díaz Plaja, Guillermo, *Estructura y sentido del novencentismo español* (Madrid: Alainza Editorial, 1975).

Díaz-Plaja, Guillermo, *Estructura y sentido del novecentismo español* (Madrid: Alianza Editorial, 1975).

Eagleton, Terry, *The Ideology of the Aesthetic* (Oxford: Blackwell, 1990).

Edel, Leon, *The Modern Psychological Novel* (Gloucester:Peter Smith,1972).

Eguizábal, Raul, 'El dueño del átomo', Suplemento CULTURAS, *Diario 16*, 2 July 1988, p.7.

Ellmann; Richard and O'Clair; Robert, *The Norton Anthology of Modern Poetry*, 2nd ed. (New York: Norton and Co, 1988).

Embarek Jedidi, Malika, 'Deambular por Ramón', Quimera, 27 (1983), 32–33.

Enrique Serrano, José, 'The Theory of the Novel in Ramón's *El novelista*', in *The Spanish avant-garde*, ed. by Derek Harris (Manchester: Manchester University Press, 1995).

Eoff, Sherman E., *The Modern Spanish Novel* (London: Peter Owen, 1961).

Espina, Antonio, 'Ramón: genio y figura', *Revista de Occidente*, no. 64 (October, 1963), 54–64.

Fernández Cifuentes, Luis, 'Fenomenología de la vanguardia: el caso de la novela', in *Anales de Literatura Española*, no. 9 (1993), 45–59.

Fernández Molina, A., 'Sobre imaginación: Diario póstumo de Ramón', *Cuadernos Hispanoamericanos*, 273 (1973), 623–625.

Flórez, Rafael, 'Gatomaquia de Madrid', Suplemento EXTRA, *El País*, 30 June 1988, p.8.

Freedman, Ralph. *The Lyrical Novel: Studies in Herman Hesse, André Gide and Virginia Woolf*, 3rd edn (Princeton:Princeton University Press,1963).

Frenk, Sue, Perriam, Chris, Thompson, Mike, 'The Literary Avant-garde: *A Contradictory Modernity'*, *Spanish Cultural Studies: an introduction*, ed. by Helen Graham and Jo Labanyi (Oxford University Press, 1995).

Friedman, Norman, 'Recent Short Story Theories: Problems in Definition', in *Short Story in Theory at a Crossroads*, ed. by Susan Loaffer and Eilyn Clarey (Boston: Luisiana State University Press, 1989), pp.51–63.

Fuentes, Victor, 'La narrativa española de vanguardia (1923–1931)', in *La novela lírica II*, ed. by Darío Villanueva (Madrid: Taurus, 1983), pp.155–163.

Fuertes Mallá, Rafael, 'Ortega y Gasset en la novela de vanguardia española', *Revista de Occidente*, no.96 (October, 1989), 27–56.

García de la Concha, Victor, 'Ramón y la vanguardia', in *Historia y crítica de la literatura española*, ed. by Francisco Rico and Víctor García de la Concha, Epoca Contemporánea: 1914–1939, 9 vols. (Barcelona: Ediciones Crítica, 1984), pp.205–215.

García Posada, Miguel, 'En el corondel de lo impreso', *ABC literario*, 2 July 1988, p.11.

Garrido, Carlos, 'Ramonscopio', *Quimera*, 27 (1983), 34–36.

Geist, A.Z. *La poética de la generación del 1927 y las revistas literarias: de la vanguardia al compromiso: 1918–1936* (Barcelona: Guadarrama, 1980).

Geist, A.L., *La poética de la generación del 27 y alas revistas literarias de la vanguardia al compromiso: 1918–1936* (Barcelona: Guadarrama, 1980).

Giménez Caballero, Ernesto. 'Paisaje en materia gris', in *Los vanguardistas españoles: 1925–1935*, R.Buckley and J. Crispin (Madrid: Alianza Editorial, 1973).

Gómez Carillo, E., 'La psicología del viaje', *Cosmópolis*, 1 (1919), 610–631.

Gómez de la Serna, Gaspar, *Ramón: obra y vida* (Madrid: Taurus, 1963).

Gómez Mesa, L., 'Boletín del Cineclub', *La Gaceta Literaria*, 95 (1930), 29–33.

González-Gerth, Miguel, 'Ramón's Faded Image', in *Essays on Hispanic Literature in Honour of L.King*, ed. by Molly Sylvia and Fernández Cifuentes (London: Támesis, 1983), pp 91–95.

―――― 'El mundo extravagante de Ramón Gómez de la Serna', *Insula*, 183 (1962), 1–2.

―――― *A Labyrinth of Imagery: Ramón Gómez de la Serna's 'Novelas de la nebulosa'* (London: Tamesis, 1986).

González-Blanco, Edmundo, 'La antropología criminal en España', *Cosmópolis*, 26 (1921), 285–399.

Granjel, Luis, 'Ramón en *Prometeo*', *Insula*, 196 (1963), 3–10.

―――― *Retrato de Ramón* (Madrid: Ediciones Guadarrama, 1963).

Haro Teglen, Eduardo, 'El espíritu del espectáculo', Suplemento EXTRA, *El País*, 30 June 1988, p.4.

Harvard, Robert, *A Companion to Spanish Surrealism* (London: Tamesis, 2005).

Harris, Derek, with Maritsany, Luis, *Luis Cernuda: prosa completa* (Barcelona: Barral Editores, 1975).

―――― *The Spanish avant-garde* (Manchester: Manchester University Press, 1995).

―――― 'Tempora Mutantur', in *Changing Times in Hispanic Culture* (University of Aberdeen, 1996), 1–5 (p.3).

Harrison, Charles, and Wood, Paul, *Art in Theory 1900–2000: An Anthology of Changing Ideas* (Oxford: Blackwell, 2003).

Henn, D., 'La Gran Ciudad Falsa: Cinelandia', *Cuadernos Hispanoamericanos*, 350 (1979), 377–387.

Hoddie, James, 'El programa solipsista de Ramón', *Revista de literatura*, no.82 (April, 1979), 131–148.

Hoyle, Alan, 'The Politics of a Hatless Revolutionary', in *Studies in Modern Literature and Art presented to Helen F. Grant*, ed. by Nigel Glendenning (London:Támesis,1972), pp.79–96.

―――― 'Towards an understanding of *El secreto del Acueducto*', in *Studies on Ramón Gómez de la Serna*, ed. by Nigel Dennis, Ottawa Hispanic Studies 2 (Dovehouse Editions Canada, 1988), pp.173–198.

―――― El humor ramoniano de vanguardia (Manchester: Working Papers 2, 1996).

―――― 'Ramón Gómez de la Serna: Avant-gardist Novelist Par Excellance', in Hacia la novela nueva: Essays on the Spanish Avant-Garde Novel, ed. Francis Lough (Oxford: Peter Lang, 2001), pp.61–77.

Ilie, Paul, *The Surrealist Mode in Spanish Literature: An Interpretation of Basic Trends from Post-Romanticism to the Spanish Vanguard* (The University of Michigan Press, 1968).

——— *Documents of the Spanish Avant-garde*. (Chapel hill: University of North Carolina, 1969).

Innes, Christopher, *The Avant-Garde Theatre (1892–1992)* (London and New York: Routledge, 1993).

Jameson, Fredric, *The Political Unconscious: Narrative as a Socially Symbolic Act* (London: Methuen, 1981).

Jones, Margaret F.W., *The Contemporary Spanish Novel: 1939–1975* (Boston: Twayne, 1985).

Jones, R.O., *A Literary History Of Spain: The Golden Age* (London: Ernest Benn Limited, 1971).

Kermode, Frank, *A Sense of an Ending* (London: Oxford University Press, 1968).

Lacarta, Manuel, *Madrid y sus literaturas de la generación del 98 a la posguerra* (Madrid: El Avapiés, 1986).

Lafuente, Fernando R., 'Sólo Ramón a los cien años', *Insula*, 502 (1988), 16–17.

Lafuente, Fernando, 'Entre el lujo y el desperdicio', *ABC* literario, 2 July 1988, p.10.

Lodge, David, *The Modes of Modern Writing* (London: Edward Arnold, 1977).

López, José, 'Ramón de ayer a hoy', *Insula*, 196 (1963), 4.

Lough, Francis, (ed.) *Hacia la novlea nueva: Essays on the Spanish Avant-garde Novel* (Bern: Peter Lang, 2001).

Mainer, José Carlos, Prólogo a *El incongruente* (Barcelona: Editores Picazo, 1972), pp.11–34.

——— *La edad de plata (1902–1931): ensayo de interpretación de un proceso cultural* (Barcelona: Libros de la Fontera, 1975).

——— '1915–1930: Vísperas de Gloria', *Lateral*, 24 (1996), 6–7 .

Manzoni, Alessandro, *I Promessi Sposi*, Introduzione e note di Vittorio Spinazzola, (Garzant Editore, 1966).

Manzoni, Alessandro, *I promessi sposi*, trans by Archibald Colquhoun (London: The Reprint Society, 1952).

Marcial de Onís, Carlos, *El surrealismo y cuatro poetas de la Generación de 27* (Madrid: Ediciones José Porrúa Turanzas, 1974).

Marías, Julián, 'Ramón Gómez de la Serna', *Diccionario de la literatura española* (Madrid: Revista de Occidente, 1953), pp.315–17.

Martínez Collado, Ana (ed), *Una teoría personal del arte: antología de textos literarios de estética y teoría de arte de Ramón* (Madrid: Tecnos, 1988).

May, Charles E., (ed) *The New Short Story Theories* (Ohio University Press, 1994).

Monegal-Blancos, Antonio, *Luis Buñuel: de la literatura al cine. Una poética del Objeto* (unpublished doctoral thesis, Harvard University, 1989).

Morris, C.B, *Surrealism and Spain* (Cambridge: University Press, 1972).

——— ed. *The Surrealist Adventure in Spain* Ottawa Hispanic Studies 6, (Dovehouse Editions, 1991).

Muñoz Molina, Antonio, 'Taquígrafo del alba', *ABC* literario, 2 July 1988, p.9.

Navarro, Eloy, La formación de las teorías literarias de Ramón: 1905–1912 (unpublished doctoral thesis, Northwestern University, 1994).

Newberry, Wilma, 'The Pirandellian Mode in Spanish Literature from Cervantes to Sastre', in *Contemporary Literary Criticism: Excerpts from Criticism of the Works of Today's*

Novelists, Poets, Playwrights, and Other Creative Writers, ed. by Dedria Bryfonski, Vol 9. (Michigan: Gale Research Company, 1978), pp.237,38.

Nicholls, Peter, *Modernisms: a Literary Guide* (Basingstoke: Macmillan, 1995).

Nicolás, César, 'Las paradojas del paseante', *Lateral*, 24 (1996), 11.

——— 'Ramón Gómez de la Serna y la novela española de vanguardia', *Insula*, 502 (1988), 11–13.

——— 'La resaca antivanguardista', *Diario 16*, 2 July 1988, p.3.

Nora, Eugenio G., *La novela española contemporánea: 1927–1939* (Madrid: Editorial Gredos, 1973).

Orozco Díaz, E, 'Introducción al Barroco Literario Español', *Historia de la Literatura Española* (Madrid:Guadiana,1975).

Ortega Spottorno, José, 'Encuentros con Ortega', Suplemento EXTRA, *El País*, 30 June 1988, p.5.

Ortega y Gasset, José, 'Ideas sobre la novela', *Obras de José Ortega y Gasset*, 2 edn (Madrid: Espasa Calpe, 1936).

Orwell; Sonia and Angus; Ian (eds), *The Collected Essays, Journalism and Letters of George Orwell*, Vol I (Harmondsworth: Penguin, 1970).

Otero Seco, Antonio, 'Mi amigo Ramón', *Insula*, 196 (1963), 7.

Percival, Anthony, 'Ramón Gómez de la Serna's *La mujer de ámbar*: '¿La novela libre?', in *Studies on Ramón Gómez de la Serna*, ed. by Nigel Dennis, Ottawa Hispanic Studies 2 (Dovehouse Editions Canada, 1988), pp.98–103.

Pinillos, María de las Nieves, 'Los libros de Ramón', *Cuadernos Hispanoamericanos*, 461 (1988), 39–44.

Poggioli, Renato, *The Theory of The Avant-garde*, trans. Gerald Fitzgerald (Massachussetts/London/Cambridge: The Belknap Press for Harvard University, 1968).

Ponce, Fernando, *Ramón* (Madrid: Unión Editorial, 1968).

Porter, Dennis, *The Pursuit of Crime: Art and Ideology in Detective Fiction* (New Haven and London: Yale University Press, 1981).

Pound, Ezra, 'Hugh Selwyn Mauberley', in *The Norton Anthology of Modern Poetry*, Ed. By Richard Ellman and Robert O'Clair, 2nd ed (New York: Norton and Company, 1988).

Prada, Juan Manuel (de), *Las máscaras del héroe*, 7th edn (Madrid: Valdemar, 1997).

Rey Briones, Antonio, 'Ramón y la novela', *Insula*, 502 (1988), 17–18.

——— *La novela de Ramón* (Madrid: Verbum, 1992).

Richmond, Carolyn, 'El problema de la creación literaria en la novela de Ramón', in *Historia y crítica de la literatura española*, ed. by Francisco Rico and Victor García de la Concha, Epoca Contemporánea: 1914–1939, 9 vols (Barcelona: Ediciónes Crítica, 1984), VII, pp.229–233.

Richmond, Carolyn (ed), *El secreto del acueducto* (Madrid: Cátedra,1986).

——— 'La otra cara de Ramón', *ABC* literario, 2 July 1988, p.7.

——— 'Mujeres de obsesión', Suplemento EXTRA, *El País*, 30 June 1988, p.6.

——— *Una sinfonía portuguesa: estudio crítico de La Quinta de Palmyra* (Madrid: Espasa Calpe, 1982).

Rico, Francisco (ed), *Historia y crítica de la literatura española: época contemporánea: 1914–1939*. Victor García de la Concha, 9 vols (Barcelona: Ediciones Crítica, 1984).

Roof, Gayle Elaine, *Luis Buñuel's Avant-garde artistic production:Towards a poetics of synthesis* (unpublished doctoral thesis, Princeton University, 1990), pp.348.

——— 'Gómez de la Serna as a Literary Mentor: Ramonian Aesthetics in the Early Work of Luis Buñuel', *Revista Hispánica Moderna*, 2 (1994), Vol 47, 353–366.

Rozas Manuel, Juan, 'Greguería y poema en prosa en tres novelas de la Generación del 27', *Anuario de Estudios Filológicos II* (1979), 251–269.

Ruiz, Casanova, José F. 'Un poeta no hallado' ,*Lateral*, 24 (1996), 13.

Sabugo Abril, Amancio, 'Ramón o la nueva literatura', Cuadernos Hispanoamericanos, 461 (1988), 7–27.

Safranski, Rüdiger, Nietzsche: A Philosophical Biography, trans. by Shelly Frisch (London: Granta Books, 2002).

Sofóvich, Luisa, 'Su maniquí de cera', *Lateral*, 24 (1996), 4.

Sallés de Toledo, Luis, 'El hombre es demasiado metafísico', 'El fracaso de la filosofía: apuntes para un libro de filosofía intranscendental', *Grecia*, 1 (1918), 15.

Sánchez Vidal, Agustín, 'De Ramón al surrealismo', *Insula*, 502 (1988), 13–14.

Senabre, Ricardo, 'Técnica de la greguería', in *Historia y crítica de la literatura española*, ed. by Francisco Rico and Victor García de la Concha, Epoca Contemporánea: 1914–1939, 9 vols (Barcelona: Ediciónes Crítica, 1984), VII, pp.221–226,

——— 'Ramón en pugna con el lenguaje', *Insula*, 502 (1988), 15.

——— 'Sobre la técnica de la greguería', Papeles de Son Armadans, 45 (1967), 121–145.

Shattuck, Roger, *The Banquet Years: The Origins of the Avant-grade in France*, 1885–1918 (London: Southern Cape, 1969).

Shaw, Valerie, *The Short Story: A Critical Introduction* (New York: Longman, 1983).

Shlovsky, Victor, 'Art as Technique', in *Russian Formalist criticism: Four Essays*, ed. by Lee T. Lemon and Marion J. Reis (Lincoln: University of Nebraska Press, 1965), pp.3–57.

Soldevila-Durante, Ignacio, 'Bajo la hoja de parra', Suplemento CULTURAS, *Diario 16*, 2 Julio 1988, p.2

Soria Olmedo, Andrés, *Vanguardismo y crítica literaria en España*. (Madrid:Ediciones Itsmo, 1988).

Stromberg, Roland N, *European Intellectual History since 1789* 5th ed (New Jersey: Prentice Hall, 1990).

——— *An Intellectual History of Modern Europe* (New York: Appleton, 1966).

Sypher, Wylie, *Rococo to Cubism in Art and Literature* (New York: Vintage Books, 1960).

Torre, Elías, 'Ramón y lo cursi', *Insula*, 196 (1963), 12.

Torrente Ballester, Gonzalo, 'Teatro de Ramón', *Insula*,196 (1963), 15.

Torre, Guillermo, 'El espíritu nuevo de los poetas', *Cosmópolis*, 1 (1919), 17–28.

——— 'Cinegrafía: el cinema y la novísima literatura: sus conexiones', *Cosmópolis*, 33 (1921), 97–107.

——— 'Génesis del Ulraísmo', in *Historia y crítica de la literatura española*, ed. by Farncisco Rico and Victor García de la Concha, Epoca Contemporánea: 1914–1939, 9 vols (Barcelona: Ediciónes Crítica, 1984), pp.234–238.

——— 'Cinegrafía: El cinema y la novísima literatura:sus conexiones', *Cosmópolis*, 33 (1921), 97–107.

——— 'Estética del yoísmo ultraísta', *Cosmópolis*, 29 (1921), 51–61.

——— 'Paralelismos entre Picasso y Ramón', *Insula*, 196(1963), 1.

——— 'Problemas teóricos y estética experimental del nuevo lirismo', *Cosmópolis*, 32 (1921), 585–607.

Tudela, Mariano, 'Las ciudades', Suplemento CULTURAS, *Diario 16*, 2 Julio 1988, p.5.

Umbral, Francisco, 'La escritura perpetua', Suplemento CULTURAS, *Diario 16*, 2 July 1988, p.12.

———— 'Los géneros fingidos de Ramón', in *Historia y crítica de la literatura española*, ed. by Farncisco Rico and Victor García de la Concha, Epoca Contemporánea: 1914–1939, 9 vols (Barcelona: Ediciónes Crítica, 1984),VII, pp.226–229,

———— *Ramón y las vanguardias* (Madrid: Espasa Calpe, 1978).

Unamuno, Miguel, *Del sentimiento trágico de la vida* (Madrid: Espasa Calpe, 1976).

Utrera, María Fernández, *Visiones de Estereoscopio: paradigma de hibridación en el arte y la narrativa de vanguardia española*, North Carolina Studies in the Romance Languages and Literatura, no 272. University of North Carolina Press, Chapel Hill, 2001.

Valle, Andriano, 'La apoteosis del cohete', in *Grecia*, 3 (1919), 3–5

Vara, José Alejandro, 'Ramón en Buenos Aires: triste, solitario y final', *ABC* literario, 2 July 1988, p.12.

Villanueva, Darío, 'La escritura ramoniana de la novela', *Insula*, 432 (1982), 7–11.

Villanueva, Darío, *La novela lírica II* (Madrid: Taurus, 1983).

Waldberg, Patrick, *Surrealism* (London: Thames and Hudson, 1997).

Waugh, Patricia, *Metafiction: The Theory and Practice of Self-conscious Fiction* (London and New York: Routledge, 1984).

Weston, Richard, Modernism (London: Phaidon, 1996).

Weisstein, Ulrich, *Expressionism as an International Phenomenon* (Paris: Librairie Marcel Didier, 1973).

Wharton, Edith, *The Writing of Fiction*, (New York: Octagon Books, 1969).

Wilde, Oscar, 'The Decay of Lying', *Complete Works of Oscar Wilde*, (London and Glasgow: Collins, 1966).

Wilson, Edmund, *Axel's Castle* (Glasgow: Fontana Literature, 1959).

Ynduraín, Francisco, 'Sobre el arte de Ramón', in *Historia y crítica de la literatura española*, ed. by Francisco Rico and Victor García de la Concha, Epoca Contemporánea: 1914–1939, 9 vols (Barcelona: Ediciónes Crítica, 1984), VII, pp.219–221,

———— 'Ramón en esquema', Suplemento CULTURAS, *Diario 16*, 2 July 1988, p.8.

Yussen de Sofóvich, Berta, 'El hacedor', Suplemento CULTURAS, *Diario 16*, 2 July 1988, p.4.

Zlotescu, Iona, '1888–1963: Ráfagas de su vida', *Lateral*, 24 (1996), 8–9 .

Zlotescu, Iona, ed. *Ramón:Obras Completas: Novelismo I [El doctor inverosímil y otras novelas 1914–1923]* (Barcelona:Galaxia Gutenberg-Círculo de lectores, 1997).